Retirement's HARSH New Realities

PROTECTING YOUR MONEY IN A CHANGING WORLD

GORDON PAPE

PORTFOLIO
PENGUIN

PORTFOLIO PENGUIN CANADA

Published by the Penguin Group

Penguin Group (Canada), 90 Eglinton Avenue East, Suite 700,
Toronto, Ontario, Canada M4P 2Y3 (a division of Pearson Canada Inc.)

Penguin Group (USA) Inc., 375 Hudson Street, New York, New York 10014, U.S.A.
Penguin Books Ltd, 80 Strand, London WC2R 0RL, England
Penguin Ireland, 25 St Stephen's Green, Dublin 2, Ireland (a division of Penguin Books Ltd)
Penguin Group (Australia), 250 Camberwell Road, Camberwell, Victoria 3124, Australia
(a division of Pearson Australia Group Pty Ltd)
Penguin Books India Pvt Ltd, 11 Community Centre, Panchsheel Park,
New Delhi – 110 017, India
Penguin Group (NZ), 67 Apollo Drive, Rosedale, Auckland 0632, New Zealand
(a division of Pearson New Zealand Ltd)
Penguin Books (South Africa) (Pty) Ltd, 24 Sturdee Avenue, Rosebank,
Johannesburg 2196, South Africa

Penguin Books Ltd, Registered Offices: 80 Strand, London WC2R 0RL, England

First published 2012

1 2 3 4 5 6 7 8 9 10 (WEB)

Copyright © Gordon Pape Enterprises Ltd., 2012

Manufactured in Canada.

LIBRARY AND ARCHIVES CANADA CATALOGUING IN PUBLICATION

Pape, Gordon, 1936–
Retirement's harsh new realities : protecting your money in a changing world / Gordon Pape.

Includes index.
ISBN 978-0-14-317922-1

1. Retirement income—Canada—Planning. 2. Retirement income—Canada.
3. Finance, Personal—Canada. I. Title.

HG179.P372 2012   332.024'014   C2011-907154-1

Visit the Penguin Group (Canada) website at **www.penguin.ca**

Special and corporate bulk purchase rates available; please see
www.penguin.ca/corporatesales or call 1-800-810-3104, ext. 2477 or 2474

To my grandchildren.
May your lives be healthy, fulfilling, and prosperous.
With love to you all, Granddad

CONTENTS

PREFACE

It has been twenty years since I wrote my first book on retirement planning. *Retiring Wealthy* was first published in 1991, but as I leafed through it again in preparation for this book, I found that it focused on many of the same themes that will be dealt with here. I also found a prescient quote in that book from a *Fortune* magazine article: "If they don't start actively planning for it, the future of retirement for the baby boomers is work."

Guess what? The first baby boomers have now reached the normal retirement age of sixty-five, and many of them are still working. A Harris/Decima poll conducted for Scotiabank and released in early 2011 found that 38 percent of Canadians expect to continue working after sixty-five because they won't have enough money to live on. That's an alarming statistic.

The poll found that, all told, more than two-thirds of respondents said they plan to keep working after reaching retirement age. I wasn't surprised. We're living longer and healthier lives, and many people aren't ready to abandon their careers just because they have a sixty-fifth birthday. I'm seventy-five as I am writing this. There is no magic number at which we suddenly lose our desire and capacity to work.

But working after sixty-five should be a matter of

choice, not necessity. That's why it troubles me that many Canadians believe they won't be able to get by financially unless they stay on the job. In some cases, those jobs will involve menial labour, like bagging groceries at a local supermarket. We've already seen signs of that. No one should be forced into doing work they don't want and don't enjoy. And as the baby boomers continue to age, the trend will likely accelerate.

There were several other worrisome findings in surveys that were published during the 2011 RRSP season. For example, the Scotiabank poll also found that 55 percent of those planning to retire completely have saved less than $20,000 over the past five years. At that rate of saving, they'll need government handouts to survive. A TD Waterhouse survey discovered that 67 percent of baby boomers are worried they won't have enough money to retire; only 15 percent feel comfortable about their situation. And a Royal Bank study concluded that only 39 percent of Canadians between the ages of eighteen and thirty-four have opened an RRSP, the lowest level in almost a decade and a sharp contrast to the 62 percent who responded positively to the same question in 2006.

And here's the most frightening statistic of all: 5 percent of the people who answered the Scotiabank poll said they were counting on a lottery win to fund their retirement. You have to wonder how much of their potential savings they're blowing on tickets!

If the poll numbers are anywhere near accurate, they tell a disturbing story that portends badly for the future. Despite years of warnings, exhortations, and incentives, far too many Canadians are still unwilling or unable to take the action necessary to protect themselves from years of financial distress in later life. And this is despite the fact that this country offers some of the best government-sponsored savings programs in the world.

In the past, some critics have accused me of scare-mongering. If that means using fear as a means to goad people into taking positive action, I plead guilty. But I hope the end justifies the means. Not every Canadian faces the prospect of a delayed and/or uncomfortable retire-ment. But it appears from the surveys that many are in that position—or at least are worried they might be.

So here I am, twenty years later, with basically the same message: only *you* can ensure your financial future. The difference is that my message has become even more urgent because of the harsh new realities we face in the twenty-first century.

This will almost certainly be my last book on this subject. I don't expect to be around to do a follow-up in another twenty years. So I hope that this time, the message is loud and clear: it's time to act. Tomorrow will come faster than you think.

PART ONE
THE HARSH NEW REALITIES

HARSH REALITY 1
THE BOOMERS ARE GETTING OLD

During the summer and fall of 2010, millions of protesters poured into the streets of France in a series of demonstrations and strikes that almost paralyzed the country and made headlines around the world. Schools were closed by student sit-ins and teacher walkouts. Most of the country's oil refineries were shut down by strikes, leaving motorists with empty tanks. Mail went undelivered. Public transportation was disrupted. To the dismay of tourists, even the iconic Eiffel Tower was closed to visitors when staff walked off the job.

In cities across the country, marchers chanted slogans and waved placards denouncing the nefarious policies of the government of Nicolas Sarkozy. Truckers, ambulance operators, and armoured car drivers used their vehicles to set up blockades, snarling traffic in the process. There were clashes with police.

Officials watched nervously. Street demonstrations had brought down French governments before. Was it about to happen again? A huge rally in the Place de la Bastille, where the French Revolution began, sent shivers down the spines of government ministers and their supporters. They became even more nervous when polls revealed that two-thirds of their countrymen supported the marchers.

What cause was great enough to bring the French people into the streets six times in less than two months? Starvation? Human rights violations? Wide-scale government corruption? War?

No, none of these traditional flashpoints was the cause. In a historic first, the French were protesting over retirement! It had never happened before, or at least not on such a huge scale. But be assured, it *will* happen again—soon and often.

People in North America could scarcely believe what they were seeing on television and reading in the newspapers. France was in revolt over a government plan to raise the minimum retirement age from sixty to sixty-two! For Canadians and Americans, that was still three years short of their traditional retirement age. But the French had different expectations. They had become accustomed to stopping work early and living their retirement years in comfort, thanks to generous pensions. In some cases, they actually ended up collecting more money in retirement than they had when they were employed. French workers saw it as a birthright. The government saw it as a fiscal liability—one that was about to become uncontrollable as the baby boom generation reached the age of retirement. In the end, Sarkozy and his ministers hung tough and the measure was passed into law. However, intransigent union leaders, claiming they are defending the rights of future generations, have vowed the fight will continue.

The protests in France drew the most attention, but the

same issues are being played out in many other countries. Germany passed legislation in 2007 to increase the retirement age from sixty-five to sixty-seven. Spain, faced with an urgent debt crisis, took similar action in January 2011 after a middle-of-the-night deal with key unions averted a general strike. That accord, born out of desperation, did not stop angry protesters from vandalizing banks and clashing with police, however. Old entitlements die hard.

The reason governments feel they have no choice but to act now can be summed up in one word: demographics. Time is running out on the baby boom generation, which shaped the second half of the twentieth century and will have a similar impact on the first half of the twenty-first, albeit in a different way. The first boomers have reached sixty-five (most American demographers identify baby boomers as those born between 1946 and 1964). The number of boomers in the U.S. alone is estimated at 79 million.

According to *The Canadian Encyclopedia*, the baby boom period in this country ran from 1946 to 1965. During this period, the birth rate jumped from 24.3 per 1,000 people in 1945 to 27.2 per 1,000 the following year, as the boys came home from war. The birth rate stayed high until 1959, at one point reaching 28.5 per 1,000, after which it started to fall. (In 2011, the birth rate was estimated to be down to 10.28 per 1,000.) The encyclopedia estimates that the baby boom produced an extra 1.5 million Canadians, the great majority of whom are still here.

No one knows with certainty how many baby boomers were born around the world, or how many are still around and approaching retirement. The simple answer is "a lot"—hundreds of millions of them. Past governments were able to ignore the approaching crisis because it was not an immediate drain on the public purse. The warnings of economists and demographers were ignored in the heat of more pressing political battles.

Well, no more. The baby boomers are no longer coming. They're here, and they have brought with them a hornet's nest of problems that will shape public debate over the next two decades. Pensions. Retirement age. Health care. Elder care. Government support. Tax breaks. Estate planning. Assisted suicide. All these issues—and more—are about to take centre stage in the public forums.

The angry reaction that boiled over into the streets of France in 2010 was just the beginning. We are about to experience a series of wrenching changes in our retirement system as governments, corporations, and individuals struggle to cope with a tidal wave of harsh economic, demographic, and social realities. Dealing with them will challenge the most astute minds in this and other countries, and will force us all to consider alternatives and make compromises.

It will be a difficult time, but not a hopeless one. There are solutions, although they won't meet with universal approval. But in the end, it will come down to each person adapting to the harsh new realities of twenty-first-century retirement. The world has changed dramatically from our parents' day, and it will continue to do so in the years to come. We have no choice but to change with it.

WHERE WE'RE GOING

It won't come as any surprise to learn that our population is getting older. What may come as a shock is how quickly it is happening. In 1956, people sixty-five and older represented 7.7 percent of Canada's population. Half a century later, in 2006, that figure had almost doubled, to 13.7 percent. These trends are projected to continue for the next three decades at an accelerating pace. According to a study carried out by PricewaterhouseCoopers for Infrastructure Canada and published in April 2008, the median Canadian age is projected to reach 43.3 years by 2026 (it was 27.2 in 1956). By that point, 21.2 percent of the population will be in the sixty-five-plus cohort. By 2051, these figures are expected to increase to 46.8 years and 26.4 percent, respectively.

Canada is not alone by any means. The whole developed world is getting older. In fact, Canada has one of the youngest populations among the G8 countries; only the U.S. has a lower proportion of people sixty-five and older, at 12.4 percent. (The report refers to them as "elderly," an increasingly dated term that many in this age group would flatly reject.) Japan, Germany, and Italy have the world's highest proportions of "elderly" persons, with approximately one in five already sixty-five or older.

"As the boomers enter their senior years," the report says, "evidence suggests that they will be relatively healthier, more independent, better educated, wealthier, and lead more active lifestyles than any senior population to precede them." This will lead to a significant shift in public priorities. Access to shopping, public transportation, and highways (trends show that older people prefer to drive their own cars) will become more important as Canadians age. The need for health care services will increase. Fewer younger people will translate into a diminished need for schools. The result will be political battles over spending priorities and budget allocations, as well as a growing squeeze on government assets. No one can predict with certainty how much the net cost will be, but one estimate quoted in the report puts it in the vicinity of $300 billion over the next fifty years.

The greatest pressure will almost certainly be in health care. Obviously, the older we get, the more likely we are to need the services of doctors, nurses, and other health care professionals. The cost implications of this are staggering. The Infrastructure Canada report found that the average per capita provincial/territorial health spending was about $2,630 in 2004. But the average for those between sixty-five and sixty-nine was about $5,016, and for those aged eighty to eighty-four it was roughly $11,902—about 4.5 times the national average for all age groups.

"The current generation making intensive use of the health care system is the relatively small group born during the 1930s Depression, allowing Canada a window of preparation before the boomers start to cause high growth in demand on the health sector throughout the 2020s and 2030s," the study said.

These are not just problems for the future. They are real and immediate. We are already experiencing a "rationing" of health care that is having a direct impact on the quality of life of thousands of people.

For example, in February 2011 *The Globe and Mail* reported that several orthopaedic surgeons who specialize in joint replacement had been forced to take an unwanted holiday because funding for hip and knee replacements was drying up. With the March 31 end of their fiscal year looming, many hospitals had used up most or all of the money allocated by the federal and provincial governments for joint replacement. The operations cost between $10,000 and $12,000 each on average.

Although the Infrastructure Canada report did not touch on the issue, we can expect a contentious debate in the next few years over whether private health care services should be allowed to exist in parallel with the public health system, along the lines of the British model. An aging and wealthy population is not going to tolerate compromises to health because of a rationing system that limits access not only to elective treatments but even in some cases to potentially life-saving ones. For example, most people are unaware that new techniques for the treatment of prostate cancer can significantly increase the chances for a cure while minimizing the undesirable side effects (including incontinence and erectile dysfunction). And even fewer know that age can be the deciding factor in whether a person is accepted into the program. Because funding is limited, radiation oncologists are forced to pick and choose who will get the treatment, and with a few rare exceptions, they give priority to younger men with longer life expectancies.

Defenders of our medicare system argue that allowing

private practices would compromise the level of treatment offered to the general population. But reality is catching up with us quickly. I predict this will be the number-one political issue in Canada within five years.

WE'RE GETTING OLDER, BUT ...

You'll sometimes hear older people say that age is catching up to them. Well, guess what? It's not! If anything, it's running away from them. Let me explain.

For most of recorded history, the lifespan of the average individual has been increasing. During some periods—for example, in Europe during the Black Death—the progress has been very slow or has even temporarily stalled. But the pattern of increasing longevity eventually resumed, and in recent years it has accelerated at an astounding pace.

According to a fascinating table that can be found on Wikipedia under the heading "Life expectancy," a baby born during the Neolithic period would live an average of only twenty years. Think about that for a moment—by the time people reached their mid-teens, they were elders in their communities.

During the period of the Roman Empire, the average life expectancy for a citizen had increased to about twenty-eight years. It was several centuries before there was any meaningful advance from that level; in medieval Britain, the average life expectancy at birth was still only thirty. By the early twentieth century, the average was between thirty and forty-five, depending on which part of the world you were born in. That's when the great leap forward began. A century later, in 2010, the average world life expectancy was estimated to be 67.2 years. Advances in medical science, the development of vaccines, and a big drop in infant mortality rates combined to trump two world wars and a flu pandemic that killed tens of millions of people prematurely over that hundred-year period.

Canadians, with their higher standard of living, not surprisingly fared even better. According to Statistics Canada, a baby girl born between 1920 and 1922 had a life expectancy of sixty-one years. A boy born in the same period could expect to live to fifty-nine. A decade later, at the start of the Great Depression, life expectancy for each sex had increased by only one year. But after the Second World War, it took a big jump: a baby boy born in Canada between 1950 and 1952 could expect to live to sixty-six, while a girl would survive to seventy-one.

The second half of the twentieth century saw more big gains. Baby girls born between 2000 and 2002 have a life expectancy of eighty-two years, eleven years longer than half a century before. Boys also gained eleven years, to a life expectancy of seventy-seven. The rate of increase has slowed somewhat since then, but the trend is still in place. Baby girls born between 2005 and 2007 have a life expectancy of eighty-three years, while boys have reached seventy-eight.

And the older you are, the greater your life expectancy. Statistics Canada found that in 2007, the average sixty-five-year-old could expect to live another 19.8 years (18.1 years for men and 21.3 years for women). This means that people who reach what was once considered the normal retirement age need to have adequate financial resources to sustain them well into their eighties. Unfortunately, many Canadians are coming up short and only just realizing it. And they're worried!

They should be. In a study prepared for the Institute for Research on Public Policy and published in April 2011, Dr. Michael Wolfson of the University of Ottawa concluded that a high percentage of baby boomers are likely to experience a significant decline in their standard of living after retirement. Dr. Wolfson, who was previously assistant chief statistician at Statistics Canada, warned that about half of all middle-income Canadians born between 1945 and 1970 can expect to have at least a 25 percent drop in disposable income once they stop work. (Middle income is defined in the study as an average lifetime income of between $35,000 and $80,000 annually.) Dr. Wolfson believes that any reduction in disposable income from pre-retirement levels will result in "a substantial decline in living standards." Furthermore, he warns that none of the public pension changes being considered by the federal and provincial governments will fix the problem, and he argues for "much more ambitious reforms" to be put forward.

WHAT THE POLLS ARE SAYING

Each year during RRSP season, we are deluged with retirement-planning surveys prepared for major financial institutions. The motive is to shock people into putting more money aside for their post-employment years, thus adding to the fees collected by the banks and brokerage firms for managing accounts and facilitating trades. But even if we discount the bias towards depicting us as being in terrible financial shape, the results of some of these polls are disquieting.

The Scotiabank survey I mentioned in the preface also asked Canadians how much money they felt they needed to save for a comfortable retirement. The results were all over the map. The study found that 56 percent of respondents believed they would be able to get by with less than $1 million, and half of those put the figure at under $300,000. At the other extreme, 28 percent said they would need between $1 million and $2 million, and 16 percent believed they would need $2 million or more to fund their ideal retirement.

Scotiabank senior vice-president Gillian Riley said that while there is "no magic number" for people to aim for, Canadians should be "realistic about how they plan to spend their retirement and how much it will cost." She went on to say: "Whether it be $250,000 or $1,000,000, it can be daunting to think about needing such a large sum of money, so it is equally important for Canadians to consider how much they can afford to put away for retirement and understand what that amount will mean for them down the road."

SO HOW MUCH IS ENOUGH?

Ms. Riley is absolutely correct: there is no magic formula. I have lost track of the number of times I have been asked, "How much money do I need to retire comfortably?" I wish it were a question I could answer! Unfortunately, there is no easy response and no silver bullet. The only honest response I can give is "It depends." There are so many variables to consider that the answer will be different for everyone.

Start with your planned retirement age. At one time sixty-five was the standard, but not anymore. Retirement has become a moving target, with an increasing number of people working into their seventies. About the only thing we can say with any certainty is that the idea of retiring young—the old "Freedom 55" slogan of the London Life advertising campaign—has become an elusive dream for most people. Of course, the longer you plan to work, the less you need to save for retirement. The equation is simple: more years of employment income and pension credits equals fewer years of living off those pensions and your savings.

Next, think about your retirement lifestyle. It will almost certainly be more active than that of your parents and grandparents, thanks to advances in medical care and greater awareness of the importance of nutrition and exercise. The Scotiabank poll found that an amazing 86 percent of Canadians plan to travel after they stop work.

Then there's the question of how long you'll be around. Many people worry about outliving their money, and they're right to do so. As we saw earlier in this chapter, the average life expectancy has increased at an almost unbelievable rate in the past century and continues to do so. Of course, the longer you live, the more money you'll need to carry you through. In an ideal world, we'd die on the day our money ran out, but that's not the way it works.

All of this reinforces my "It depends" answer to the question of how much money you'll need. Since I cannot offer a meaningful number, let me go at it another way. I've devised what I call a Retirement Worry Index, and you can find it on pages 124 to 127. That will at least be a start towards answering the "How much do I need?" question. I hope very few of you will fall into the High or Extreme categories. But unless you are at the Very Low level, you need to take some action to improve your financial prospects after retirement. Otherwise, you may have to keep working for a lot longer than you planned.

HARSH REALITY 2
PENSION PLANS ARE DYING

On January 14, 2009, Nortel filed for bankruptcy protection. It was the culmination of the decline and fall of what once was Canada's largest corporation and the international jewel in our high-tech crown. And it was a disaster for some twenty thousand people who are still trying to figure out what happened to their pensions.

The end did not come as a surprise. Nortel had been in a downward spiral for years and was surviving only with money received from issuing high-yield junk bonds. The company, which was spun out of Bell Canada in the 1990s, had been instrumental in the construction of the Internet, expanding internationally in the process. But the high-tech crash that began in early 2000 brought everything to a screeching halt. Business dried up, and Nortel's profitability vanished along with it. The stock, which at one time made up more than one-third of the market capitalization of the Toronto Stock Exchange, plunged from over $120 a share to pennies.

Most companies go into bankruptcy protection with a view to reorganizing and emerging as leaner, meaner, and more profitable on the other side—think General Motors, Chrysler, and some of the big U.S. banks. That was not to be the case here. Nortel is done, finished, gone. All that remains is for the bankruptcy trustees to liquidate whatever assets remain and pay off creditors to the extent possible. That process will take years.

When the end came, the company was on the hook for as much as US$30 billion in claims against its assets (the exact amount is still being determined by auditors as this is written). It is estimated that Nortel will have only US$7 billion to be disbursed—US$3 billion from cash on hand and another US$4 billion from asset sales.

First in line for a share of that money will be the banks that kept Nortel afloat well after the company's "best before date" had expired. Then will come the lawyers (they always make sure they get their fees), other secured creditors, bondholders, and suppliers. Who is missing from this picture? The company's approximately twenty thousand pensioners and four hundred former employees on long-term disability.

Nortel's pensioners enjoyed the advantages of a defined benefit pension plan (DBPP). These are the Cadillacs of pension plans because they provide a guaranteed (in theory) income after retirement, usually based on a combination of average salary and years of service. By contrast, defined contribution pension plans (DCPP) offer no such guarantees; an employee's retirement income is dependent upon total contributions credited to his or her account, plus the investment returns on that money during the working years. As a result, DCPPs are much less of a drain on corporate finances.

After the company's bankruptcy, Nortel employees

were financially stranded and faced losing a major portion of the benefits they'd expected to receive. That's because their pension plan was allowed to fall into fiscal disrepair and is in deficit to the tune of at least $1.5 billion. It is expected that when all the calculations have been done, former Nortel employees will lose as much as 50 percent of their pension income, as well as the health care benefits they expected to receive in retirement. Even worse off are the people on long-term disability. They were cut off at the end of March 2011 after receiving a payout of 10 percent of the money that remained in the Nortel Health and Welfare Trust.

THE NORTEL PENSIONERS

Who are these people? Ordinary folks who could be living next door. Slightly more than half were unionized workers, while the rest were managerial and professional people, many of whom worked in research and development. The average age of Nortel pensioners is about seventy-four, and many are now in their eighties. Some had been receiving a full pension for years prior to the bankruptcy. Let's meet two of them.

Robert Dowson, Iroquois, Ontario

I started at Nortel in the Bramalea plant in 1961. At that time the company was owned by Bell Telephone and was called Northern Electric, and I started in the shop as a basic assembler. The work was exciting and the foreman was a great guy.

I was happy to work in this great enterprise because they were extremely busy and the chances for promotion were everywhere. I felt I had a job for life and could buy a home, raise a family, and then enjoy the fruits of my labour. I was thrifty and did everything right while preparing for my retirement.

After I moved up into management at age twenty-four, the older fellows training me talked about savings and Northern Electric's pension plan. It was offered to us as part of our wage "package," which included medical benefits and life insurance. We would get a letter about once per year outlining our wage package and the benefits. The pension was always part of this package plan. I didn't have to contribute to the pension plan, as the company looked after the contributions as part of my wages. My wife would be cared for with a survivor pension after I was gone.

I was a first line production manager for twenty-seven of the thirty-two years that I worked there. It was an exciting career, as we sent our products across Canada and then all around the world. I was retired at age fifty-two in 1993. I was shocked in January 2009 when I heard that Nortel had let my pension fund go down and had stopped making the promised contributions. It was then that I began to learn about the Bankruptcy Insolvency Act and its lack of protection for twenty thousand Nortel retirees. We thought that in a country such as Canada, our elected government would step in and help us out.

We very peacefully protested on Parliament Hill, and I was in the House of Commons when our Minister of Industry stood up and answered an Opposition question by stating loudly that [the] Nortel pension was an Ontario problem, and that we should go to Queen's Park to protest. I was stunned, because I knew that the Bankruptcy Act was in his portfolio, not that of Queen's Park. We needed federal help.

My wife, Marilyn, and I started a series of meetings with our MP, to no avail. He knew less about the act than I did; however, he assured us that we were worrying for nothing, as the Minister of Industry was working hard on our behalf. I was hopeful but leery. This was the beginning of a long two-year campaign to stir up our federal government.

Our meetings with our provincial MPP went much better and we got excellent results with him. He took our plea and our NRPC [Nortel Retirees and former employees Protection Canada] plan right to the Premier, who wrote us a letter accepting it. The plan was later accepted by the Finance Minister of Ontario.

Two years later and many meetings, phone calls, and letters to all the MPs, we have no action from our government. They have stonewalled us all the way. This has caused a heavy strain on our household. All our annual trips were cancelled and our retirement spending has halted, as we don't know how much the impending pay cut will be. We may have to sell our retirement home ten years before our planned time frame. It is not hard to feel depressed these days, as it seems our lives are on hold and the future is bleak. I hate the word "survive," but I guess that is what we can look forward to. This pension debacle is a sad way to live out one's golden years.

William (Bill) Nickerson, Winnipeg, Manitoba

I joined Nortel in June 1964 and worked for the company in Brampton, Ottawa, and Winnipeg for twenty-nine years. I retired in 1993 with the position of Manager, Quality Function. I am now seventy-four.

I joined the company pension plan and expected to retire with full benefits plus health and dental coverage, as well as life insurance.

When I retired, I received a pension of $25,034 a year, which, with the health insurance plan and some personal savings, was enough to maintain our lifestyle. I was diagnosed with Parkinson's disease sixteen years ago, but I have been able to cope reasonably well thanks to medication procured under the Nortel plan. I take pills seven times a day at an estimated cost of $22 a day, of which 80 percent was covered under the Nortel plan in conjunction with the Manitoba Pharmacare plan.

Nortel health coverage has now been withdrawn, and I understand that my pension will be cut by about 40 percent. It is too early to tell how the reduced pension, coupled with the increased medical expenditures, is going to affect our lifestyle. We will need at least a year before we can verify the effect on our daily living. However, the high cost of personal health insurance (about $4,600 per year for premiums alone from Manulife Financial) will certainly have a serious financial effect on us. Further adding to the financial strain is the fact that my wife has macular degeneration and has lost sight in her right eye, with her left eye also affected and *degenerating. She also has osteoporosis. Dental expenses will probably increase too.*

Understandably, all this has been extremely stressful for me and my family, and we are very disappointed in the failure of the government to help us. I can only wish that other Canadians do not have to experience the difficulties that we are trying to cope with when they retire.

THE FIGHT TO RECOVER PENSION MONEY

The fight to recover at least some of the pension money is being waged by a lobby group with the rather awkward name of Nortel Retirees and former employees Protection Canada (NRPC). Its leaders face massive obstacles, not the least of which is that because Nortel was an international company, claims are being made against it from all parts of the world. Moreover, virtually all the cash that Nortel had left in the end is being held outside of Canada, while money from the sale of assets goes directly into a "lockbox" in the United States.

Governments aren't helping much, NRPC says. They claim that bankruptcy laws in Canada encourage employers to neglect their pension obligations, in contrast to legislation in the U.S. and the U.K. In those countries, Nortel pensioners and those on long-term disability will receive virtually everything they are owed. NRPC's request that Ottawa amend federal bankruptcy laws to grant former employees preferred status among unsecured creditors has so far been rebuffed on the grounds that it would discourage foreign investment in Canada and force more businesses into bankruptcy.

The organization has also pressed the Ontario government to create an agency that would take over abandoned pension plans in a manner similar to the Pension Benefit Guaranty Corporation in the U.S. Queen's Park has shown no interest, even though the idea was recommended in 2008 by the Ontario Expert Commission on Pensions. The reason is a familiar one these days: such an agency would expose the province to an unacceptable degree of financial risk when the next economic downturn hits.

NRPC has targeted Ontario in particular because it believes the province is responsible, at least in part, for the plight of Nortel's pensioners today. "Ontario's loose funding rules and the lax oversight by the Financial Services Commission of Ontario led to the Nortel plan being significantly underfunded for several years before the company filed for bankruptcy," charges Anne Clark-Stewart, an NRPC board member and the organization's media director. "Part of the problem has been the 'too big to fail' syndrome leading governments to give companies excessive leeway in meeting their pension obligations.

"Furthermore, a major systemic problem lies in the way in which plans are valued. Typically the valuation is done on the assumption that the sponsoring company will stay in business. No allowance is made for the plan to be wound up by conversion to annuities in a bankruptcy, as most provincial rules require. In practice, as Nortel pensioners are discovering, this can cost them at least a further 20 percent of the value of their pensions."

In late 2010, NRPC successfully fought off a move by the Ontario government to force a mandatory wind-up of the pension plan in that province and convert the assets to non-indexed annuities at a time when interest rates were at near-record lows (low rates translate into reduced annuity payments). The organization claimed the action would cost retirees about one-third of their pensions (which had been indexed) and asked instead that the approximately $2.5 billion in assets be managed by private financial institutions, and that employees be offered other income choices. The province's finance minister, Dwight Duncan, initially rejected the proposal, saying he wasn't prepared "to risk making an already difficult situation worse by subjecting $2.5 billion in retirement savings to an untested capital markets model." But after Nortel retirees, most of them white-haired and some in wheelchairs, staged an embarrassing rally in front of Queen's Park, he retreated and promised to introduce legislation that would enable pensioners to opt out of the province's wind-up plan, have their money privately managed, and invest in life income funds, or LIFs (the equivalent of RRIFs).

NORTEL IS NOT UNIQUE

Unfortunately, the Nortel story is anything but unique. Similar situations are occurring with depressing frequency all across Canada and the United States. It's not always a case of a company going bankrupt either.

In November 2010, U.S. Steel Canada, which purchased

Stelco a few years ago, locked out nine hundred employees in Hamilton, Ontario, after they refused to accept changes to their pension plan, the costs of which the company claimed made its Canadian plants "uncompetitive." U.S. Steel wanted to close the existing defined benefit pension plan and direct new employees to a less lucrative defined contribution plan, a move the union said would have the effect of transferring all the risk from the company to the workers. That was bad enough, but the real sticking point was a bid to end cost-of-living indexing for some nine thousand retirees. That, said the union, was just plain mean. It carried its fight to the streets of Hamilton in January 2011, with thousands of people turning out in support. At the time of writing, the workers were still locked out and the impasse had not been settled.

Air Canada hasn't moved to cut benefits to retirees— at least not yet—although it has issued warnings that anything is possible if changes aren't made, noting that twenty-six thousand employees are now supporting twenty-nine thousand retirees. In the spring of 2011, the company said that its defined benefit pension plan was in deficit to the tune of $2.1 billion, which a spokesperson said was "not sustainable" and "puts at risk both the viability of the company and the pensions of all employees." Ominous words indeed, especially in light of what happened at Nortel.

Air Canada asked its unions to accept proposals that would see all new hires switched to a much cheaper defined contribution plan. The company, which began life as a Crown corporation, said it had accumulated $13 billion in pension liabilities in its seventy-five years of existence and was facing funding obligations amounting to hundreds of millions of dollars annually for the next several years. At the time of writing, the company's customer service employees were on strike in a desperate attempt to persuade Air Canada to back off.

Many companies have already gone down the path that U.S. Steel Canada and Air Canada want to follow by converting to the less expensive defined contribution pension plans. According to the most recent survey by Statistics Canada, as of 2008 about 4.5 million people, or 75 percent of those with a registered pension plan, were in a defined benefit plan. "The rate of participation in these plans has declined constantly from more than 85 percent a decade earlier," the agency said.

StatsCan said that while membership in defined contribution plans was virtually unchanged from the year before, "membership in other types of pension plans, including hybrids and combinations ... showed high gains, increasing by 29.9 percent to 565,400 in 2008. This growth came mainly from sponsors in the private sector who added a defined contribution component to their defined benefit plans for new entrants."

There was one more number worth noting: the agency said that about 38 percent of employees had a pension plan in 2008, about the same as the previous three years. However, the division between the public and private sectors is dramatic. In the public sector, there's a coverage rate of 84 percent, compared to about 25 percent in the private sector, which is down slightly from 2007.

There is no doubt that the move by the private sector to DCPPs is accelerating. The 2011 Pension Risk Survey, published by the human resources consulting firm Towers Watson, reported that 51 percent of private-sector defined benefit plan respondents have now converted their plans to defined contribution for current or future employees. That was up from 42 percent in 2008, and a press release issued by the company said there is no indication the trend is relenting.

Towers Watson asserted that defined benefit plans were at "a tipping point" and said that private-sector employers have "crossed a pension Rubicon." Ian Markham, Canadian Retirement Innovation Leader at Towers Watson, added: "This year's survey results show that employers planning a conversion to DC are intent on doing so regardless of whether economic conditions improve, or a more sponsor-friendly legislative environment appears, or even in lieu of less dramatic changes to plan design or investment strategy."

In at least one case, a company was later sued after employees figured out that converting to a DCPP wasn't such a great deal after all. In that action, brought against Tolko Industries of Vernon, British Columbia, a group of employees claimed that the company and its actuary incorrectly calculated how much money would be transferred to the new plan, and that Tolko made "unreasonable" predictions of the value of future pensions, all of which the company denied. The case was still before the courts at the time of writing.

I expect there will be more lawsuits like this as people discover that defined contribution plans do not provide any guarantees of future income, and that the value of the eventual pensions will depend in large part on the financial acumen of the employees—most of whom have little or no skill in this area.

CANADA IS NOT ALONE

Pension woes are not confined to Canada by any means. Nor are workers in the public sector immune. In 2009, the pension fund for city employees in Prichard, Alabama, ran out of money, just as actuaries had been predicting it would. The town responded by cutting off pension cheques to some 150 retirees, breaking a state law in the process. Prichard is a small community, but the situation was so unique at the time that *The New York Times* assigned two reporters to write about it, bringing the case to national attention. The poignant story by Michael Cooper and Mary Williams Walsh about the hard times the retirees were experiencing shocked readers. A sixty-eight-year-old retired fire department dispatcher had been forced to declare bankruptcy, while a retired police captain was being supported in part by the proceeds from bake sales. The worst case was that of a retired fire marshal who passed away in June 2010. "When they found him, he had no electricity and no running water in his house," the article quoted a friend as saying. "He was a proud enough man that he wouldn't accept help."

Sad, yes. Unfortunately, there will be many more stories like this if current trends continue. And it appears almost certain that they will, as governments at all levels in the U.S. come under increased financial pressure and are forced to make decisions that would have been unthinkable a decade ago.

Several states have already moved to end defined benefit plans for public employees and switch them into defined contribution plans as a means to control costs. With defined contribution plans, cash-strapped state governments will not be on the hook for any future funding shortfalls because pensions will be based on the returns earned on the invested money. In Utah, which decided to make the move after the stock market crash of 2008 caused the deficit in the state's plan to swell to US$6.5 billion, it is estimated that the cost of retirement contributions for new employees will be reduced by 50 percent. Kentucky, Alaska, Michigan, Ohio, Georgia, and Colorado are among the other states that have made similar changes, in whole or in part. These moves will undoubtedly save state governments some money, but it means an uncertain future for public employees whose pensions will now be dependent on the fortunes of the markets.

Those public servants who are fortunate enough to have defined benefit pension plans can expect to pay more for them. In February 2011, Americans were treated to the bizarre spectacle of fourteen Democratic Wisconsin state senators going into hiding in neighbouring Illinois in an effort to deprive the Republican-controlled senate of the quorum needed to pass a controversial bill that, among other things, would require public servants to contribute 5.8 percent of their salaries to their pension plan. Previously, the plan had been funded entirely by taxpayers.

We have not experienced this kind of assault on public pensions in Canada, but it may be coming if governments start looking for ways to cut costs. There has already been criticism of the gap between private-sector plans and what are perceived as "rich" public-service plans, funded with taxpayer dollars. In a 2010 report on our pension system, the Certified General Accountants Association of Canada (CGA-Canada) said: "The present pension system in Canada has produced pension 'haves' and 'have-nots'—at one end of the spectrum are public-sector employees who enjoy the security of government-guaranteed DB pension plans and on the other end of the spectrum are some private-sector employees having no income or retirement security whatsoever."

It is not inconceivable that a political party would choose to make this a major issue in a future election, with the hope of winning votes from private-sector workers who feel they are being short-changed.

THE COST OF GUARANTEEING PENSIONS

The plight of private-sector pensions in the U.S. is highlighted every year by the annual report of the Pension Benefit Guaranty Corporation (PBGC), a federal government agency that bails out members of failed plans. During the 2010 fiscal year, the agency reported that it had paid out about US$5.6 billion to retirees and surviving beneficiaries because their own pension plans were unable to meet their obligations to them. As of September 30, 2010, the PBGC reported single-employer liabilities of US$99.4 billion, up by US$10.2 billion from the close of the previous fiscal year. Against this, the agency had single-employer assets of US$77.8 billion, leaving a massive deficit of US$21.6 billion.

"In part, this financial position is the result of inadequate plan funding and misfortunes that have befallen plan sponsors," the report said. "In part, it is a result of the fact that the premiums PBGC charges are insufficient to pay for all the benefits that PBGC insures, and other factors.

"Since our obligations are paid out over decades, we have more than sufficient funds to pay benefits for the foreseeable future. Nonetheless, we cannot ignore PBGC's future financial condition any more than we would that of the pension plans we insure."

In Canada, only Ontario has an agency similar to the PBGC. It is called the Pension Benefits Guarantee Fund (PBGF), and it's administered by the Financial Services Commission of Ontario. It provides a limited guarantee of pension benefits in situations where a defined benefit plan is unable to make payments because an employer is insolvent and cannot fund deficiencies. Coverage is for the first $1,000 a month, plus an "excess amount" based on the wind-up value of the plan.

Like its U.S. counterpart, the Ontario program has come under increased financial pressure in recent years, with big-time bankruptcies such as those of Algoma Steel and Nortel resulting in thousands of new claims. The taxpayers of the province have been required to come up with hundreds of millions of dollars in bailout money to keep the program solvent. It's no wonder that Queen's Park does not want to expand coverage, and that other provinces are not rushing to create similar agencies to assist retirees.

We are looking at a growing problem that has no easy solutions. More pension plans, both public and private, are failing. But the political will to help those affected is not there, and won't be. In these financially difficult times, governments are struggling to find the money to pay for essential services, and taxpayers are unwilling to be stuck with the tab for bailing out retirees who were left in the lurch when their pension plans failed.

That's not what these increasingly desperate folks want to hear. But it's today's harsh reality.

HARSH REALITY 3
WE'RE ON OUR OWN

I recently went on a cruise out of Fort Lauderdale, Florida, visiting several ports in the eastern Caribbean. As you would expect, most of the people on board were Americans. One day at lunch, I was seated next to a woman who introduced herself as Anne. Although she was in her seventies, she still worked writing children's books and had an opinion about any subject you might think of. One of those opinions was that governments are inherently bad and the less they intrude on people's lives, the better.

She was particularly contemptuous of "Obamacare," the legislation pushed through by President Barack Obama that, among other things, requires all Americans to have health insurance. It was nothing more than "socialized medicine," she said, and then proceeded to tell me how lousy the Canadian health care system is because "the government runs it." Every Canadian she knows hates it, she asserted.

When I mildly suggested that not all Canadians believe our medical system is terrible, she bristled. "Then why do you think they all come down here to go to the Mayo Clinic and places like that for treatment? They don't want to wait months and months for a hip replacement or whatever."

There was no arguing with her. The government should keep its fingers out, period! "Americans want to be free to make their own choices. They don't want to be told what to do by the politicians!"

That last line neatly sums up one of the fundamental differences between the way Canadians and Americans think. A majority of Americans feel that less government is better government. A majority of Canadians believe the opposite to be true. Many Canadians would agree that our health care services could be made more efficient. And from my own family experience, I can attest that the facilities and services in top-level American hospitals are far superior to what most medical institutions in this country provide. That said, few Canadians would advocate scrapping the existing system and starting over with one based in the private sector. We've seen that model in the U.S., and we don't like it. Plus, it is outrageously expensive!

Health care is only one of many areas touching our personal lives in which the government is greatly involved. Another is retirement planning and income support.

THE GOVERNMENT AND YOUR RETIREMENT

The federal government has created a dazzling array of programs to help us save for retirement and to ensure a steady stream of income after we stop work. Some are mandatory, notably the Canada Pension Plan (CPP) and its counterpart, the Quebec Pension Plan (QPP). Every working Canadian must contribute to one or the other; there is no opt-out privilege.

To encourage private savings, the Liberal government of Louis St. Laurent created the Registered Retirement Savings Plan (RRSP) in 1957. It was its last major accomplishment, as the Liberals were swept from office a few months later by John Diefenbaker's Progressive Conservative party. It was more than fifty years before another powerful savings tool was brought in, the Tax-Free Savings Account (TFSA), which was introduced by Stephen Harper's Conservatives in the 2008 budget and became effective in January 2009. So both the Liberals and Conservatives can claim some credit for the generous tax-sheltered plans available to Canadians today.

Once we reach age sixty-five, other government programs kick in. Everyone who has been in Canada a certain number of years can collect Old Age Security (OAS), which, unlike CPP or U.S. Social Security, is a non-contributory program. Ottawa deposits several hundred dollars in your bank account just because you're alive—you don't have to do anything to earn it beyond completing an application form. If OAS, CPP, and your private savings aren't enough, the federal government has another pot you can dip into, the Guaranteed Income Supplement (GIS). It makes monthly payments to people whose income falls below a certain level. Ottawa doesn't want any of its seniors to be poor—well, not *too* poor.

This level of government intrusiveness would be anathema to many Americans, but rarely have I heard any

Canadians complain about it. We don't simply tolerate it—we welcome it. If anything, we want more.

That's why it didn't surprise me when the immediate reaction to studies showing that a significant percentage of Canadians approaching retirement haven't saved enough was to expand the CPP. Finance Minister Jim Flaherty initially supported the idea, and according to a poll released by the Canadian Union of Public Employees (CUPE) early in 2011, the majority of Canadians agreed with him. It showed that 76 percent of respondents wanted the CPP to be extended. However, the results must be considered in context, because they happen to reflect the position of both CUPE and the Canadian Labour Congress.

But Mr. Flaherty then did an about-face, announcing in December 2010 that there would be no expansion of the CPP. He apparently backed off in the face of ideological opposition from key provinces like Alberta, which prefers a private-sector solution, and from the business community.

One of the problems with expanding the CPP is the cost it imposes on business. Contributions constitute what amounts to a payroll tax because employers are required to match employee payments dollar for dollar. This results in a disincentive to hire new staff, especially in periods of economic recession—exactly the time when job creation is especially important.

In fact, the financial burden imposed on employers by the CPP goes beyond simply matching contributions. They are frequently required to overcontribute but receive no tax credits for doing so. This can happen, for example, in cases where part-time workers hold two or more jobs and contribute to the CPP in all of them. The worker will receive a refund of any overcontributions collected over a year; the employers will not. The extra money they pay amounts to a hidden tax. This is especially hard on small businesses and helps explain why owners of these companies tend to resist any expansion of the CPP/QPP. The Canadian Federation of Independent Business, the main lobby group for this sector, has consistently opposed any mandatory increase in CPP premiums.

There are other implications in an expanded CPP, and these were highlighted by William B.P. Robson, president of the C.D. Howe Institute, in a June 2011 report titled "Don't Double Down on the CPP: Expansion Advocates Understate the Plan's Risks" (available as a PDF on the C.D. Howe Institute website). In the study, Mr. Robson writes that the CPP is not a fully funded defined benefit plan, as most Canadians believe. Target payouts can change if the plan's financial situation deteriorates, which in fact has happened in the case of the Quebec Pension Plan. "The CPP is a gamble, not a guarantee: expanding the plan would raise the stakes on a bet most Canadians do not know they have made," he says. "It is misleading to tell Canadians that the CPP is fully funded and could reliably deliver richer benefits on the same basis."

As an alternative to enhancing the CPP, Jim Flaherty embraced the idea of creating a privately run program that would be available to small businesses with no pension plan, the self-employed, and anyone else who wants to join. This Pooled Registered Pension Plan (PRPP) would be voluntary and would be operated as a defined contribution plan.

This is a critical difference from the CPP; as I explained in the previous chapter, defined contribution plans provide no guarantee of future income. The eventual pension will depend on how well the investments in the plan perform.

The defined contribution approach appeals to governments and plan sponsors because it means no one is on the hook for anything. If the market crashes and pensions are reduced as a result ... well, that's the way it goes. The flip side is that these plans, by their nature, create what may turn out to be an unacceptable degree of uncertainty for participants.

DELAY RETIREMENT AND GET PAID MORE

The 2011 study by the Institute for Research on Public Policy, which I referred to in the first chapter, contends that the retirement challenges facing middle-income Canadians are so serious that only "ambitious reforms" to the existing system can deal with them. Believe me— those reforms are *not* going to happen. Now that the Conservatives are firmly entrenched with a majority government, the best we can expect is the implementation of the PRPP and some nibbling around the edges, such as the recent funding increase for the GIS. What we have in place now is about as good as it's going to get.

In fact, we could see a gradual diminution in the generosity of existing plans as retiring baby boomers place them under increased financial strain. Not only is Ottawa unwilling to enlarge the CPP, but it is implementing measures to discourage Canadians from starting to draw benefits early.

Although a full CPP retirement pension is not payable until age sixty-five, Canadians have been able to begin collecting benefits at a reduced rate as early as sixty provided they meet a few not very rigorous conditions. Until recently, the payments were reduced by 0.5 percent for each month prior to a contributor's sixty-fifth birthday. So someone who applied to receive payments immediately after turning sixty would get 30 percent less than if she had waited five years.

When the CPP was launched in 1966, actuaries underestimated the percentage of contributors who would make use of this early retirement option. As a result, the plan paid out far more money than expected in the early years, which forced a series of federal–provincial meetings to deal with a growing financial crisis. The result was a dramatic increase in contribution rates. The CPP is now stable but could face increased pressure in future unless people are persuaded—or forced—to delay applying for benefits.

The first step has been to create a disincentive to begin early withdrawals and an added inducement to wait. Under rules that are being phased in now, the penalty for claiming benefits early will increase to 0.6 percent a month, or a maximum of 36 percent for those who want payments from age sixty. If you choose to delay, you'll receive a bonus of 0.7 percent (8.4 percent a year) for each month after your sixty-fifth birthday, up from 0.5 percent (6 percent a year). These bonuses can accumulate until age seventy, at which time you would receive 42 percent more than if you had begun withdrawals at sixty-five.

The government's goal is obvious—as the country ages, Ottawa wants to discourage us from retiring early and reward those who remain in the labour force by sweetening the pot that will await them when they finally decide to stop work.

It's part of a growing trend in developed countries, all of which have aging populations. France, Spain, Great Britain, and Germany are all raising retirement ages, some with more urgency than others. The United States is in the process of gradually increasing the age for drawing full Social Security benefits from sixty-five to sixty-seven. Anyone born before 1937 will still qualify for the full payment at sixty-five, but those born later will have to wait longer. Those born in 1960 or later will not be eligible for full benefits until they reach sixty-seven.

Even as these changes are being phased in, a bitter controversy has erupted in Washington over a proposal to raise the age again, to sixty-eight. The proposal was made in late 2010 by a special committee appointed by President Obama to formulate a plan to rein in the runaway U.S. federal deficit. The committee also recommended reducing cost-of-living indexing for Social Security benefits. The idea was immediately dismissed as "provocative" by one Republican congressman, and President Obama avoided endorsing the plan. But some experts believe that raising the age to at least sixty-eight is inevitable to ensure the future viability of Social Security. The U.S. already has a program in place that rewards people who wait until seventy to claim benefits.

It's a similar story for other government programs. Old Age Security payments are increasing at an alarming rate as the population ages. During the seven years between 1993 and 2000, for example, annual payments under the program increased from $19.5 billion to $23.8 billion, or just over 22 percent. Over the next seven years, to 2007, they grew by 33.6 percent, to $31.8 billion. No government is going to want to exacerbate that financial drain by adding more goodies to the plan. The challenge in the coming years will be to maintain the benefits we already have, especially if inflation becomes a significant factor. The payments are indexed, so increases in the cost of living increase the financial drain on Ottawa—and since OAS is non-contributory, there is no easy fix for that other than raising taxes.

Nor can we expect any significant increase in GIS benefits beyond those that were announced in the 2011 budget. These payments are designed to provide financial assistance for low-income seniors to keep them above the poverty line, but evidence is growing that they are not succeeding in that objective. According to figures released in late 2010 by Campaign 2000, a non-partisan anti-poverty public education organization, the number of older Canadians with incomes below Statistics Canada's poverty line grew from 204,000 to 250,000 between 2007 and 2008, an increase of almost 25 percent.

The take-away from all this is that when it comes to government financial support for retirees, what we have now is all we should expect. Ottawa has clearly indicated that it has no taste for expanding the CPP, and accelerating costs make it unlikely that OAS and GIS payments will increase in future beyond cost-of-living hikes. This is not to suggest there is anything inherently wrong with these programs. But they provide only a basic level of financial support, and there is no more where that came from. If we want more than a subsistence-level income, we have to provide it for ourselves.

HARSH REALITY 4
OUR SAVINGS RATES ARE PITIFUL

Here's an alarming statistic: 38 percent of Canadians expect to continue working after sixty-five because they won't have enough money to live on. Why is more than a third of the population in such dire straits? The answer is simple: we aren't saving enough. In fact, not only are we collectively spending almost everything we earn, but we're making matters worse by maxing out our credit cards and piling up debt that we may still be carrying when we would normally stop work.

In a February 2011 report titled "The Current State of Canadian Family Finances," the Vanier Institute of the Family reported that Canadian savings rates have fallen dramatically in the past two decades. (The report is available as a PDF on the Vanier Institute website.) In 1990, the average family in this country was able to put aside about $8,000 a year, which worked out to a savings rate of 13 percent. The average family debt at that time was $56,800, which translated into a debt-to-income ratio of 93 percent.

By 2010, the amount of annual savings per household had fallen all the way to $2,500, for a rate of 4.2 percent. Meanwhile, the debt-to-income ratio ballooned to a record 150 percent and the average family debt grew to a staggering $100,000. This obviously does not bode well for the future.

The Vanier Institute's report also confirmed the Harris/Decima finding about older Canadians working longer. "Both men and women aged 55 and up continued to experience job increases during the recession, albeit at a reduced rate," the report stated. "Job growth picked up pace during the recovery period (July 2009 to December 2010). The 55+ group, [which] comprised only 16 percent of all job holders in October 2008, had no net job losses during the downturn, and still captured 57 percent of the jobs created during the recovery period up until December 2010.

"The increase in employment among older workers points to significant anxiety concerning their readiness for retirement within the near to medium-term future. A poll conducted for Investors Group found that 30% of baby boomers believe they won't have enough money to pay for their *basic* living expenses once they retire."

An analysis of the sources of income of Canadian seniors (those sixty-five and older) shows the boomers are right to be fearful. According to Statistics Canada, the total income of this group in 2007 (the latest year for which data were available at the time of writing) was $144.8 billion. Government transfers (OAS, CPP, etc.) were the major source of that income, at $58.3 billion (40.3 percent). About $18 billion (12.4 percent) was investment income, not quite as much as seniors earned from employment ($18.7 billion). Only $2.6 billion (1.8 percent) came from RRSPs. Private pension payments accounted for $41.6 billion (28.7 percent).

The increase in the employment income figure since 2003 is startling. In the space of only four years, that figure grew by almost 60 percent. The pattern is clear: more people are working past what used to be the normal retirement age, either by choice or because they otherwise would not have enough money to live on.

SAVE MORE: BANK OF CANADA

Mark Carney, the governor of the Bank of Canada, has repeatedly warned that our low savings rate is putting households at ever-greater financial risk. During a speech in Toronto in December 2010, he told the Economic Club of Canada that after a series of analyses, the central bank concluded that "households are increasingly vulnerable to an adverse shock, and that this vulnerability is rising more quickly than had been previously anticipated …

"Credit continues to grow faster than income. In some regions, lower house prices have begun to weigh on personal net worth. Without a significant change in behaviour, the proportion of households that would be susceptible to serious financial stress from an adverse shock will continue to grow."

He said a "stress test" conducted by the bank found that an increase of just 3 percent in the unemployment rate would result in a doubling of the number of household loans that were three months or more in arrears. "Even if the growth in debt continues to slow, the vulnerability of Canadian households is unlikely to decline quickly given the outlook for subdued growth in income," he concluded. His advice: pay down debt and save more.

The Certified General Accountants Association of Canada (CGA-Canada) has also weighed in on this issue, saying in a recent statement: "The rapidly deteriorating situation of the household sector's balance sheet should be viewed as alarming." But despite all the admonitions, debt levels continue to grow. The Vanier Institute report concludes that one million families are in a "vulnerable" position, and it says that number will increase if we hit another economic downturn.

Most, although not all, pension experts believe that Canadians must ramp up their savings if they are going to have any hope of maintaining their standard of living when they retire. Former Bank of Canada governor David Dodge is one of those firmly in the "save more" camp. Writing for a study prepared by the C.D. Howe Institute (co-authored by Alexandre Laurin and Colin Busby), Mr. Dodge warned that Canadians must put aside between 10 and 21 percent of their pre-tax earnings every year for thirty-five years in order to live post-retirement in the style to which they have become accustomed. That's more—a lot more—than most people think is needed. "This fraction is likely far higher than many Canadians believe," he wrote. "It is also higher than the effective contribution over time of employer-sponsored defined benefit plans. And for high-income earners, it exceeds the annual limits placed on RRSP contributions."

People over thirty-five who are just beginning to save will need to put aside even more than 20 percent of their income or resign themselves to working past sixty-five. "Our findings provide Canadians with a reality check about the saving rates required to meet their retirement goals and inform the choices they could have to make between working longer or consuming less and saving more," Mr. Dodge said.

WHAT IT MEANS TO YOU

So what do Mr. Dodge's numbers *really* mean in terms of how much money you have to put aside? He wrote about the need for Canadians to perform a "reality check" on their retirement goals, so I've constructed some fictional scenarios to help you do that. I've kept all the numbers in constant dollars for simplicity, although in the real world, inflation would have to be factored in to the calculations. This has several implications. For example, it's important to gradually add to the amount of money saved each year to at least keep pace with the rising cost of living. Over time, this will have the effect of significantly increasing the amount being put aside. Assuming you add just 2 percent annually to your savings, after twenty-five years you'll be contributing $1,641 to your retirement plan for every $1,000 now. Add a little more and you should be able to offset the loss of purchasing power over the years.

Now let's look at my fictional scenarios. In all cases, the people have no pension plan and their savings are held in tax-free RRSPs and TFSAs.

We'll start with Catherine Lapointe, who works for

an advertising agency. She is thirty years old and earns $45,000 a year. She has taken to heart all the admonitions to start saving for retirement early and intends to put 10 percent of her gross income into her RRSP each year. That's at the bottom end of what Mr. Dodge says should be committed to retirement savings.

Catherine begins by contributing $4,500 a year to her plan. Assuming an average annual compound rate of return of 6 percent and no increases in contributions over time, Catherine's RRSP will be worth about $532,000 when she turns sixty-five. Is that enough?

The answer is probably, depending on how much income she wants after she stops work. If her target is 80 percent of her pre-retirement gross, she will need $36,000 annually (remember, we are dealing with constant dollars). Assuming her RRSP continues to earn an average of 6 percent a year, she can withdraw about $32,000 annually without encroaching on her capital. After she adds her Canada Pension Plan and Old Age Security payments, she should have as much money as she needs with perhaps a little left over for luxuries.

The danger for Catherine is that after age seventy-one, when she has to convert the RRSP to a RRIF, the amount of money that must be withdrawn each year sharply increases. By the time she's seventy-five, the government requires her to take out 7.85 percent of the plan's value; by eighty, that has increased to 8.75 percent. This means her capital will gradually be eroded. If she's smart, she'll put some of that extra income from these withdrawals into a TFSA to protect her financial position.

Next we'll look at Charles Wong. He is a forty-year-old computer programmer and he's done nothing about retirement planning until now, so he's starting from scratch. He's currently making $65,000 a year, and his retirement income target is the same as Catherine's—80 percent of gross. So he will need $52,000 a year at age sixty-five. Like Catherine, he commits to saving 10 percent of his income, or $6,500 annually. His average annual compound rate of return is also 6 percent. How does he fare?

Not well! Even though Charles is saving much more than Catherine each year, the value of his retirement fund at sixty-five is only $378,000. That's about $150,000 less than she accumulates. Those ten years of zero savings have had a huge impact. At a withdrawal rate of 6 percent, Charles will receive only $22,680 in annual income. CPP and OAS won't come close to making up the difference. Charles is heading for trouble!

What if he increases his savings rate to 15 percent, or $9,750 a year? This will give him $567,000 at retirement, which will generate about $34,000 a year in income—still not enough. According to my calculations, Charles will need to save about $11,700 a year—18 percent of his gross income—if he is to come close to his target. That will generate about $40,800 a year and CPP/OAS should make up the difference.

Finally, let's consider the predicament of Ali Ross. She is the marketing manager for a small business and has recently turned fifty. Her milestone birthday got her thinking about the future, and she realized with a shock that the normal retirement date is just fifteen years away.

She has no savings and decides she'd better do something about it. Her current income is $80,000 a year, and her goals are the same as those of Catherine and Charles. Ali swallows hard and makes a big commitment. She will put 21 percent of her annual income—$16,800 a year—into RRSPs and TFSAs. That's at the upper end of Mr. Dodge's range.

Unfortunately, she has delayed too long. Even at that high savings rate, she will be able to accumulate only $414,500 by age sixty-five. That won't even produce half the income she needs. Ali must make some hard decisions: save even more, plan to work longer, or accept a reduced standard of living when she retires. None are palatable options, but her many years of procrastination have placed her in this uncomfortable position.

So what should we take away from these scenarios?

First, it's essential to start saving early. Time is really on our side here. But it's not an easy commitment to make when you're young and retirement seems forever away. There are too many other priorities, from feeding the family to buying a home. The reality is that very few people under forty ever think seriously about retirement. By the time they get around to it, many valuable years of savings have been lost.

Second, the longer you wait to begin, the greater the percentage of your income you will have to save. As we saw in our examples, the thirty-year-old ends up in a good financial position at sixty-five even though she saved only 10 percent of her income. The fifty-year-old is way behind even though she contributes 21 percent.

Saving is not easy, especially in this era of effortless credit and rampant consumerism. But collectively we should be doing better than we are. A national savings rate of 4.2 percent is going to leave many people in financial difficulty when the time comes to stop work. That's a harsh reality every Canadian needs to address.

HARSH REALITY 5
WE DON'T KNOW WHAT WE'RE DOING

Not long ago, I received an email from a confused reader. He wrote, in part: "I am sixty-seven years old and I want to continue contributing to an RRSP. I was told that I can't because of my age. I am still working and I am afraid I will be paying a fair amount of tax next year. What can I do to avoid this?"

As I read over the message, I became increasingly angry. Whoever told him that he couldn't contribute to an RRSP because he is too old obviously knew nothing about the rules. We can only wonder if it was a well-meaning but ignorant friend or, much worse, a poorly trained professional.

Anyone with a basic knowledge of RRSP rules would have told the gentleman that he can contribute to his RRSP until the end of the year he turns seventy-one, as long as he has "earned income" (usually from employment) or carry-forward room. Since he was still working at the time, he obviously would have had the earned income needed.

In fact, I would suggest that this is something the writer should have known himself. The information is easy enough to find—all he had to do was to check his most recent notice of assessment from the Canada

Revenue Agency. We can only assume that he was so financially uninformed that he had no idea where to look for guidance.

He's not alone. Millions of Canadians are in the same situation, often without even realizing it. And those who do understand that they are financially illiterate don't know what to do about it. Here's another email I received at about the same time:

> My frustration at my lack of knowledge regarding stocks, bonds, mutual funds, etc., has led me to write this email. I am a forty-year-old professional, I have my own business, have a family of three, yet the only thing I know to do with my money is save it. I am afraid of investing it because I have no understanding of what to do, where to start, whom to trust (frankly, I don't trust anyone). But basically and most importantly, I don't understand any of it! How can I put my money in something I don't understand? Yet I feel like I am wasting time sitting on it.
>
> My question to you is: How do I learn what I need to know? Maybe the real question is, How do I determine what I need to know? I have read a few books on finance, but I find them too generalized and they don't get into defining what bonds or mutual funds or ETFs exactly are and how you would incorporate them into a "diversified" portfolio.
>
> Can you recommend a good book (that gets into specifics yet is still reader-friendly to someone who knows nothing about the subject matter), or a

continuing education course (preferably online) that
I could consider taking? Thank you.

Surveys aimed at learning how much Canadians really
know about money confirm that our level of knowledge
is woefully low. For example, an online poll conducted
in March 2011 by Léger Marketing on behalf of BMO
Investments found that barely half of those questioned
(51 percent) understood how to use securities to generate
income. What was especially surprising was that only
57 percent knew they could use guaranteed investment
certificates (GICs) for cash flow, while 52 percent knew
that bonds pay interest income. The poll identified a real
thirst for more financial information among Canadians,
with 73 percent saying they would like to learn more.

Another poll released in April 2011 by the Autorité des
marchés financiers (AMF), Quebec's financial services
regulatory body, concluded that people are not very good
at identifying deals that are potentially high risk or even
fraudulent. The survey found that only about half of
respondents were sceptical about buying a security that
offered a return of 2 percent monthly, which would be
worth about 27 percent annualized. Of course, any investment with a return like that would likely be a rip-off,
which may explain why so many people fall prey to investment scams each year.

TASK FORCE ON FINANCIAL LITERACY

There can be no doubt that the paucity of financial knowledge is a serious and growing problem in this country. In an attempt to come to grips with it, Ottawa created a Task Force on Financial Literacy, which released its report early in 2011. (The report is available as a PDF on the task force's website.) It had some worrisome things to say about the ability of Canadians to deal with even basic money management issues.

"Canadians today have to make an ever-larger number of financial decisions, at an ever-younger age—and these decisions are increasingly complex and fraught with consequences," the report said. "Yet too many people remain underequipped when it comes to understanding money matters, and some groups are particularly vulnerable in this regard."

The report continued: "Canadian and international polls, surveys and studies have consistently shown that many consumers—young and old, rich and poor—have real challenges with financial literacy, from reading financial statements to managing credit cards to planning for retirement."

To support these assertions, the report cited the following findings from the 2009 Canadian Financial Capability Survey, conducted by Statistics Canada:

1. Only 51 percent of Canadians have a budget.

2. Almost one-third of the population (31 percent) is struggling to pay the bills.

3. Of those Canadians who plan to purchase a house, 48 percent had saved less than 5 percent of the cost of the home and 52 percent were not expecting to incur any costs other than the down payment.

4. A surprising 70 percent of Canadians were fairly or very confident that their retirement income would provide the standard of living they hoped for. But only 40 percent had a good idea of how much money they would need to save in order to maintain their desired lifestyle.

5. Financial advisors are the most common source of information (at 54 percent) among people seeking advice on investment matters.

"Our review of the evidence makes it clear that Canada must move to address deficits in financial literacy in a more focused way, and that the time for action is now," the task force concluded. "The status quo is no longer an option."

To this end, the report contains "an integrated set" of thirty recommendations. They all make good sense and reflect a thorough and carefully designed strategy. The first is that the federal government appoint an individual, directly accountable to the minister of finance, to serve as the national leader in implementing the program. He or she is to be supported by an advisory council, also to be appointed by Ottawa. But this new financial literacy czar will face a huge challenge in persuading the provinces and other major stakeholders to follow his or her lead.

The report explicitly recognizes the need to get the provinces onside with its fourth recommendation, which reads: "The Task Force recommends that all provincial and territorial governments integrate financial literacy in the formal education system, including elementary, high school, post-secondary education and formalized adult learning activities."

The challenges here are both costs and priorities. Any educator will tell you that it is almost impossible to add a new element to the curriculum without dropping something. So what goes out? Art? Geography? Music? Careers? Then there's the problem of finding accredited teachers, since financial courses are still rare in this country. "Historically, financial literacy has not been a significant part of school curricula in Canada, and so there was no requirement or incentive for teachers to acquire the necessary background," the report says, adding that such training should now become a priority. At the time of writing, British Columbia was the only province that had made financial literacy a mandatory part of its education program. The task force recommends that other provinces draw on the teacher resources that have been created there.

Another area of focus is the business community, which the task force asserts is not doing enough to educate employees about money matters. Why should this be an issue? Because an increasing number of employers are offering defined contribution pension plans and group RRSPs. In both cases, participants are required to make sophisticated decisions about investing their contributions, and I know from personal experience that the great majority feel overwhelmed by the process.

To encourage employers to be more proactive in this regard, the task force recommends tax incentives for financial literacy programs in the workplace. It also suggests that employers offer automatic savings programs for employees, presumably along the lines of the old Canada Savings Bonds payroll deduction plan. Both are worthwhile proposals, although with no matching employer contributions, the level of participation in the automatic savings programs may be small.

I'm not so sure about the recommendation that "financial services providers put a strong emphasis on delivering educational information and ensuring that it is fully understood by Canadians at 'teachable moments' so that Canadians can make responsible financial decisions." The marketing objectives of financial institutions are often in conflict with the best interests of their customers. With all due respect to the task force chairman, Donald Stewart, who recently retired as CEO of Sun Life Financial, insurance companies have a long history of creating products and designing marketing materials that are almost impossible for an untrained individual to comprehend in a meaningful way. And try comparing one insurance plan with that of a competitor! Significantly, the task force specifically states that one of the goals should be to make comparison shopping and decision making "easier and accessible" for more people. The insurance companies are the place to start.

But banks are not squeaky clean either. Posted interest rates are frequently negotiable, although an uninformed client may not realize it. Some products, such as index-linked GICs, are promoted as "risk-free" when in fact they are anything but that. Credit card interest rates and how they are calculated are mysteries to most people. Advisors may sometimes recommend investments that are more profitable to their employer than to a client.

But in all fairness, it must be said that financial institutions already publish educational materials and sponsor a variety of programs. Often these are part of a marketing effort, however, and are designed to encourage a specific action from the reader.

One of the questions I am most often asked is how to find a good financial advisor. There is no simple answer. Recommendations from family and friends are the best source of intelligence, in my view, since they come from people who presumably have no interest in steering you in the wrong direction. Otherwise you are pretty much on your own.

As a result, I was pleased to see that one of the recommendations in the report is that the government should "provide tools to help Canadians become better informed about the role and benefits of professional financial advice, as well as how to choose a financial practitioner." But while the concept is laudable, I was disappointed that the task force didn't offer any specific ideas on how to implement it. Financial advisors who sell products are basically in a conflict of interest, which is one reason why some people mistrust them. If a solution could be found to that issue, it would go a long way towards raising the credibility of the profession and encouraging a greater number of people to seek help.

The report is worth reading if you care at all about the sad state of financial knowledge in this country, and it should certainly stimulate discussion. Whether any of the recommendations will actually be implemented is another matter. Politics, costs, and plain inertia are going to make it difficult to come anywhere close to the ideals set out by the task force. The political hurdles alone are formidable, and the report may just end up gathering dust on a shelf, like so many others before it.

HARSH REALITY 6
THERE IS NO SAFE PLACE FOR YOUR MONEY

I have lost count of how many times I have been asked this question or some variation of it: "Where can I put my money where it will earn a decent return and be safe?"

In the past, a target rate of return of 10 percent was often given. Now most people realize that a 10 percent average annual return is a pipe dream unless they are willing to take a lot of risks. But they still hope to earn 6 percent, and sometimes more, risk-free.

It's not possible, and anyone who says otherwise either is too ignorant to know better or, more likely, is trying to sell you something. But people keep searching for the Holy Grail—the investment that offers a great return while guaranteeing you can never lose.

In reality, every investment implies risk of some sort. You can't even escape it by hiding money under your mattress. Yes, it will be safe (assuming no one discovers it), but the purchasing power of your sequestered cash will decline as the years go by. With an annual inflation rate of 2 percent (the official target of the Bank of Canada), every $1,000 that you tuck away today will buy only $817 worth of goods and services a decade from now. Suddenly the mattress doesn't seem quite so safe anymore!

Don't misunderstand me. There is nothing wrong with being prudent when it comes to investing. Multi-billionaire Warren Buffett neatly summed up the value of caution when he identified the two most important rules for financial success. "Rule number one: Never lose money," he said. "Rule number two: Never forget rule number one." But telling people not to lose money and providing them with a means of achieving that goal are two different things. Even some of Mr. Buffett's investments have turned out to be losers—proof that nobody's perfect.

Although there is no such thing as a riskless investment, promoters make a lot of money by convincing people that there is such an animal, and that they have it. Some of these promoters are con artists who would sell you a unicorn if they thought you would buy it. But some are legitimate, respected businesspeople. Even our largest financial institutions, including the banks, are guilty of promoting the idea that some of their products are risk-free. In fact, financial companies have become remarkably successful at spinning out new products almost before people realize they want them.

It wasn't always this way. A generation ago, the financial services industry in Canada consisted of little more than the good, grey banks and insurance companies and several third-rate stock markets. People kept any extra money in cookie jars or savings accounts. For those who were adventurous enough to "invest," the most popular securities were guaranteed investment certificates (GICs) and Canada Savings Bonds.

No one worried too much about saving in those days.

Just earning enough to meet day-to-day living expenses was challenging enough. Retirement planning was almost unheard of. If you lived long enough to earn a gold watch, the company pension plan would take care of you. Failing that, the kids could pitch in.

Well, the world has changed. Now we are confronted with a dazzling array of investment options. Simplicity has given way to opacity as people struggle to understand the many choices available in the financial marketplace and try to decide which ones are best suited to their needs. Blame the Bay Street innovators and their complicit marketers for this state of affairs. They have become experts at inventing clever new products and then hyping the hell out of them.

In recent years, these market manipulators have begun to realize that the pursuit of safety had become the main financial objective for older people, many of whom saw their assets shredded in the market plunge of 2008. It marked the second major crash in less than a decade (the high-tech collapse at the start of the century was the other) and left many Canadians traumatized. That made them classic candidates for anyone with a believable risk-free, or at least low-risk, approach to investing.

Bay Street was quick to oblige. Here are some of the choices currently being offered.

MARKET-LINKED GICS

Market-linked guaranteed investment certificates (GICs) have been around for about twenty years, but they found a new level of popularity after the 2008 crash. They were originally created in response to the steady decline in interest rates through the mid-1980s and into the 1990s. Faced with falling yields, people began to cash in their GICs and move their money into mutual funds. Because GICs had been a huge business for the banks, they knew something had to be done to stop the bleeding. The response was the market-linked GIC, which based its return not on interest rates but on the movement of an underlying stock index, such as what was then known as the TSE 300, over the term of the note.

Like regular GICs, market-linked GICs guarantee the investor's principal at maturity. But unlike traditional GICs, which pay a fixed rate of interest, market-linked GICs offer no certainty of return. If the benchmark index does well over the term, you make money. If it drops, you get your principal back but nothing more. So it is possible that you could tie up your capital for five years or longer with zero profit at the end.

That's exactly what happened to people who bought these securities in the late 1990s or in early 2000. Using a calculator on the Royal Bank's website, I found that a five-year investment made on March 31, 2000, in RBC's Canadian or global market-linked GICs would have returned zero at maturity. Think about that—five years and nothing to show for it. Sure, you would have received your money back, but the purchasing power would have been reduced by five years of inflation. That's no way to build wealth.

Of course, if your timing was better, the story would

have been different. A three-year investment in RBC's Canadian market-linked GIC made on March 31, 2003, just as a new bull market was gaining traction, would have produced a profit of 18.33 percent at maturity in 2006. But that's total return. On an average annual compounded basis, your money would have earned only about 5.8 percent a year. By comparison, one of the bank's more conservative mutual funds, RBC Balanced Fund, posted annual gains of 14.4 percent, 8.1 percent, and 14.7 percent during the same period. Yes, there was a risk of loss, but it was small compared with the returns. Still, that small risk was enough to convince a lot of people that the market-linked GIC was preferable.

All the banks offer a wide range of market-linked GICs from which to choose. Clearly, there is a high investor demand for these products. At the time of writing, CIBC had seventy-one unmatured older issues and eight new issues on offer, including one based on the CIBC Monthly Income Fund, which was being offered in three- and five-year terms. At maturity, investors receive 60 percent of the return of the fund over the period of the note. If the fund loses money, their principal will be returned.

Sounds good, doesn't it? If the fund makes money, you make money, and if it loses money, you still retain what you put in. But before you rush off to invest, consider this: the three-year average annual compound rate of return for the CIBC Monthly Income Fund as of May 31, 2011, was 1.65 percent. That means the fund had a total profit of $50.32 for every $1,000 invested over the period. The GIC pays 60 percent of that, or $30.19. That works out to an average annual return on the GIC of only 1 percent. A high-interest savings account is actually better!

Of course, the CIBC Monthly Income Fund might do much better in the next three years. But it also could do worse. It's a crapshoot. A true low-risk investor would choose an old-fashioned interest-paying GIC and be done with it.

PRINCIPAL PROTECTED NOTES (PPNS)

In recent years, many of the same people who invested in market-linked GICs have moved on to the much more complex world of principal protected notes in the hope of better profits—still with the expectation of zero risk, of course. A PPN is a hybrid product that offers a chance at big gains while theoretically ensuring that you won't lose your capital if things go wrong. It's something like sitting down at a roulette table with a guarantee that your stack of chips won't be any smaller when it's time to go to bed.

Investors seem enthralled with the idea of being able to place a bet on the future direction of the stock market— or on a bundle of mutual funds or commodity indexes— without really seeming to risk anything. Greed with safety! How can you go wrong?

Easily! PPNs are a terrific invention for brokers and underwriters, many of whom pad their bank accounts with fat sales commissions and fees. For everyone else, they're a crapshoot. And yes, you can lose on these things if you take inflation and the time value of money into account.

Like market-linked GICs, a simple PPN will track the performance of a recognized stock index, such as the S&P/TSX Composite or the Standard & Poor's 500, which is made up of the largest five hundred companies in the United States. And again, like market-linked GICs, PPNs tie up your money for three or five years, at the end of which you receive a return based on the performance of the index over that period. Nothing all that different so far.

However, unlike market-linked GICs, PPNs come with a lot of extra costs. In fact, the only sure winners are the underwriters of the issue and the broker or dealer who sells it to you. They get their fees and commissions right off the top—typically 3 to 5 percent of the total amount raised, but sometimes more. If the commission is 5 percent, only $95 out of every $100 you invest actually goes to work for you. Of that amount, a significant percentage—perhaps as much as 70 percent of the total—goes to purchasing the strip bond or forward contract that provides the "guarantee" of your capital. The organization that gives the guarantee is known as the "counterparty"—a term you need to understand if you invest in PPNs.

Your upfront cost is probably not your only expense. Most PPNs also have annual fees and expenses. I have seen management expense ratios (MERs) as high as 2.65 percent. Some of that money is paid as a trailer fee to financial advisors, thus providing them another incentive to sell the product.

The majority of PPNs track a benchmark index. But many base their returns on one or more mutual funds, a basket of stocks, one or more commodities, a hedge fund, a collection of indexes, a hot stock category, or just about anything else you might imagine. Each note has a maturity date, which is usually three to ten years from the date of issue (a few are longer), and is on sale for only a limited time. The investor's principal is guaranteed—if there is no profit at the maturity date, the capital is refunded.

There are literally hundreds of these notes out there. If you click on the Miscellaneous (Other) category on globefund.com, you'll find more than eleven hundred entries, most of which are PPNs. The Bank of Montreal and CIBC are by far the major issuers among the banks. As of mid-2011, CIBC had 361 outstanding PPN issues, tracking everything from major indexes to foreign exchange, while BMO had about 300. Both banks were continuing to promote new issues.

If you scan through the performance numbers, you'll find that many of these PPNs show a negative return since inception. If that continues, investors will receive only their principal at maturity, nothing more. For example, the CIBC Callable Global Financials Deposit Notes, Series 2, were issued on August 29, 2007, and mature on August 29, 2013. Their return is based on the results of a portfolio of ten international bank stocks, including Bank of America, Wells Fargo, BNP Paribas, Barclays, and Royal Bank of Canada (the only domestic bank included). These stocks were all hammered during the financial crisis of 2008–2009, so it will come as no surprise that the note was showing an annualized loss of 1.37 percent as of mid-2011 and was trading at about ninety-five cents on the dollar.

Investors faced an unpalatable choice: sell early at a loss (if a buyer could be found) or hold until maturity and, in all probability, receive only their principal back. That would mean six years of zero return on their money! That's hardly what I would call "safe"!

This is not an isolated example. Although a few PPNs have turned out to be winners—such as the CIBC Callable Equity Deposit Notes, Series 4, which were showing an average annual compound rate of return of 12 percent as of mid-2011—they're the exception. Most PPNs have generated little or no return for investors and are best ignored.

PORTFOLIO FUNDS

Portfolio funds (also known as packaged funds and funds of funds) are also being aggressively sold these days. They are pitched not as risk-free but rather as risk-management tools—a way for people to invest in a fund portfolio that is suitable for their risk profile. An advisor determines this by having a client fill out a questionnaire that is then used to assign a risk category. In ascending degree of risk, these categories are typically labelled as very conservative, conservative, moderate (or balanced), aggressive, and very aggressive.

I consider this to be an imprecise and potentially dangerous way of determining risk, especially for people an advisor may not have done business with in the past. But that has not stopped the rise in popularity of packaged funds. They are hot items. In fact, they are outselling traditional stand-alone mutual funds, and new products are appearing almost every week as companies battle for a larger share of a growing market. The growth rate has caught even seasoned professionals off guard. "Frankly, we've been surprised by the demand," said Glen Gowland, CEO of Scotia Asset Management. "It's come out of nowhere."

Industry statistics show that the movement to packaged funds is accelerating. According to the Investment Funds Institute of Canada (IFIC), portfolio fund net sales for member companies totalled almost $19.4 billion for the twelve months to the end of April 2011, compared to only $590 million for stand-alone funds. Investors are voting with their money, and packaged funds are the clear winners.

IFIC members reported total fund-of-fund assets under management (AUM) of slightly over $150 billion at that point, up 23.6 percent from the previous year. Individual funds still dominate, with AUM of $514 billion, but their market share shrank from 79.4 percent in April 2010 to 77.3 percent a year later. It's pretty obvious where the momentum is.

This is great news for financial advisors who prefer to offer their clients off-the-shelf fund packages rather than having to spend time building personalized portfolios. Many do-it-yourself investors also like funds of funds because of their simplicity and diversification. The challenge for both advisors and individual investors is trying to figure out which packages are best. The Canadian Investment Funds Standards Committee (CIFSC) does not group these funds—except for target date portfolios—into a single category. They are scattered throughout the fund universe, making apples-to-apples comparisons very difficult in most cases.

Even for target date portfolios, the results so far aren't encouraging. In the 2010 target date grouping, the Scotia entries, launched in June 2005, have been around the longest. There are two of them, both made up exclusively of Scotiabank funds. The Vision Aggressive 2010 Portfolio was showing, since inception, an average annual compound rate of return of 2.47 percent as of May 31, 2011. The Vision Conservative 2010 Portfolio did slightly better, at 2.58 percent, but neither of those numbers is going to impress people very much.

The Fidelity ClearPath 2010 Portfolio, launched in November 2005, had performed somewhat better to that point, with a five-year average annualized gain of 4.05 percent (B units). But the old-fashioned stand-alone Fidelity Canadian Balanced Fund did much better over the same period, with a five-year average annual compound rate of return of 6.66 percent (also B units). A check of all the other target date categories (2015, 2020, and 2020+) showed the same pattern. Not a single one has a three- or five-year annual rate of return that even comes close to that of Fidelity Canadian Balanced.

I searched through the Globefund database in an effort to find portfolio funds that are producing better returns than Fidelity Canadian Balanced. In the Canadian neutral balanced category, where the Fidelity fund is slotted, not a single fund of funds did better. A few stand-alone entries had higher returns, such as the Dynamic Power Balanced Fund, which has a 7.57 percent five-year average annual compound rate of return. But the portfolio funds were shut out. It was the same story in the Canadian equity balanced and Canadian fixed income balanced categories. The portfolio funds simply don't match up in terms of profitability.

These results raise some serious questions as to why people are investing billions of dollars in portfolio funds. Convenience is all well and good, but the results to date prove that there are many stand-alone balanced funds that are more attractive, carry about the same level of risk, and are just as easy to buy if one-stop shopping is the goal.

COUCH POTATO INVESTING

People seem to love the idea of "couch potato" investing, and I can understand why. Who wouldn't be attracted to a plan that is easy to comprehend, doesn't cost much, requires minimal time, is relatively low-risk, and makes money over time? Those are the benefits touted by proponents of this approach, and they can be very passionate about it.

I recently received an email from a reader asking for my views on this approach to managing money. "What are your thoughts on 'couch potato' investing through ETFs?" he asked. "Would you agree this strategy is better than using mutual funds?"

The couch potato concept is generally credited to Scott Burns, then a financial writer for *The Dallas Morning*

News. In 1987, he wrote a column in which he suggested that readers set up a very simple portfolio using only two securities. Half the money would be invested in an index fund that tracked the S&P 500 Index, the other half in a fund that tracked the bond market. Every year, the portfolio would be rebalanced to retain the 50–50 split. That's it!

The idea has been massaged over the years to add foreign exposure (there is more to investing than the U.S. market) and to vary the asset allocations to suit the objectives of each individual. But the fundamental concept remains the same: set up an investment portfolio using a few broadly based exchange-traded funds (ETFs) or indexed mutual funds and then sit back and watch it grow.

ETFs are increasingly the securities of choice in these portfolios. They were originally created to offer investors a cheap and efficient way to track the performance of major indexes such as Canada's S&P/TSX Composite Index or New York's Dow Jones Industrial Average. They have become extremely popular in recent years. As of March 31, 2011, we had invested more than $41 billion in Canadian-based ETFs, an amount that had more than doubled since the end of 2008. In the U.S., ETF assets under management (AUM) were expected to reach US$1 trillion by the end of 2011. Globally, the figure is projected to be US$2 trillion at the end of 2012. This is a huge and growing business!

Advocates of using ETFs to build what is known as a "passive portfolio" can be very persuasive. They point out that once the portfolio is in place, there are no further buy/sell decisions. Investors are not constantly forced to deal with complex choices; in fact, the whole idea behind this approach is not to make any change in the securities, regardless of what the markets are doing. Over time, the theory says, the historic long-term rise of the stock market will be reflected in your returns.

True believers contend that this is a much better and cheaper approach than trading stocks or investing in mutual funds. They point to the fact that studies consistently show that most active fund managers don't beat their benchmark indexes on a regular basis.

In fact, neither do ETFs or indexed mutual funds. The management fees and expenses, however low, ensure that returns will be slightly less than those of the index being tracked. For example, if an ETF with a 0.5 percent MER perfectly tracked an index that gained 10 percent, the investor would net 9.5 percent after the costs were deducted.

I agree that the couch potato concept is easy to understand. I'll also concede that ETFs and index mutual funds are cheaper—they have much lower MERs than actively managed mutual funds, which means that you pay less to the people who are looking after your money. The savings go straight to the bottom line in the form of higher returns.

But simplicity and cost savings aren't the whole story. The real questions are how safe the investment is and how much you will end up earning on your money by adopting a passive strategy. I think the couch potato approach fails on both counts, for two reasons: time horizon and human nature.

TIME HORIZON. Passive investing requires taking a long-term view, ten years or more. The concept assumes that over time, stock prices will rise and you will benefit. Short-term ups and downs will average out over the years, the theory goes, leaving the investor ahead of the game. The problem is that many people, especially those over fifty, aren't comfortable with the idea of waiting many years for a decent return. They need to see profits sooner. This is especially true for those who depend on their investments to generate income.

HUMAN NATURE. As we have seen in recent years, markets can be extremely volatile, with big gains one year and stomach-churning losses the next. For example, in 2008 the S&P/TSX Composite Index plunged 35 percent, while the Dow dropped 33.8 percent. How many couch potato investors would have had the fortitude to stick with the plan through that debacle? The fear factor certainly would have taken over in many cases.

In 2009, the markets rebounded, with the TSX rising 30.7 percent while the Dow gained 18.8 percent. But those who bailed out during the height of the collapse and retreated to GICs would not have benefited. Even investors who held on would be only marginally ahead at this point, and I can prove it. At the beginning of 2008, I set up a couch potato ETF portfolio for readers of the *Mutual Funds/ETFs Update* newsletter. I wanted to test how well such a portfolio would perform in the real world to see if I should in fact recommend it.

I took a balanced approach, putting 40 percent of the

portfolio into bonds and 60 percent into stocks. I chose four mainstream ETFs, as follows:

1. iShares DEX Universe Bond Index Fund (TSX: XBB): This ETF tracks the performance of a broad range of Canadian government and corporate bonds. It received a 40 percent weighting.

2. iShares S&P/TSX Capped Composite Index Fund (TSX: XIC): I decided to devote half the total equity weighting of 60 percent to Canadian stocks. This ETF, as the name suggests, tracks the performance of the leading stocks on the Toronto exchange. Its portfolio weighting was 30 percent.

3. iShares S&P 500 Index Fund (TSX: XSP): All portfolios should have some exposure to the U.S. market. This ETF, which is hedged back into Canadian dollars to eliminate currency risk, represented 15 percent of the portfolio.

4. iShares MSCI EAFE Index Fund (TSX: XIN): Finally, we needed some exposure to stock markets in other parts of the world. This currency-hedged ETF tracks the Morgan Stanley EAFE Index, which covers markets in Europe, Australasia, and the Far East. It was also given a 15 percent weighting.

This is a classic couch potato portfolio. It provides global diversification, currency protection, low costs, and a conservative asset allocation. It's the sort of portfolio that most investors would probably feel comfortable with. So how has it fared?

Not well! Remember that this portfolio was launched in January 2008, six months before the start of the worst stock market crash since the Great Depression. Despite the 40 percent bond cushion, it had at one point in early 2009 lost about 25 percent of its value. It subsequently recovered, but as of the end of April 2011, it was only marginally ahead—and that was mainly due to the bond component. Below are the results to that point. The book value represents the original amount invested, while the current value combines the market price at the time of the review with all cash distributions received.

COUCH POTATO ETF PORTFOLIO

FUND	WEIGHT	BOOK VALUE	CURRENT VALUE	RETURN
XBB	40%	$4,019.40	$4,805.99	+19.6%
XIC	30%	$3,015.30	$3,215.80	+6.6%
XSP	15%	$1,489.94	$1,281.23	−14.0%
XIN	15%	$1,500.40	$1,078.84	−28.1%
Totals	100%	$10,025.04	$10,381.86	+3.6%

As you can see, the bond fund was by far the biggest gainer over the three-plus years, which reinforces the importance of always retaining a significant fixed-income weighting in a portfolio. Among the equity-based ETFs, only the one that tracks the TSX was ahead. The U.S. and international ETFs were both deeply in the red, and it will likely be a long time before they return to break-even.

Overall, the portfolio showed a gain of only 3.6 percent in more than three years—and that's total return. On an annualized basis, that works out to 1.06 percent. Most people would not be happy with that, and with good reason. But this is the reality of couch potato investing—timing counts for a lot. If you set up a portfolio a few months before a market plunge, it will take years to recover.

Perhaps this explains why I am not a fan of the couch potato concept. While it's true that you might do worse by actively managing your money, at least you, and not the markets, are in control of your financial fate. And the performance of the portfolio during the 2008 market crash shows that this approach is not risk-free or even low-risk.

THERE ARE NO SAFE HAVENS

The bottom line is that there is no place where your money can be completely safe. There is an element of risk in every investment, just as there is in life. The best you can hope for is to manage that risk effectively.

The starting point is to realize that the higher the projected return on any investment, the more risk it entails. No one gives away something for nothing. If a bond is paying 10 percent interest at a time when normal rates are running at half that, there is something seriously wrong with the company or government that issued it.

In June 2011, for example, yields on Greek ten-year bonds hit 17.5 percent, but few people were willing to buy them, even though they were guaranteed by the government. Why? Because investors were convinced that Greece would default on them in the face of an unprecedented national financial crisis. What good is a high interest rate if the money isn't paid?

If you want to minimize risk, you must be willing to accept a low return on your money. The two are inseparable. Don't waste your time searching for that magic investment that will pay big bucks while guaranteeing you'll never lose. It doesn't exist!

HARSH REALITY 7
THE TAX SYSTEM IS STACKED AGAINST US

You would be amazed at the number of retirees who are unhappy because they are making too much money! As a percentage of the sixty-five-plus cohort they may be a small group, but they are very outspoken. I regularly receive emails in which these folks lament the heavy tax burden they face each year. Some even say they wish they could go back in time and take back all the contributions they made to their RRSPs over the years. It's the old "If I had known then what I know now" syndrome.

One reader from Kingston, Ontario, angry at the tax she is paying on RRIF withdrawals, wrote: "It just seems so unfair when I scrimped and saved to provide myself with a retirement income—just as the government told me to do. Interest rates were high enough then for the percentage they insist I take out each year, but that sure doesn't work now. I have considered refusing to pay taxes on that amount and going to jail—a real martyr—but I really don't want to devote all that energy to the issue. If you have any ideas that might push the powers that be to pay attention to all us aging widows, please let me know."

A man from Maple Ridge, British Columbia, also wrote to complain about taxes on his RRIF. "I always understood in theory that when I retired I would have to pay income tax on my RRSP withdrawals, but I did not foresee the practical consequences of it until it actually happened," he said. "After I retired, my wife and I found that we could meet all our regular living expenses from our combined pensions. Some years we even had as much as $1,500 left over to donate to charity. Now that I have to draw down my RRIF, my taxes have increased by $2,700 a year even though my real income has not changed. Our spare $1,500 plus another $1,200 taken from savings is being sent off to keep the taxman happy—and our charitable donations have dropped to zero. Is this what the government had in mind?"

It could be argued that these people should stop whining and enjoy life. So they have to pay more taxes— they are still far better off than many Canadian seniors. According to a 2011 report from Campaign 2000, about 250,000 seniors were living below the poverty line in 2008, a 25 percent jump from the previous year. The majority of these were women.

But the suggestion that better-off seniors should keep quiet about their taxes breaks down when we take a close look at the many ways the federal and provincial governments rip them off. The system is structured in such a way that even middle- and lower-income people are penalized for having had the foresight and discipline to put money aside for their retirement. There's something very wrong with this picture, but to date no government has shown a willingness to fully confront the problem. The Conservatives, to their credit, made some valuable changes by restoring the age at which RRSPs must be converted to income vehicles to seventy-one and introducing pension income splitting. But the tax system is still stacked against older Canadians, even those who have only a basic income. Here are some examples, starting with the issue that sparked the two complaints quoted earlier.

RRIF WITHDRAWALS

Canadians can make contributions to an RRSP until the end of the year they turn seventy-one. At that point, the plan is deemed to "mature." That means you must do one of three things with the money: take the cash (and pay a bundle in taxes), buy a life annuity, or move the RRSP assets into a Registered Retirement Income Fund (RRIF). Most people choose the RRIF because it offers the greatest flexibility and keeps the capital in the family. (An annuity purchase requires you to hand over all your savings to a life insurance company in exchange for a guaranteed income.)

However, there is one RRIF rule that is completely inflexible: the minimum annual withdrawal. The federal government requires you to take a certain amount of money from your RRIF each year, and this money is fully taxable at your marginal rate. There is no legal way around this. The method of calculating the minimum withdrawal requirement depends on your age. If you are under seventy-one, apply the following formula:

$$\frac{\text{Value of RRIF at start of year}}{90 - \text{your age at start of year}} = \text{Minimum withdrawal}$$

So if you had $100,000 in a RRIF at the beginning of 2012 and you were seventy, the minimum withdrawal would be calculated as follows:

$$\frac{\$100,000}{90-70} = \frac{\$100,000}{20} = \$5,000$$

For the record, I do not advise converting to a RRIF earlier than the law requires because of the minimum withdrawal rule. If you need money from an RRSP sooner, you can make a lump-sum withdrawal. It will be taxable, but you have control over the amount and the timing.

Once you reach seventy-one, the formula no longer applies. Instead, the required minimum withdrawal is a percentage of the capital in the plan at the beginning of each year, as shown in the table on the next page.

At age ninety-four, the minimum annual payment reaches 20 percent of the value of the RRIF at the start of each year, and it remains at that level for the rest of your life. Although this ensures that there will be money available after ninety, the formula poses another problem. The large percentage of the assets that must be paid out each year will quickly erode the capital base of the RRIF. As a result, the amount you'll receive annually will steadily decline as you reach your mid-nineties.

When the RRIF withdrawal rates were set back in the early 1990s, interest rates were higher than they have been in recent years. So it was easier to invest RRIF assets in relatively low-risk fixed-income securities and generate enough income within the plan to replace a significant

MINIMUM RRIF WITHDRAWAL

AGE	MINIMUM WITHDRAWAL
71	7.38%
72	7.48%
73	7.59%
74	7.71%
75	7.85%
76	7.99%
77	8.15%
78	8.33%
79	8.53%
80	8.75%
81	8.99%
82	9.27%
83	9.58%
84	9.93%
85	10.33%
86	10.79%
87	11.33%
88	11.96%
89	12.71%
90	13.62%
91	14.73%
92	16.12%
93	17.92%
94+	20.00%

part, if not all, of the money taken out. That is no longer feasible. In order to meet the minimum withdrawal requirement of 7.38 percent at age seventy-one, a person must choose higher-risk securities. The alternative is to see the value of the RRIF quickly diminish, potentially leaving the plan holder in a precarious financial position by the time he or she reaches eighty.

This is bad public policy, but no government has been willing to address it, presumably because of the impact on tax revenue. RRIF holders have been growing increasingly impatient with the government's intransigence on the issue, to the point that some have resorted to questionable schemes, such as RRSP strips, in an attempt to short-circuit the system.

The situation became so serious that in his 2011 budget, Finance Minister Jim Flaherty proposed measures to stop such practices, which the budget notes said "continue to evolve, and to be marketed, often with unexpected and undesirable outcomes for taxpayers." Those "undesirable outcomes" include onerous fines and penalties.

Mr. Flaherty would have been better advised to address the core issue: the unrealistically high minimum withdrawal rates. Not only do they have the effect of eroding a RRIF's value prematurely, but they also force some retirees to take out money they don't need and to pay taxes on it.

When the Canadian Association of Retired Persons (CARP) polled its members prior to the 2011 budget asking what specific measures they would like to see, an end to mandatory RRIF withdrawals topped the list. As the population ages, that pressure is going to build. Count on it.

OAS CLAWBACK

From the time Old Age Security was introduced in 1952, payments were treated as ordinary income for tax purposes. But in 1989, the Progressive Conservative government of Brian Mulroney decided that "rich" retirees, as they were referred to at the time, should have some or all of their OAS benefits taxed back. The social benefits repayment, as it is officially called, was introduced to achieve that. People whose net income is above a certain level are subject to a special tax of 15 percent on all income above the threshold, which is indexed to inflation.

The net income threshold for 2011 was $67,668 for an individual. OAS recipients (people age sixty-five and older) whose income exceeds that figure are hit with the 15 percent clawback until all their benefits are repaid. For example, if a person's net income is $80,000, the amount subject to the clawback using the 2011 threshold is $12,332. The additional federal tax payable is therefore $1,850. The full OAS pension is clawed back when a person's net income reaches $109,607, again using 2011 numbers.

This means that seniors who are subject to the clawback face the highest tax rates of all Canadians. The normal federal tax rate for someone with an income of $80,000 a year is 22 percent. However, an OAS recipient with that income faces a marginal tax rate of 37 percent—and that does not include the provincial share. Seniors' organizations contend that the clawback is blatantly unfair, especially since in many cases a significant portion of the income is derived from years of RRSP savings. In effect, people are being penalized because they made personal sacrifices to put money aside for retirement.

The clawback issue was further complicated by the introduction of pension income splitting by the Harper Conservatives. Although the plan was intended to relieve the tax burden on older people, it can have the effect of increasing the income of one of the spouses to above the clawback level. This compromises the effectiveness of the concept and is a disincentive to maximizing income splitting in these cases.

DIVIDEND TAX CREDIT

The same money should not be taxed twice. As any taxpayer will attest, that's only fair. The dividend tax credit (DTC) is designed to achieve that goal by giving people a credit for the tax that has already been paid on a company's profits.

That seems straightforward enough, but the method of calculating and applying the DTC is unfairly stacked against the taxpayer. As a result, an Old Age Security recipient can end up paying tax on money he or she never receives, the age and GST credits may be cut or eliminated, and other federal and provincial tax benefits may be lost.

The convoluted calculation for determining the amount of the DTC can result in what amounts to "phantom income" for the purposes of determining eligibility for various tax credits and liability for the OAS clawback. That happens because the first step in the process is to inflate the dividends actually received through a process called the "gross-up." The result is that the amount of money included in net income is much more than you ever actually took to the bank.

Here's how it works. Eligible dividends (generally, those received from public Canadian companies) are subject to a gross-up of 38 percent. This means that for every $100 of eligible dividends you are paid, you must record income of $138 at line 120 of the tax return. That figure is then multiplied by 15.02 percent to calculate the dividend tax credit. The extra $38 is never actually received—it is a completely artificial number. Unfortunately, people can end up paying tax on it.

That's because the figure at line 120 is included in the calculation of net income at line 236. That number determines both whether you are over the OAS clawback threshold and how much you can claim for various tax credits. (Note that the gross-up for dividends from small businesses is only 25 percent because they pay a lower rate of corporate tax.)

Although many people regard the inclusion of grossed-up dividends in the net income calculation as blatantly unfair, the government has no plans to change it. In a 2008 reply to a complaint from a taxpayer, Finance Minister Jim Flaherty wrote that if the gross-up were not used in the determination of income-tested benefits, it would distort the tax system. "Because of the DTC, a taxpayer's after-tax income from a dollar of dividend income is generally higher than it would be for a dollar of income from other sources," he said. "It is appropriate that the measure of income used to determine income-tested benefits takes this into account."

The minister went on: "While some recipients of dividend income may have their income-tested benefits reduced by an enhanced gross-up, the tax reduction provided by the DTC for those taxpayers will generally outweigh the reduction in benefits by a significant amount."

Note the word "generally" in the last sentence. As Mr. Flaherty is obviously aware, in some cases the DTC gross-up will result in higher taxes, especially when the OAS clawback is triggered.

One final thought on this subject: It is possible for one spouse to claim all the dividends paid to a couple if by doing so he or she would be able to claim the spouse or common-law partner amount (see line 120 in the General Tax Guide). This could reduce or eliminate the negative effect of the gross-up. A tax software program will enable you to experiment with the various options to see which works best.

DIVIDENDS PAID TO REGISTERED ACCOUNTS

The dividend tax credit does not apply to payments made to a registered plan, such as an RRSP, a RRIF, or a TFSA. In the case of the TFSA, it doesn't matter because no tax is payable when money is withdrawn from the plan. It's a different story with retirement plans, however.

All withdrawals from RRSPs, RRIFs, LIFs, and the like are taxed at your marginal rate. This means that dividends paid into those plans are indeed taxed twice: once at the corporate level and again when the money is taken out. That flies in the face of the whole concept of tax fairness, but the government has shown no indication that it is prepared to change the rules. As a result, my advice is to hold dividend-paying securities in a TFSA, where they won't be taxed at all, or in a non-registered account, where the DTC will apply.

CAPITAL GAINS

The dividend gross-up isn't the only type of phantom income that can push someone into OAS clawback territory. I received the following email from a reader who drew my attention to another problem: "Have you had any complaints about the treatment of capital losses for seniors whose income puts them in clawback territory for Old Age Security (OAS) payments?" the writer asked. "The computer program used by the Canada Revenue Agency credits capital losses against taxable income rather than against capital gains. The result is that seniors in the clawback region pay tax on income they never received. As an extreme example, if you have a $50,000 capital gain offset by a previous $50,000 loss and you are in the clawback area for OAS, you will pay $4,676 in taxes. If you are not over sixty-five, then the capital gains offset the losses and you pay no taxes on this transaction. Also, if your income is above or below the clawback zone, you pay no taxes on this transaction."

Although I have for years been looking closely at the tax system as it relates to OAS recipients, this is a wrinkle I hadn't come across. I checked it out and found that the reader had pinpointed yet another serious flaw in the net income calculation. Those potentially affected are people with capital losses from previous years who want to apply them against current year gains.

Here's how it works. As mentioned earlier, net income is calculated at line 236 of the income tax return. The deduction for net capital losses of other years comes at line 253. This means that 50 percent of all capital gains are included in net income for purposes of the clawback calculation, but any offsetting capital losses from other years are not deducted until later in the return. The end result is the same as it is for the dividend gross-up—line 236 is inflated by phantom income to the point that it could push some OAS beneficiaries into clawback territory.

OAS recipients aren't the only ones affected by the inflated net income formula. Some federal tax credits are determined by net income, including the age credit, the medical expense credit, the caregiver credit, and the credit for infirm dependants over eighteen.

AGE CREDIT

Let's take a close look at the age credit, which is available to taxpayers sixty-five and over. The maximum age amount (the figure on which the actual credit is calculated) was $6,537 for 2011 (it is indexed to inflation). The federal tax credit is worth 15 percent of the age amount, or a maximum of $980.55 for the 2011 tax year.

However, people with a net income of more than $32,961 will have their age amount reduced by 15 percent of the excess. So someone with net income of $40,000 would have her age amount cut by $1,055.85 ($40,000 − $32,961 = $7,039 × 15 percent = $1,055.85). The revised age amount would be $5,481.15 and the actual tax credit would drop to $822.17. The result is a federal tax increase of $158.38. Since the provinces also allow the age credit in the calculation of the taxes they collect, the effect of this is magnified.

Because the net income threshold for the age credit is less than half that for the OAS clawback, many more people are potentially affected by it. At this level, even relatively small amounts of investment income from dividends and capital gains can end up costing hundreds of dollars in increased taxes for money never actually received.

GIS RULES

How's this for a bizarre situation: an elderly senior with little income sees her government support payments cut because she saved a little money in an RRSP during her working years. Sadly, it happens all the time.

The reason is that withdrawals from RRSPs and RRIFs are considered "income." Anyone eligible for the GIS ends up losing fifty cents in benefits for each dollar of income received over $3,500. Talk about a savings disincentive!

The GIS is paid to low-income people who are eligible to receive Old Age Security. The maximum payment to a single person in the second quarter of 2011 was $665 a month. To qualify, you must report all income received from such sources as the Canada Pension Plan; RRSPs, RRIFs, and LIFs; employer pension plans; investments; employment; etc. Benefits will be reduced accordingly until a person's income reaches $15,960 (indexed to inflation), at which point he or she is cut off.

The entire approach was sharply criticized by Dr. Richard Shillington in "New Poverty Traps: Means Testing and Modest-Income Seniors," a 2003 report published by the C.D. Howe Institute. In it, he wrote that millions of people who are at or approaching retirement age "are victims of a fraud, however unintentional," because they were constantly urged to save using RRSPs. "The primary beneficiary of this saving will be the federal and provincial governments because most of the income from it will be confiscated by income-tested programs and income taxes," he wrote.

Almost a decade later, the system remains virtually unchanged and the criticism still applies. The major difference now is the availability of Tax-Free Savings Accounts—withdrawals from TFSAs do not count as income for the purposes of calculating GIS benefits. But any modest-income seniors who listened to the advice and put money into RRSPs are out of luck.

The Standing Senate Committee on Banking, Trade and Commerce called on the government to change this policy in a report on RRSPs and TFSAs published in the fall of 2010 and available as a PDF on the committee's website. "We were particularly struck by the negative implications, for low-income Canadians, of RRSP withdrawals being treated as income for purposes of obtaining government benefits," the committee said. "While we agree that withdrawals from RRSPs should be treated as taxable income, we believe that such withdrawals should have no impact on eligibility for, or the amount of, such government programs as Guaranteed Income Supplement benefits or income-tested tax credits.

"In the Committee's view, an end to the practice whereby RRSP withdrawals compromise eligibility for, or the amount of, government benefits would make RRSP contributions a more attractive option for low-income Canadians, thereby perhaps enhancing their standard of living in retirement. It would also remedy what we consider to be somewhat discriminatory treatment, since withdrawals from Tax-Free Savings Accounts do not have a negative effect on such government benefits."

So far, there has been no response from the government.

An overhaul of the system to eliminate these inequities is long overdue. In 2006, Finance Minister Flaherty justified the killing of income trusts by introducing what he called a "Tax Fairness Plan." It's time he extended that fairness to older Canadian taxpayers.

HARSH REALITY 8
WE DON'T KNOW WHO TO TRUST

Investors are constantly being encouraged to find a "trusted advisor" to work with. In principle, it's a good idea. The problem is that many Canadians don't trust financial advisors, sometimes with good reason.

In part, it's the Bernie Madoff syndrome. If the poster boy for Ponzi schemes can rip off some of the world's richest people for $50 billion, who can you trust? Madoff had an impeccable background and was utterly convincing in his role as a financial confidant to the rich and famous. People believed in him implicitly, even referring him to their relatives and friends, who willingly provided more money for his massive con game. Even some banks were caught up in the collapse, which left a trail of financial ruin that affected luminaries such as Steven Spielberg and left the New York Mets baseball team teetering on the brink of bankruptcy.

Madoff is perhaps the greatest con artist the world has ever seen, but there are plenty of others, including some Canadians, who have tried to emulate him, albeit on a smaller scale. In February 2010, one former "trusted" financial advisor, Earl Jones (who was actually unlicensed), was sentenced to eleven years in prison by a Montreal court after he pleaded guilty to two counts of fraud. Among the victims of his twenty-year, $50-million Ponzi scheme was his own brother, Bevan Jones, who after the sentencing bitterly said: "He can rot in hell."

The Jones case was only one of several financial frauds that have rocked the province's investment industry in recent years. In 2005, the Quebec Provincial Police raided the offices of the Norbourg Financial Group after the Autorité des marchés financiers, the province's securities regulator, discovered that $130 million supposedly held in the company's client accounts could not be found. It turned out that the money was being skimmed off by Norbourg's founder, Vincent Lacroix. More than nine thousand investors were bilked in the fraud, which began in 2003. Lacroix was eventually charged, found guilty, and sentenced to thirteen years in prison.

In June 2011, Quebec Provincial Police arrested Pierre Jolicoeur, the director of BMT Capital Corporation, and charged him with fraud in connection with the disappearance of $12.5 million of investors' money. Financial regulators alleged that having promised investors returns of 15 to 30 percent, Jolicoeur misappropriated their money for his personal use. The case was still before the courts at the time of writing.

Investment scams are not exclusive to Quebec by any means. In February 2011, the Canadian Foundation for Advancement of Investor Rights (FAIR Canada) released a scathing report titled "A Decade of Financial Scandals." (The report is available as a PDF on the FAIR Canada website.) In it, the organization said that as of July 2009, an estimated 1.3 million Canadians had been the victims of financial frauds.

"In many cases, investors lose a significant part of or their entire life savings," the report said. "The impact on their lives is devastating and irreversible. These crimes impact the financial, emotional, psychological and physical health of the victims and seed doubts about the security and fairness of our financial system."

The study reviewed fifteen cases of investment fraud over the past decade, with total losses to investors of $1.9 billion. The main targets were the elderly, FAIR concluded, citing such cases as that of Ian Thow, a British Columbia financial advisor who "promised 'secure, high-yield investments' to a number of elderly investors, many of whom remortgaged their homes to invest. The loss to investors was $32 million." Thow was eventually convicted and sentenced to nine years in jail.

The report found that there is a widespread perception in Canada that securities frauds go unpunished both by regulators and by police, and that when prosecutions are launched they drag on for years. It said that part of the problem stems from the "complexity and fragmentation" of securities regulation and enforcement. As a result, "no one agency has ultimate responsibility for combating investment fraud."

FAIR recommended the creation of a national system that would enable investors to check the credentials of financial advisors, based on this rationale:

The complexity of the regulatory regime and the fact that multiple sources must be consulted can make background checks, or even determining if someone is registered or not, a difficult and confusing exercise for a retail investor. Even when investors are aware that they should "check" the registration information of a firm or individual, the system of registration currently in place in Canada is so complex that it would be difficult for most investors to understand exactly what and where they should check to get the basic information they need.

To remedy this problem, FAIR Canada recommends that Canadian regulators provide an informative, comprehensive, "one-stop" national system for investors to check registration and background information (including proficiency and disciplinary history) and SRO [self-regulatory organization] membership for all firms registered with securities regulators and SROs and to identify non-securities licenses for individuals licensed under different regimes with different sponsoring firms. This system should include plain language explanations of the information provided and be searchable under business names as well as proper legal names.

It's a great idea, but realistically, it will be many years before it becomes operational, if it ever does.

SOME PERSPECTIVE

Let's hit the Pause button for a moment. So far, this chapter has dealt with scams and frauds. Let me be very clear: these are the exception, not the rule. According to Statistics Canada, there were about 288,000 financial advisors operating in 2008, and most have the best interests of their clients as their top priority. They should—it is to their advantage. A happy client is a source of ongoing commissions and fees, and may also refer new business.

The problem is that most advisors are in a conflict of interest that is endemic to the financial services industry. Because of this, they constantly find themselves between a rock and a hard place when it comes to making recommendations. Let me explain.

Most advisors earn their living from sales commissions and fees. The commissions are generated by the buying and selling of securities. A stockbroker earns a commission every time you place a trading order; the amount shows up on your confirmation notice so you can see exactly how much the transaction cost you.

Mutual funds are a little different. You pay no commission at all when you buy no-load fund units, although the advisor may be compensated in another way—more on that in a moment. When you buy load funds, you are usually given a choice of purchase options. You can opt to pay a commission at the time you buy—this is known as a front-end load. Or you can choose a deferred sales charge (DSC) option, also known as a back-end load. If you select the DSC units, no commission is payable immediately, but if you sell within a certain period of time (typically seven years), a charge will be applied.

The compensation paid to financial advisors depends on which type of units you purchase. Front-end load units may cost as much as 6 percent (the maximum varies among companies), although the rate is negotiable with the advisor. For DSC units, a sliding scale is applied depending on how long you hold them. For example, AGF Management charges 5.5 percent if you sell the units within the first two years. The commission declines gradually to 1.5 percent during the seventh year. After that, no DSC applies.

If you choose the front-end load option, your financial advisor receives whatever commission has been negotiated with you. In the case of DSC purchases, the fund company pays a commission directly to the advisor, typically 5 percent.

But that's not the end of it. When you buy a stock, the advisor earns income only when you make the trade. Mutual funds are different. Advisors receive what is known as a "trailer fee." This is an amount paid every year by most (but not all) fund companies for as long as you hold the units. The rationale is that the trailer fee compensates the advisor for servicing your account. Critics contend that it acts as an incentive for advisors to discourage switches, even though a move might be in the client's interest. Moreover, although the money comes from the fund company, you actually pick up the tab because the cost is embedded in the fund's MER. All expenses are deducted before your net return is calculated.

The amount of the trailer fee depends on the nature of the fund itself and the type of unit purchased. The AGF prospectus requires more than a page to show all the permutations and combinations. In the case of AGF, its money market and short-term funds pay a trailer fee of 0.25 percent, other fixed-income funds pay 0.5 percent, equity and balanced funds 1 percent, and portfolio funds 1.25 percent. Remember, these amounts are received by the advisor every year.

These fees represent the main conflict of interest facing advisors. Suppose you have $100,000 to invest. If the advisor recommends that all the money go into money market and short-term funds, he will receive $250 a year in trailer fees. If he advises putting half into fixed-income funds and half into equity funds, he will get $750 a year. And if he suggests putting everything into a portfolio fund, he'll receive $1,250 every year! That's five times more than if you chose short-term investments. That has to be in the back of an advisor's mind when he looks at a new account.

The fees also act as a deterrent to making an account more defensive when stock markets are going through a rough time. Moving some assets from an equity fund to a money market or bond fund during such periods is only prudent, but the advisor will be out of pocket because of the reduced trailer fee.

I have come across many instances where this inherent conflict of interest has cost an investor dearly. One such case was brought to my attention by a friend who had been looking into the financial affairs of his mother-in-law. She was in her eighties but still living independently.

She had been left a sizeable estate by her late husband, and the money had been managed by the same firm for several years.

When my friend looked at the account, he was surprised to find that a large percentage of the assets were in equity funds, much more than would normally be appropriate for a person of her age. He also felt that the income stream was inadequate for her needs, and that the fees were too high. He suggested his mother-in-law switch to another company. She was very reluctant to do so. Her advisor was a "nice young man" who came to her condo to discuss her financial needs, a service she much appreciated.

But the plain fact was that the portfolio was badly designed for her situation and appeared to be structured to maximize the fees paid to the advisor. It was only when my friend was able to demonstrate this that his mother-in-law finally agreed the service she received was coming at a very high price in terms of reduced income and elevated risk exposure, and she moved the account elsewhere.

FEE-BASED ACCOUNTS

Switching to a fee-based account mitigates this conflict of interest because you then become eligible to purchase F units. They do not have any sales commissions attached and do not pay trailers. However, you have to pay the advisor yourself, in the form of an annual fee based on the value of the account.

I received an email from a reader who was trying to figure out whether his financial advisor was charging a fair price for his services. "Please let me know if you consider a 1.5 percent fee on an RRSP valued at $268,000 to be satisfactory," he wrote. It's a reasonable question. The problem is that there is no cut-and-dried answer. The most honest response I could offer is "It depends."

I'll explain what I mean in a moment, but first some background. Fee-based accounts provide compensation for advisors through an annual assessment of the total value of the assets under management. So if, for example, your account is worth $100,000 and the fee is 2 percent, your cost for that year will be $2,000. Usually, but not always, the value of the account at the start of each year is the reference point for the calculation.

The advantage for advisors is certainty. They know exactly how much income they will receive from each account in any given year, which makes budgeting much easier. For clients, a fee-based account means that all stock trades are commission-free. Plus, the F-class mutual fund units come with zero commission and reduced management expenses. Those lower costs translate into higher returns. Also, if an account is non-registered, the fee is tax-deductible.

The move to fee-based accounts is likely to accelerate in the coming years as pressure builds to move away from the commission and trailer-fee system that has prevailed for decades. Countries such as Great Britain and Australia are implementing new rules that effectively ban commission-based advisor compensation in favour of a fee-only structure. There has been talk of similar action in Canada, but the idea is strongly opposed by Advocis, the Financial Advisors Association of Canada, in part on the grounds that it could restrict professional financial planning to the wealthy.

In any event, such a drastic change is several years away, if it ever happens. In the meantime, we have to deal with the situation in place, which brings me back to the reader's question: What is a reasonable fee for his RRSP? As I said, it depends, and the fee is usually negotiable. Several factors have to be considered.

For starters, the size of the account makes a big difference. A fee of 1 percent on a million-dollar account is much more palatable to an advisor than the same charge on a $100,000 account. Remember, advisors have costs that have to be paid out of the fees and commissions they collect, and they all want to end the year with a reasonable profit.

The next consideration is the nature of the account. It's more expensive and time-consuming for an advisor to handle an actively traded account that is invested primarily in stocks than one that is heavily focused on fixed-income securities. So for the equity-based account, 1.5 percent to 2 percent is normal. The fee for an account that keeps 70 percent or more in bonds and cash should be somewhat less. If all the assets are invested in mutual funds, some advisors charge as little as 1 percent, although 1.25 percent is more common.

Then there's the question of time—how much does the advisor have to devote to the account over the year? Time is money, after all, so the more demanding you are, the higher the fee the advisor is likely to request.

Also, don't be surprised if your advisor asks for a fee increase next year. New securities regulations have saddled brokers and dealers with an increasing amount of administrative paperwork in recent years. This means a lot more time must be spent on each individual account—time you may not be aware of because it's all behind-the-scenes stuff.

A broker told me confidentially that three years ago he had two full-time assistants, one to handle administrative matters and the other for research and order taking. He had to let the researcher go when the market crash caused business to dry up. Now he has been forced to take on a second part-time employee to help deal with the growing administrative requirements. The extra cost is coming out of his pocket right now, but at some point clients will likely be asked to foot at least part of the bill.

It all boils down to this: if you have a fee-based account, or are considering moving to one, schedule a face-to-face meeting with your advisor and discuss the cost considerations openly. The result should be a fee that both parties feel is fair and reasonable.

FIDUCIARIES

Fiduciaries are people who have a legal responsibility to place the interests of the clients ahead of their own. For example, a corporate director has a fiduciary responsibility to shareholders. The executor of an estate has a fiduciary responsibility to the heirs. However, most financial advisors do *not* have a fiduciary responsibility to their clients.

Warren MacKenzie, president and CEO of Weigh House Investor Services, says this puts advisors in a very difficult position. "Most financial advisors are highly ethical individuals but unfortunately the system in which they work makes it almost impossible for them to put their clients' interests ahead of their own," he wrote in a guest column for my *Internet Wealth Builder* newsletter. "They almost always have a conflict of interest with which to contend. For example, if they always recommended exchange-traded funds (ETFs), which do not pay an annual trailer fee, over the mutual funds which do, they might not earn enough money to stay in business." (Weigh House, which is based in Toronto, has been certified by the Centre for Fiduciary Excellence [CEFEX], one of the first organizations in Canada to achieve this independent endorsement.)

Although the idea of holding advisors to a fiduciary standard makes a lot of sense, it will be strongly opposed by the financial community. Banks and brokerage firms will line up against the concept because, as MacKenzie points out, it would force their employees to act in clients' interests at the expense of potential profits. Advisors themselves are unlikely to support the idea because it would require them to complete a new level of certification and to reorganize the way in which they do business.

In the coming years, we may see more individuals and organizations like Weigh House operating under fiduciary standards, but I don't expect the majority of financial advisors to go along with the idea.

FEE-FOR-SERVICE ADVISORS

There are financial advisors and planners who operate on a fee-for-service basis. They charge by the hour or the job for their services and do not earn commissions of any kind. They are the closest thing to fiduciaries that we have in our financial services system. The problem is finding them.

One organization that should be doing everything possible to make it easy for investors to find a financial advisor who meets their needs is the Financial Advisors Association of Canada, commonly known as Advocis. The website (see appendix 4) actually offers a feature called Find an Advisor, where people can narrow their choices using various search terms. The criteria from which you can choose include "Fee-for-service planning," but the results are so meagre as to be useless.

I checked it out again as I was writing this book. I began by asking for a list of fee-for-service planners in Toronto. I got one hit. Perhaps they're divided among the city's former boroughs, I thought, so I tried North York, Scarborough, and Etobicoke. Nothing. Mississauga produced one name, as did Barrie, Richmond Hill, and Markham. Oakville, Hamilton, and Newmarket all drew blanks.

Other Canadian cities produced similar results. There were two hits for Vancouver but none for Calgary, Winnipeg, or Halifax. However, when I changed the criterion to "Financial planning," I got fourteen hits in Halifax, forty-two in Winnipeg, fifty-eight in Calgary, fifty-two in Vancouver, and fifty-nine in Toronto. Some of these may operate on a fee-for-service basis, but there is no way of telling from the listing. You have to review each individual profile and see if you can pinpoint a fee-based planner that way. A random spot check found none.

After that frustration, I went to the website of the Financial Planning Standards Council (FPSC). It says that one of the organization's primary mandates is "raising awareness of the importance of financial planning to Canadians," and the site really helps you to do that. When you click on the tab that reads "Search for a Planner Now," you are taken to the FPSC's Directory of CFP [Certified Financial Planner] Professionals in Good Standing. Ignore it—it is just a list of names with their home city. There is no screening mechanism.

Instead, click on the line that reads "If you are looking for a practicing Certified Financial Planner professional in your area, use our Find a Local CFP Professional Google map tool." This enables you to pinpoint planners in proximity to you on the basis of their method of compensation, their specialities, and the languages they speak. For example, you can look for a Cantonese-speaking, fee-based professional who specializes in estate planning. The feature even includes a Google map that pinpoints locations. This is well worth checking out. Of course, it does not tell us anything about the quality of the planner's work. That's up to you to determine.

I also had good luck doing a Google search with the

entry "fee-for-service financial planners Toronto." I not only found the names of several companies that operate on a fee-only basis but also came across a useful feature on the *MoneySense* website that lists fee-only planners in several provinces (see appendix 4).

WHAT TO DO?

Clearly, the financial services business has a lot of problems. Some bad apples have tainted its image, and the structural conflict of interest is a serious and ongoing problem that won't be solved easily. Despite all this, the evidence indicates that people with a financial advisor generally do better with their investments than those who take a do-it-yourself approach. In a report published in mid-2010 titled "The Value of Advice," the Investment Funds Institute of Canada (IFIC) found that households that use an advisor have far more investible assets than those that do not. This held true across all income levels.

The study also found that people who use an advisor are far more likely to have RRSPs, RESPs, and TFSAs than those who don't, and that those with an advisor tend to be less conservative and have more money in the stock market. Whether that's a good thing depends on your point of view.

Asked about their comfort level relating to their retirement savings, current financial condition, and debt load, people with advisors consistently indicated they were more satisfied. They also expressed a higher degree of confidence in the future. "Having advice is strongly associated with the accumulation of financial wealth regardless of income level or age of household," the report concluded.

I agree that having a good advisor is critical to the financial health of most families. Few people outside the industry have the time and the motivation to become experts in the complex world of investing and money management. When we need medical advice, we don't (or shouldn't) try to do it ourselves; we consult a professional. It should be the same for the family finances.

But as we have seen, finding someone you can trust is not a straightforward matter and it's easy to make a mistake. Until such time as the industry deals with the problems I have described (or regulators force it to do so), we have to tread very carefully. There is no simple formula for choosing a reliable advisor, but you'll find some suggestions that may be helpful further on in this book (beginning on page 253).

HARSH REALITY 9
YOU HAVE TO MAKE SACRIFICES

I never met my great-great-grandfather, but I doubt that he worried much about retirement. Back then, few people lived to sixty-five, and those who did usually kept on working for as long as they were physically able to. After that, they depended on their children for support.

The German chancellor Otto von Bismarck is regarded as the first politician to introduce old age pensions, during the 1880s. In 1935, the United States brought in Social Security, which remains one of the legacies of Franklin Roosevelt's New Deal. However, it wasn't until after the Second World War that government pensions and retirement planning became institutionalized in Canada. Old Age Security was introduced in 1952, followed by the Canada and Quebec pension plans in 1966. During this period, more public- and private-sector employees were given access to pension plans, usually the defined benefit type. So no one worried much about retirement. Many workers had a pension plan they could count on, and CPP/OAS provided an income cornerstone for the rest.

Welcome to the harsh new world of the twenty-first century, where almost everyone is concerned about retirement. And unless you are in the military or work in the public sector, you are right to worry. As we have seen so far in this book, it is becoming increasingly difficult to ensure a decent retirement income. Without major sacrifices, many people will come up short and find themselves facing tough decisions as they approach their target retirement age.

How worried are we? The Canadian Institute of Actuaries recently published a survey titled "Retirement Risk: Defining Retirement Horizons" (available online at the institute's website). It contained some surprising revelations about the mindset of pre-retirees (defined as Canadians over forty-five who have not yet retired) and those who have already retired.

The poll was conducted by Ipsos Reid in early 2010. It found that of more than one thousand pre-retirees surveyed, 72 percent were concerned about "maintaining a reasonable standard of living for the rest of their life." Assuming this is anywhere near indicative of attitudes in the general population (the margin of error was +/–3 percent), this suggests that almost three-quarters of people in this age group believe they may run into financial problems when they stop work. Among those, 41 percent believe they may be forced to reduce their standard of living in retirement.

Ipsos Reid probed further and discovered that 62 percent of pre-retirees are concerned about having enough money to pay for adequate health care. This is a startling figure in a country where access to medical treatment is supposed to be free. When the researchers asked why, the respondents focused on the future costs of such things as nursing homes, suggesting that a significant number expect to live to an old age. "This suggests that older Canadians doubt that the current public system will make the delivery of services available to them, and that they will have to rely on private delivery at a cost that is not known," the report said.

The same percentage (62 percent) said they are worried about running out of money after they stop work at a time in their lives when they have nothing to fall back on except welfare.

Given this high level of concern, you'd think the pre-retirees would be acting aggressively to improve their financial outlook. Some are—but far too many seem to be waiting for someone to wave a magic wand and solve all their problems. The survey found that 57 percent plan to eliminate their consumer debt, while 4 percent appear content to let it ride. Only half the respondents intend to save as much as possible; 12 percent have no savings plans, and it is not clear what the rest are thinking. The study found that 46 percent intend to pay off the mortgage (16 percent don't), and 44 percent intend to cut back spending (19 percent have no such goal).

Amazingly, despite the concerns and lack of prepared-ness, many pre-retirees believe they are financially able to stop work. Clearly, these baby boomers are living in a dream world! And they don't seem to be doing much about it; only 35 percent have talked to a financial advisor about their situation, while 18 percent discussed it with their bank.

"In many ways, this survey is a story of contrasts," the report concluded. "While the majority of retirees and a significant number of pre-retirees feel confident about their financial future, a majority of both groups are concerned about maintaining a reasonable standard of living for the rest of their lives. Often there are gaps between what Canadian retirees and pre-retirees think and feel about retirement issues and what they are doing to follow through. For example, while a majority of Canadians take retirement planning and preparation seriously, only half seek financial advice from financial advisors, banks, newspaper articles, internet sites, family members, books or co-workers."

This report and others like it suggest that baby boomers are not prepared to make the sacrifices needed to ensure a comfortable retirement. As the most privileged demographic cohort in history, they have lived well and they don't want that to change now. But unless they *do* start to make sacrifices, their concerns about the future will likely become reality over the next twenty years. Here are some of the things they need to do.

FINANCIAL SACRIFICES

If there is one theme that dominates the whole retirement discussion, it is that we are not saving enough. People hear this message so often from so many sources that there is a danger it is becoming background noise.

Several years ago, David Chilton self-published a book that was eventually picked up by a publisher and went on to become a runaway bestseller, with an amazing two million copies sold in Canada. It was called *The Wealthy Barber*, and it focused on one simple theme: pay yourself first. It's a concept that's as old as civilization. As the great Roman orator Cicero put it: "Men do not understand how great a revenue is economy." Chilton dusted it off and popularized it by advising his readers to put aside 10 percent of their income and invest it for the future before they spend a cent.

Understandably, publishers were after him to write something else, hoping that lightning would strike twice. He consistently resisted the idea because, as he said on his website, "luck played such a huge role in *The Wealthy Barber*'s success that I didn't want to tempt fate."

But finally he changed his mind and wrote a sequel, titled *The Wealthy Barber Returns*. Why? Frustration with the failure of people to do anything to safeguard their future, he says. "After watching Canadians' savings rates plunge, debt levels skyrocket and investment returns consistently disappoint over the last decade, I was pulling my hair out," he writes. "I wondered, 'How can I help?'"

The sequel, which was published in the fall of 2011, quickly made the bestseller lists. Whether it will actually change anything remains to be seen.

As I pointed out in the chapter titled "Our Savings Rates Are Pitiful," boomers who have procrastinated until now may find that putting aside even 10 percent of income may be nowhere near enough. They may be looking at 15 to 20 percent or more, depending on their age and situation. That's a huge commitment, especially for someone who is starting from zero.

The high debt load that many families are carrying only makes matters worse. When 15 percent or more of household income is already committed to debt servicing, saving seems almost impossible.

Unpalatable as it may be, you must come to grips with some hard decisions if you are in this situation. Get rid of high-interest debt (e.g., credit cards) and start socking away at least 10 percent of your income. If you're over forty, make it a minimum of 15 percent. If this is a sacrifice you are not prepared to make and you don't have a top-tier pension plan, then you better win a lottery or inherit a lot of money. Otherwise, retirement is going to be as bleak as many people fear it will be.

LIFESTYLE SACRIFICES

In all likelihood, you won't be able to make the financial sacrifices needed without some changes in your lifestyle. Very few people can suddenly start saving 10 or 15 percent of their income without missing a beat. Something's got to give.

Only you and your family can decide what that something is. But it can't be a one-time purchase. Forgoing that new fifty-inch high-definition television set won't do the job. You need to free up money every month, for years to come. That will be hard on everyone. Children won't understand why they have to give up hockey or ballet lessons. They'll complain even more when you cut back to basic cable. You may have to take public transit to work and leave the car in the garage. Two dinners a week may be meatless. If only one spouse is working, that may have to change.

Does this sound like an austerity program to you? It is—domestic style. It's the same kind of stark reality that was imposed on the Greeks in 2011, and it is coming to other countries that have lived beyond their means for years. Households must face up to the same economic truths.

There is no way to sugar-coat this. If you've let the savings slide with a perpetual promise to get to it next year, time has run out. Look at your life, decide what the priorities are, and start taking action.

TIME SACRIFICES

There is no escaping the fact that, collectively, we are financial dolts. The Federal Task Force on Financial Literacy returned to this theme repeatedly in its report, although its language was much more polite. The survey commissioned by the Canadian Institute of Actuaries found the same thing, noting that few Canadians have read a retirement-planning book, researched the subject on the Internet, or even talked to family members about the matter. It's almost as if we don't want to know.

In one of my early books, I used the analogy of baking a cake. Just putting flour, sugar, eggs, baking powder, and milk into a bowl will produce nothing more than a gooey mess. You need to know what proportions to use, how to prepare the pan, and how long to bake it. In short, you need a recipe. It could come from your mom's old cookbook, or you may find it in a magazine or online, but if you don't have a step-by-step guide, the cake will probably be inedible.

Money management is the same. You need a recipe. In fact, like any good cook, you need many recipes—one for budgeting, one for handling the mortgage, one for saving, one for investing, one for getting out of debt—a whole book of them.

In short, you need to educate yourself about money. That takes commitment and time. Can you spare one hour a day? Before you say no, think about how much time you spend in front of the television set or playing video games. If it is more than an hour a day, you *do* have the time. It's only a matter of reallocating it.

No one likes being told they have to make sacrifices. And sometimes they don't have to be as extreme as those I've described here. For example, a defined contribution pension plan that I looked at recently offered members the option to contribute 4, 5, or 6 percent of their income. The employer matched the amount. So by increasing her personal contribution from 4 to 6 percent, an employee was actually moving from 8 to 12 percent in terms of total savings. Assuming a $50,000 salary and a 6 percent average annual compound rate of return, this would add another $158,000 to her pension pool over thirty years. At an 8 percent average annual return, the gain is almost $227,000. That's a pretty nice bonus for an extra 2 percent contribution.

So the starting point is to look at all your options and choose the least painful ones first. It may turn out to be easier than you think—and the kids can still have their hockey and ballet lessons.

PART TWO
THE SOLUTIONS

SOLUTION 1
MAKE A PLAN

Ask yourself the following question: In the past year, did I spend more time planning the family vacation or planning for retirement? If you're honest and you're like most Canadians, the answer is probably the former.

It's understandable. Planning a holiday is fun—in fact, it's sometimes more fun than the vacation itself. You can visit potential destinations online, check out the hotels, schedule the trip around local festivals, see what activities are available for the kids, and compare prices. And gratification comes soon after the planning stage ends.

Retirement planning is a slog. You have to wade through myriad details, crunch numbers, and do some serious thinking about the future. To make matters worse, gratification is many years away. It's hard to get excited about a payoff that may be twenty-five or thirty years down the road.

But here's the problem: the vacation is over in a couple of weeks. If you didn't plan it well, you only have to endure the consequences for a short time. A bad or non-existent retirement plan, however, will make your life miserable for many years. Maybe it's time to shift priorities.

According to a survey released by Sun Life Financial in

March 2011, only about two Canadians in ten (21 percent) have a financial plan. The study found that of those with a plan, 84 percent are confident about being able to meet their basic living expenses in retirement; only 48 percent of those with no plan are similarly confident. You have to wonder why that group is so complacent!

Another revealing finding was that the average Canadian now expects to retire at sixty-eight. That's three years later than the finding in the previous year, and it suggests that the market crash of 2008 was a wake-up call for many.

So how concerned should you be about your retirement? I've devised a Retirement Worry Index that should help you figure that out. Read through it and decide which category you fit into. Then we'll discuss what to do about it.

YOUR RETIREMENT WORRY INDEX

WORRY INDEX: VERY LOW. You have a generous defined benefit pension plan sponsored by a senior government (federal or provincial), the military, the police, or a powerful union (e.g., teachers). You also have personal savings, own your own home, and have little or no debt.

Analysis: You're in great shape. Enjoy your retirement years.

WORRY INDEX: LOW. You have a defined benefit pension plan from a corporation or a junior level of government (e.g., a municipality). You have some personal savings, own your home, and have little debt.

You are probably in good shape, but even though your pension is "guaranteed," it could be at risk if the sponsor runs into financial problems. It happens—as we saw in the case of the Nortel pensioners, who have been in a protracted battle to get at least some of the benefits they expected. This loss of pension rights used to be almost unheard of. But the Great Recession of 2008–2009 changed a lot.

Analysis: Protect yourself by adding to your savings.

WORRY INDEX: MEDIUM. You have a defined contribution pension plan, some personal savings, little debt, and you own your own home. A defined contribution plan does not guarantee a specific level of pension at retirement, but it is better than nothing, especially if the employer is matching your contributions. These plans are structured in such a way that you invest your own personal pool of cash in the many options that are offered.

Analysis: The amount of your pension will ultimately depend on how well your investments perform, so it is essential to pay close attention to that money and manage it carefully.

WORRY INDEX: ELEVATED. You have no pension plan. You have some RRSP/TFSA savings, but not as much as you think you need. You own your home and have modest debts. This is not a hopeless situation by any means, but it requires some immediate action.

Analysis: You need to pay off the debts and begin to boost your savings rate. The more years you have left until your planned retirement, the less of a financial strain this will be—as long as you don't procrastinate.

WORRY INDEX: HIGH. You have no pension plan and limited RRSP/TFSA savings, and you still have a mortgage and are carrying credit card debt. If you aren't worried about what will happen when you stop work, you clearly don't understand the situation. You're probably thinking that a combination of the Canada Pension Plan and Old Age Security will provide for your needs. They will certainly help, but unless you plan to scale back your lifestyle considerably, they won't be enough.

Analysis: You need to pay off your credit card debt as fast as possible and then cut up the card so you don't incur any more. Once that is done, direct all the money that went to the monthly card payments to an RRSP and use the tax refund to pay down the mortgage. Depending on your age, you may have to postpone your target retirement date for a few years.

WORRY INDEX: EXTREME. You have no pension plan, hardly any savings, a big mortgage and other debts, and you're supporting other family members, such as an aged parent. This is almost a desperation scenario.

Analysis: You should seek the help of a financial planner to get your affairs on track, but if you are within ten years of your planned retirement age, your options may be limited. You may be forced to depend on income-tested programs such as the Guaranteed Income Supplement (GIS) to make ends meet after you stop work. If that appears to be a possibility, don't put any savings into an RRSP because withdrawals count as income and will reduce your GIS payments. If you are able to save anything, use a TFSA instead.

I hope you don't fall into the High or Extreme categories, although I know that many people will if they are honest with themselves. But unless you are at the Very Low level, you need to take some action to improve your financial prospects after retirement. Otherwise, you may have to keep working for a lot longer than you planned.

HOW MUCH WILL YOU NEED?

As I said back in the first chapter, there is no simple answer to the question of how much money is needed to retire comfortably. You have to look at all the variables and make some choices.

Start with your planned retirement age. At one time, sixty-five was the standard, but not anymore. Retirement has become a moving target, with an increasing number of people working into their seventies. About the only thing we can say with any certainty is that the idea of retiring young—the "Freedom 55" slogan of the London Life advertising campaign—has become an elusive dream for most people. But of course, the longer you plan to work, the less you need to save for retirement. The math is simple: more years of employment income and pension credits mean fewer years of living off pensions and savings.

Next, think about your retirement lifestyle. It will almost certainly be more active than that of your parents and grandparents, thanks to the advances in medical care and our awareness of the importance of nutrition and exercise. An active lifestyle is a lot more fun than staring at the TV all day, but it costs money to travel, play golf, and spend winters in the Sunbelt.

Then there's the question of how long you'll be around. In an ideal world, we'd die on the day our money ran out, but that's not the way it works.

All of this reinforces my "It depends" answer to the question of how much money you'll need.

THE STARTING POINT

You can't plan for the future unless you know what you want the future to be. So the starting point is to cast your mind forward and ask yourself four questions about your retirement. The answers may evolve as the years pass, but you need to begin somewhere. Here are the questions:

WHAT IS IT? By this, I mean what does retirement mean to you? Do you see yourself stopping work completely and just kicking back? Some people like that idea, especially when they are young and under a lot of career pressure. But I can tell you from experience that the older you get, the less likely you are to want to opt out entirely. Most people I know who are nearing retirement age and are in good health tell me that they are afraid they would be bored within a few months if they cut themselves off completely from their job. They talk about working part time, consulting, or setting up a home business. Those who don't want to stay employed often choose to do volunteer work.

WHEN IS IT? You need to set a target date for ending your working career, or at least this phase of it. You don't have to stick to it; circumstances may change as the years pass. But without a target retirement date, you can't do any meaningful financial planning.

HOW LONG WILL IT BE? Many people worry about outliving their money, and they're right to do so. As I pointed out in the first chapter, life expectancy has increased at an almost unbelievable rate in the past century and continues to do so. A man who makes it to sixty-five now can expect to be around for another eighteen years, a woman for twenty-one. Of course, the longer you live, the more money you'll need to carry you through. Since there is no way of predicting how long that will be, I suggest assuming the best-case scenario and planning for at least thirty years in retirement.

HOW WILL I LIVE IT? This is perhaps the most difficult question to come to grips with. What do you *really* want to do with those retirement years? The answer may not become clear until after you stop work, but you have to make a stab at it because a large part of your planning will depend on your desired lifestyle. You may want to travel more—take those dream vacations that you never had time for while you were working. You may want to play more golf or tennis. You may want to spend more time with the grand-children—but not twenty-four hours a day. (One of the guilty pleasures of being a grandparent is being able to hand the kids back to Mom and Dad when they get too rambunctious or throw a temper tantrum.)

In fact, a comprehensive retirement plan begins with a clear understanding of the lifestyle to which you aspire once you stop work. Everything else, including the financial projections, flows from there. Simply saying that you want to live comfortably when you retire isn't enough. You must have an understanding of what that will mean in terms of your lifestyle, and what it will cost to achieve and maintain it.

So use your imagination. You know what you like and don't like. Your tastes and your dreams are probably not going to change a lot as you grow older, but even if they do, there is plenty of time to make adjustments. To give you a personal example, my wife and I knew from the time we were married that we would one day like to live by the sea. That wasn't possible through most of my working career, but we never lost sight of that goal. We finally achieved it in 1997, with the purchase of a winter home in Florida that looked out over a bay teeming with dolphins, aquatic birds, fish, and even manatees. To us, it was paradise, and we enjoyed it together for fourteen years before her ill health no longer made it feasible to winter there. What do you want when you retire? Something similar? A ski chalet in Whistler? A cottage in Muskoka or the Laurentians? None of the above? This is not an exercise in idle dreaming. It is the first stage of a long-range plan that will help you decide how you would like to spend your later years and enable you to build the financial resources needed to achieve your goals.

To help get you started, I devised a Personal Lifestyle Planner for my book *The Retirement Time Bomb.*

Many people have told me they found it very useful, so I have included it in this book as well. You'll find it in appendix 1. Spend an evening or two going through it with your spouse or partner. You may discover some common hopes and desires that you never knew about before.

Finally, you and your spouse or partner should decide which of the following statements best describes how you hope to live in retirement:

a) We want to maintain our current standard of living.
b) We want to have a higher standard of living with enough money to spend on luxuries.
c) We have modest needs and will not need much income to be comfortable in retirement.

WHAT WILL IT COST?

Settling on a future lifestyle is an important starting point, but now you have to move from daydreaming to math. That involves putting a price tag on the way you want to live. Yes, that means some work, but it will be time well spent. Giving up a few hours of television now may change your entire way of living in future years.

There are two ways to estimate your retirement income needs. One is the quick method and the second is the Expense Estimator at the back of this book. The quick method simply involves using your current family before-tax income as a base and multiplying by a target percentage to calculate your post-retirement income. What percentage should that be? In the past, the federal government and many actuaries used a figure of 70 percent, based on the theory that expenses will decline after you quit work. It now seems that's not the case.

Statistics Canada looked at household spending and income patterns from 1982 to 2008 and came up with some surprising numbers. It turns out that people in their early seventies spend only 5 percent less than they did when they were in their forties. Unfortunately, their income fell by 16 percent. The patterns changed—less money went to food and clothing, more to health care and residential costs—but overall, people were spending almost as much to live after retirement as they did before. If you haven't planned for that, you're in trouble!

Based on this, I suggest you try to ensure that you will receive 95 percent of your pre-retirement income after you stop work. In that case, my quick and easy formula would be this:

$$\frac{\text{This year's family}}{\text{gross income} \times 95\%} = \text{Retirement spending needs}$$

If your household income this year is $70,000, you'd need $66,500 in today's purchasing power to maintain your standard of living after retirement if your spending pattern is similar to that in StatsCan's findings.

Of course, if you know you'll be able to get by on less you can aim lower, but you'd better be very sure of your calculations. I prefer to err on the high side—it is always better to have too much money than too little. So I suggest your goal should be to bring in 100 percent of your pre-retirement income, if that is at all feasible.

If you want more precise figures, you'll have to do some additional work. You'll find the second, more detailed way to calculate your post-retirement needs in the Expense Estimator, which appears in appendix 2. It will help you prepare a more accurate projection of your anticipated costs when you stop work.

THE INFLATION FACTOR

The amount of money you'll need when you stop work will be directly affected by the increase in the cost of living between now and then. The more years you have until retirement, the greater the inflationary impact will be. If you don't account for that, you could face problems down the road. An RBC survey published in early 2011 found that within the previous twelve months, 41 percent of retirees had gone back to work, full or part time. In many of these cases, it was because inflation had eroded their purchasing power to the point that they could not make ends meet.

In recent years, inflation has been under control, held down by the Great Recession of 2008–2009 and the slow economic recovery. The Bank of Canada has a target range of 1 to 3 percent for annual increases, although 2 percent is the preferred figure. If there is a danger that inflation will rise above that band, the bank will normally raise interest rates to control it.

The table in appendix 3 enables you to convert today's dollars to a future purchasing power value, based on the number of years to retirement and the expected inflation rate. For example, if you have thirty years remaining until retirement and inflation averages only 1 percent annually, you must increase your cost projection by more than one-third to maintain the purchasing power in today's dollars. At a 2 percent average inflation rate, you will need to increase your estimate by 72 percent. So if you think you will need $50,000 of post-retirement income in today's dollars, that will really be $86,000 in thirty years' time.

So how do you cope with this situation, especially since we don't know what will happen to the inflation rate in the years to come? Here are some suggestions.

First, assume a higher rate of inflation than you actually expect. Let's go back to Ottawa's 1 to 3 percent range. In effect, the federal government is telling us that it won't switch back into a strong anti-inflation mode until the CPI (the consumer price index) starts to move towards the upper end of that band. So under present conditions, the 2 percent figure looks like a decent average to work with. The prudent planner will want to build in a cushion, however, and I recommend you use 3 percent as your average annual inflation target. If inflation comes in below that, you will have some extra spending money available.

Second, determine how much of your anticipated retirement income will be protected against inflation. All of the main government support programs (CPP, OAS, and GIS) have built-in inflation adjustors. If that policy is maintained, that part of your income will be secure in terms of purchasing power. Some pension plans also offer inflation protection, especially for those working in the public sector. If you are a pension plan member, find out the policy in this regard. If your plan does not have inflation protection now, it's unlikely to be added in the future because of the high cost involved. If you design a RRIF or a LIF to make payments under the government's minimum withdrawal formula, the amount you receive will increase each year, as long as the capital base isn't eroded. However, if inflation returns to higher levels, the annual increases may not be enough to compensate. There are also inflation-indexed annuities available, although they are expensive.

Once you are able to estimate how much of your retirement income will have built-in inflation protection, you will have an idea of what percentage is fixed and therefore vulnerable to rising prices.

Third, develop a plan to ensure that your income will rise according to your needs. There are several possible ways to increase retirement income. They include the following:

POSTPONE CPP PAYMENTS. Although you become eligible for full payments at sixty-five, you don't have to start collecting Canada Pension Plan benefits until age seventy. As of 2013, every month that you wait will increase the amount of your pension by 0.7 percent, or 8.4 percent annually. If you wait until seventy, your pension will be 42 percent more than if you'd started drawing it at sixty-five. So if you don't need your CPP immediately to make ends meet, put it off.

When you start to draw it, that extra income should more than compensate for inflation in the intervening years.

POSTPONE CONVERTING RRSPS. You don't have to close your RRSP until the last day of the year in which you turn seventy-one. If you don't need the money in your plan immediately, leave it alone. The longer the assets continue to grow tax-sheltered, the more capital you will have to draw on when it's needed. If you need only some of the RRSP income now, arrange for a partial withdrawal. You'll obtain immediate cash flow while the balance continues to grow.

MANAGE YOUR RRSP/RRIF FOR CONTINUED GROWTH. Just because you've retired doesn't mean your RRSP savings need to stagnate. Although you should put a greater emphasis on safety at this stage, don't go overboard. Retain a significant growth component in your RRSP—and in your RRIF, when you move on to that stage—so your capital base can increase.

IF POSSIBLE, CONTINUE INVESTING. You may find yourself in the fortunate position of having more income than you really need in your early retirement years. Believe it or not, it does happen. Take advantage of this by investing the surplus, starting with maxing out your TFSA. This will increase the capital available for income generation later.

There are many ways to beat the inflation problem. But you need to have a plan that takes it into account.

WHERE WILL THE MONEY COME FROM?

Once you have an idea of how you want to live in retirement and how much it will cost, you'll have to focus on the sources of your future income. Where is that money going to come from? There are six possibilities, not including windfalls like a lottery or a big inheritance.

1. *Government retirement programs.* Basically, we're talking about Old Age Security and the Canada and Quebec pension plans here. The amount of the CPP retirement benefit will depend on how many years you contributed to the plan and your income during that time (with some exceptions for low-income years and maternity leave). Everyone sixty-five and older gets the same OAS payment provided they have been residents of Canada for at least forty years. (Those who have been here for between ten and forty years qualify for a reduced payment.) Both OAS and CPP payments gradually increase over time because of indexing. However, these programs will provide a relatively small part of your total retirement income needs—about 38 percent of pre-retirement earnings for an average worker making $45,000. The higher your income, the lower the percentage that will be replaced by CPP/OAS.

2. *Guaranteed pension plans, also known as defined benefit pension plans.* If you don't work for a government, you are unlikely to have a luxury plan of this type. The private sector is increasingly turning to defined contribution plans.

3. *Non-guaranteed pension plans.* These include defined contribution plans, group RRSPs, and (if approved by Parliament) the proposed pooled registered pension plans (PRPPs). None of these programs guarantee you a specific amount of money when you retire. Your income will depend on the total contributions you made to the plan and the returns earned on the portfolio.

4. *Personal savings.* This money will mainly be invested in RRSPs, TFSAs, and non-registered investment accounts. Depending on what other income is available, this could be a critical source of your retirement funding.

5. *Employment.* As we have seen, an increasing number of retirees are going back to work on a full- or part-time basis. Some do so because they want to keep active, but for many the driving force is financial necessity.

6. *Welfare.* I hope no one who reads this book will need to draw on this option, but many Canadians will. The GIS and the Allowance (paid to people between sixty and sixty-four) are the main federal government welfare sources. Of course the word "welfare" is never used, but that is what these payments really are—support for low-income seniors who would otherwise slip below the poverty line. Provincial and municipal governments also offer welfare benefits, as do some charities.

Taking all this into account, here are the key components of a comprehensive retirement plan:

- a well-planned savings program
- an estimate of income/expense needs
- a debt-reduction strategy
- pension plan knowledge
- an RRSP
- a TFSA
- the right securities
- an appropriate asset mix
- good risk management

We have already dealt with the first two points; the rest will be discussed in upcoming chapters.

PLANNING ISN'T EASY

In its final report, the Task Force on Financial Literacy acknowledged that retirement planning is "a significant challenge for some Canadians." The report cited several reasons for this, including:

- lack of awareness about the importance of saving for the future;
- poor understanding of the public and private pension systems;
- the "multitude and complexity" of retirement savings choices and pension plan features;

- the difficulty of accurately estimating life expectancy and retirement income needs; and
- behavioural factors that lead to failure to take action soon enough.

These are difficult to overcome, but it is certainly not a hopeless situation. The first three problems are educational. This book and others like it can provide significant help, as long as people are motivated enough to read them.

The fourth challenge—estimating life expectancy—is impossible to do in specific terms. But it is certainly feasible to estimate how long you'll be around by using the sophisticated life expectancy tables and calculators now available. Take your projected life expectancy, add five years to be conservative, and you'll have a reasonable figure to use in calculating the savings you will need.

An interesting life expectancy calculator can be found on the website of E.E.S. Financial Services (see appendix 4). You are asked to fill in your current age, height, and weight, and to answer a few questions (such as whether you have had a traffic accident in the past three years, how much you drink, whether you are a smoker, how high your blood pressure is, and whether there is a history of diabetes or cardiovascular problems in your family). The calculator then tells you how long you can expect to live. The only problem is that it is based on 1986–92 mortality tables published by the Canadian Institute of Actuaries. They're out of date by now, which is why I suggest adding a few years.

One interesting thing I discovered when I played around

with the variables was that losing fifteen pounds did not add a single year to my life expectancy. But reducing the number of alcoholic drinks per day to two added more than three years to my projected lifespan. Becoming a teetotaller didn't help at all, however; in fact, it cost me almost two years.

The behavioural problem is the most challenging, especially for younger people. In this age of consumerism, we are constantly being urged to spend, especially by such powerful forces as television advertising. It's difficult for those under thirty-five to take the concept of saving for retirement very seriously when there are more urgent priorities, such as buying a home and having children.

Recognizing these biases, the Task Force on Financial Literacy proposes that governments introduce more options to make the savings process easier, if not automatic. One idea is to give people the option of having tax refunds "automatically transferred into a personal savings account, RRSP or Tax-Free Savings Account, with a checkbox on tax forms to simplify and automate this process." The report justifies this type of approach by saying: "Behavioural research has shown that lump-sum transfers may be more prone to savings because individuals mentally account for these funds differently from regular income flows, seeing them as surplus or bonus funds that can be saved. People tend not to save money they have in their possession; rather, they are more willing to commit future earnings or windfalls to a saving mechanism."

I don't like the idea of forced saving, but options such as this make sense, as long as they are voluntary.

I wish I could say this whole planning process is easy. But that would be a lie. It requires some careful thought, hard work, and a genuine commitment to see the plan through. All I can do is show the way and try to make it as straightforward as possible. You and your family are the ones who will have to make it happen.

SOLUTION 2
PAY OFF DEBT

There was a time when the idea of carrying debt into retirement was almost unthinkable. It made no sense whatsoever. Paying off old debts at a time when income will probably be lower is a recipe for financial disaster. Everyone used to know that.

Well, they don't anymore. In April 2011, the Royal Bank published its second annual Retirement Myths and Realities Poll. The findings were unsettling. Only 56 percent of Canadians retire debt-free, down from 61 percent in 2010. This means that almost half the population is going into retirement carrying a debt load. That makes retirees extremely vulnerable to rising interest rates in the future.

The reasons for this vary, but a lot of it has to do with the way in which the baby boomers lived. They spent their adult years in a time of easy credit, when you could buy a luxury car with almost no money down and a house with a down payment of only 10 percent. It was, and is, a comfortable lifestyle, but it comes at a cost if you aren't able to clear the debts by the time you stop work.

The RBC poll, conducted by Ipsos Reid, was based on a sample of 2,245 adults aged fifty and over with household assets of at least $100,000. The findings showed that the types of debt most frequently carried into retirement are a home mortgage (23 percent), a line of credit (22 percent), and consumer debt including credit cards (15 percent).

Asked what they would do if money became tight as a result, many said they would stay in their homes but live more frugally and perhaps sell off some assets. The poll also found, however, that a surprising 41 percent of retiree respondents said they are returning to work because they need the money. That was a big jump from 32 percent the previous year. This is especially significant because the sample group was reasonably affluent.

When I wrote my first book on retirement back in 1991, I described what I called "The Four Pillars of Independence" on which a good plan should be based. Number one was Freedom from Debt. Nothing has changed in the more than twenty years since, except that the debt problem has become more serious. I have not been able to find any statistics on the number of people who retired with debt back then, but I would bet my house that it was a lot lower than it is today.

Let me make this crystal clear: carrying debt into retirement is dangerous and puts you at grave financial risk if interest rates rise. And the larger the debt load, the greater the risk.

One of the prime objectives of a retirement plan should be to eliminate all debt before you end your career. If that means working an additional year or two, so be it. You should aim to pay off all outstanding mortgage balances on your primary residence and on any vacation property you own. Five percent of the respondents to the Royal Bank poll said they were still carrying mortgages on second properties in retirement.

Beyond that, you need to pay off all credit cards, retire any investment loans, and get rid of any consumer loans you may still be carrying. Going into retirement debt-free will place you in a much more comfortable financial position, for three reasons.

First, interest payments are a drain on what will likely be a reduced income flow once you retire. If you must put aside a large chunk of money every month to service old debts, you may find yourself having to compensate by reducing your living standard.

Second, loans are more difficult to pay off after you retire. If your income drops, you'll find it harder to put money aside to reduce your outstanding principal. Nor will there be any windfalls, such as an annual bonus, to put towards debt repayment.

Third, and perhaps most important, carrying debt into retirement puts you at extreme risk. Interest rates have been unrealistically low in recent years as central banks responded to the Great Recession by slashing their target rates—in the U.S., effectively to zero. As of fall 2011, the target overnight rate set by the Bank of Canada was 1 percent. The prime rate used by commercial banks was 3 percent.

YOUR FINANCIAL RISK

Here's an example of the financial risk you will face when interest rates move higher, as they inevitably will. Let's assume you have a $100,000 home equity line of credit, which you have fully drawn against for renovations. These are variable rate loans, where the interest rate moves up or down to reflect any changes in prime.

Let's say your bank was charging you prime plus one-half percent interest, or 3.5 percent as of 2011. If you make no payments against the principal, the annual interest expense is $3,500. (It is actually slightly more than that because you are making monthly interest-only payments, but let's keep things simple for purposes of this illustration.)

The average prime rate in this country over the past decade is about 4.25 percent. If the rate should move back to that level, the interest rate on your line of credit would increase to 4.75 percent. The cost of servicing the debt would rise to $4,750 annually, a hike of 36 percent.

But historically, when central banks begin to raise rates, they don't stop at the average. There's a reason they are pushing rates higher: the economy is overheating and inflation is becoming a major concern. High interest rates are intended to take some of the steam out of the economy by making it more expensive to borrow money.

According to the Bank of Canada website, the prime rate was as high as 6.25 percent in the summer and fall of 2007 as economic growth surged in the years following the 2000 high-tech crash. We could easily see those levels again in the next few years as the world recovers from the recent series of financial shocks.

With prime at 6.25 percent, the interest rate on your line of credit would be 6.75 percent, which means it would cost you $6,750 a year to carry—and that's in after-tax dollars. That's almost double what you paid in 2011. But now you're retired and there is no extra money coming in to cover that expense. That would put a big strain on your retirement budget. Do you have any idea where that extra money would come from?

That's why part of your retirement plan must be directed to debt elimination. Set up a repayment program to ensure that all your loans are paid off by the time you plan to stop work (or even sooner, if at all possible).

THE FIRST PRIORITY

Your first priority should be non-tax-deductible debt carrying the highest interest rate. For most Canadians, that means credit card balances. Unpaid credit card bills are one of the most expensive forms of consumer loans available, and the interest rates charged by the card companies tend to be very slow in coming down, even when rates generally are very low.

In mid-2011, when prime was at 3 percent, the interest rate on balances carried on most Royal Bank cards was 19.99 percent. Three premium cards were as high as 20.5 percent. Those rates border on usury, but they are the norm for most bank credit cards. Those issued by retailers tend to be even more expensive. The rate quoted for my latest Hudson's Bay Company MasterCard was 28.8 percent!

Step one in getting rid of credit card debt is to move the balance owing to a less expensive card or, if possible, a line of credit. At the time of writing, the Capital One SmartLine Platinum MasterCard was offering an interest rate of 5.99 percent on new purchases and balance transfers for three years, as long as you paid your bills on time. After that, you would be charged a variable rate of prime plus 4.99 percent.

Competition among the card companies is very intense. To find the lowest rate available right now, go to RedFlagDeals.com, then click on Financial Services, Credit Card Comparisons, and Low Interest Credit Cards. By reducing the interest rate on your credit card debt, you will free up more money to pay down the principal and retire the loan faster. Just don't make the mistake of continuing to add to the debt load. The goal is to eliminate it.

AFTER THE CREDIT CARDS

Once the cards have been dealt with, use the money that has been freed up to attack other high-interest loans. A car loan, if you have one, should probably be next on your list. Once all your non-deductible consumer loans have been retired, go after your mortgage. Take advantage of any prepayment clauses in your contract and make the maximum penalty-free payments you can afford.

Remember, you can pay off any amount you want with no penalty at each renewal date.

Your final target, once all other debt has been eliminated, should be any tax-deductible loans you've incurred for business, education, or investment purposes. The reason for leaving these until last is simple—once the tax advantages are taken into account, they're the cheapest form of borrowing available to most people.

Some young people make the mistake of paying off student loans while running up credit card debt at the same time. This can be very costly. Student loan rates are usually quite low, and the interest is tax-deductible. For example, loans under the Ontario Student Assistance Program (OSAP) carry an interest charge of prime plus 1 percent and don't have to be fully paid off until fifteen years after graduation. This is cheap money. It makes no sense to exchange it for more expensive credit card debt.

I'll give the last word on this to Lee Anne Davies, the head of Retirement Strategies for RBC. "To help make your retirement dreams a reality," she says, "our advice is to start early and prepare a comprehensive financial action plan that will keep you focused on paying down debt and saving, as well as establishing a budget for both your pre- and post-retirement years."

Right on!

SOLUTION 3
KNOW YOUR PENSION PLANS

Imagine celebrating your sixtieth birthday without a clue how much you can expect to receive in pension income when you retire. Sounds implausible, doesn't it? Yet many people who will end their working career in a few years are in precisely that situation. They may be in for an unpleasant surprise.

It's impossible to create a meaningful retirement program without a thorough understanding of the pensions you can expect to receive when you stop work. For some people—those with what are often referred to as "Cadillac plans"—their pension will be the primary source of retirement income. But in many cases, pensions will account for less than half of after-work income.

We have two types of pension plans in Canada, public and private. You need to understand the technicalities of each and what you can reasonably expect from them when you retire.

PUBLIC PENSION PLANS

We have one national public plan, called the Canada Pension Plan (CPP); it covers people in all provinces except Quebec, where the Quebec Pension Plan (QPP) performs a similar function. We also have two national income support programs—Old Age Security (OAS) and the Guaranteed Income Supplement (GIS). These are not pension plans, in that they are non-contributory, but one or both will supplement your income in your later years.

For purposes of this book, I will focus on the details of the CPP, OAS, and GIS. If you live in Quebec and want complete information about the QPP, go to the plan's homepage (see appendix 4).

The Canada Pension Plan

The CPP was created by the Liberal government of Lester B. Pearson in 1966. At the time, I was Quebec City bureau chief for *The Gazette* of Montreal, and I vividly remember the strong opposition to the concept from Quebec premier Jean Lesage. He wanted the vast pool of money that would be accumulated from Quebecers to be under the province's control and was prepared to scuttle the whole venture if Ottawa didn't cave in.

After a series of sometimes acrimonious meetings, Lesage got his way, which is why Quebec is the only province with its own program. The Quebec legislature created the Caisse de dépôt to invest the contributions collected by the QPP, and it eventually expanded to manage money for other large pension plans and corporations. As of the end of 2010, it had $151.7 billion in assets under management and had invested in over five hundred Quebec businesses. The Caisse has been subject to criticism and controversy over the years, but it fulfilled Lesage's goal of keeping Quebec's money at home.

When the CPP and QPP were created, the contribution rate was set at 1.8 percent of "pensionable earnings," to be shared by employers and employees. The deductions at that level were so low that few people noticed, much less complained. But it was unsustainable. There was no way that the funds accumulated at that rate could pay for the coming retirement costs of the baby boom generation.

Over the years, the contribution rate edged steadily higher as a series of federal–provincial conferences came to grips with the reality of an aging population. It now stands at 9.9 percent of pensionable earnings, a figure that would have likely made Pearson and his cabinet colleagues think twice before forging ahead. As of 2011, pensionable earnings were between $3,500 and $48,300 a year. Employers and employees were each required to pay a maximum of $2,217.60 to the plan. A self-employed person was on the hook for the full amount, or a maximum of $4,435.20. The required contribution increases each year because of indexing.

So what do you get for all that money? For most people, the most important payment is the retirement benefit. You can begin to draw it as early as age sixty or as late as seventy—the longer you wait, the greater the payment will be.

The amount is indexed to inflation, so your payment will gradually increase each year. In 2011, the maximum benefit for a sixty-five-year-old was $960 a month, or $11,520 a year. However, most people don't receive the maximum because their income was below the ceiling and/or they don't have enough contribution years. The average monthly payment as of March 2011 was $512.38, or $6,148.56 annually.

Even those who qualify for the maximum are replacing only a small portion of their income. The 2011 payment was only about 24 percent of that year's maximum pensionable earnings. Those earning more than the maximum pensionable earnings receive no additional credits. So someone who retired in 2011 earning $70,000 would have only about 16 percent of that lost income replaced by CPP benefits, assuming they received the maximum payment.

You can increase the amount of your pension by postponing your application. As a result of recent amendments, in 2012 your CPP payment will increase by 0.64 percent for every month you delay drawing benefits after you turn sixty-five. In 2013, the monthly increase moves up to 0.7 percent (8.4 percent a year). You must begin drawing benefits by age seventy. If you wait until then, you'll receive 42 percent more than if you had applied at sixty-five.

Conversely, if you apply early you'll pay a penalty. In 2012, that will be 0.52 percent for each month prior to your sixty-fifth birthday. The penalty will increase gradually over the next four years until it reaches 0.6 percent a month in 2016. At that point, a person who starts receiving benefits on her sixtieth birthday will receive 36 percent less than if she had waited until sixty-five.

If we apply those percentages to the 2011 maximum retirement benefit, the person who waits until seventy would get $1,363.20 a month, or $16,358.40 a year. Someone who begins to collect at sixty would receive $614.40 a month, or $7,372.80 a year. That's less than half the amount a seventy-year-old would collect. The government's message couldn't be clearer—hold off on collecting CPP and we'll reward you handsomely.

In another recent change to the CPP, the government increased the number of low-income years that can be dropped out of the pension calculation from 15 to 16 percent in 2012 and to 17 percent in 2014. This change will be advantageous to just about everybody.

Someone who starts contributing to the CPP at eighteen and continues until sixty-five has a career span of forty-seven years. Since the retirement benefit is calculated on "average career earnings," the more low-income years you record over that period, the smaller the payment. Under the 15 percent rule, a person who contributed for forty-seven years could drop the seven lowest-income years from the calculation. At 17 percent, eight years can be dropped.

An Unexpected Wrinkle

The CPP changes that received royal assent in December 2009 contained one wrinkle that no one had expected. Now people are becoming aware of it, and they are not happy. They've figured out that the changes, which took effect at the start of 2012, are going to cost them hundreds or even thousands of dollars a year.

At the time the amendments were announced, Canadians were assured that they would not affect anyone who began drawing CPP benefits before 2011. But it turns out that is *not* the case. There is one very significant exception, and it will hit many CPP recipients under sixty-five.

In the past, once you began drawing CPP benefits you were no longer on the hook to make contributions. Technically, you were "CPP-exempt." That's the reason both my wife and I applied for our benefits as soon as we turned sixty. Between us, we were paying thousands of dollars a year into the fund (we had to pick up both the employee and the employer shares). By collecting our pensions as soon as we were eligible, we were able to cut off that cash drain immediately.

Now that will no longer be possible. Anyone between sixty and sixty-five who draws CPP benefits while continuing to work will be obligated to carry on making contributions to the plan at the same rate as everyone else. There is no grandfather clause to exempt those who applied before the new rules took effect. For example, if you applied for benefits in 2008, when you were sixty, and are still earning income, you are required to start paying into the CPP again as of January 1, 2012.

Ironically, the government has actually made it easier to draw an early pension and keep working. In the past, you had to stop work for a short period of time in order to apply. Now there is no work-cessation test. It appears that Ottawa is quite happy to have you take reduced benefits at age sixty while continuing to pay money into the pot.

The realization of what this means in hard dollars prompted some outraged emails, such as this one from Peter B. in Mississauga, Ontario:

I turned sixty on June 22, 2010. I applied for early CPP and received my first cheque in December. I am self-employed and will continue to work until the age of sixty-five. As I am self-employed, I paid my personal portion of CPP as well as the employer portion.

Now I must pay into CPP once again even though I received my first pension payment in 2010. Had I known this, I would not have elected to take my early CPP. As a matter of fact, I would elect to return any payments received to the government and retire with my full pension at sixty-five.

These rules need to be grandfathered. As it stands, I have reduced my pension by 30 percent for the rest of my life and now I am being obliged to pay the maximum CPP for the next three years.

To be fair, you do get some credit for those extra contributions. The government has introduced a post-retirement benefit (PRB). Each year of work will provide an additional PRB "that will begin the following year and will be paid for life," according to the CPP website. The PRB will be added to your retirement pension, even if the maximum pension amount is already being received.

After reading all this in my *Internet Wealth Builder* newsletter, Norm B. from Ottawa wrote: "That letter … is likely to inflame many sixty-year-olds across Canada, like me, who feel we've been snookered. When I applied for early CPP, this PRB was not one of the listed side-effects. All I really cared about was the fact that I could finally stop contributing. Now, it seems the rules have changed. The government can call it a PRB, but it sure sounds a lot like a modified CPP. And we all thought we were done paying into that for good."

I asked the Department of Finance for an official explanation of exactly how the PRB will work. Here is what they had to say:

> The contribution rate for working beneficiaries will be 9.9 percent of earnings between the basic exemption of $3,500 and the year's maximum pensionable earnings ($48,300 in 2011), or $4,435.20, split equally between the employee and employer. Self-employed workers will pay both the employer and employee share. This is the same contribution rate paid by all other workers and their employers.
>
> Individuals making these contributions, including those already receiving a "maximum" CPP pension, will see an increase in their CPP retirement benefit. Working beneficiaries will accrue further CPP benefits for their contributions at a rate of 2.5 percent of the maximum CPP pension amount ($11,520 at age 65 in 2011), adjusted for earnings and age. The increased CPP pension amount will be paid annually and will be indexed for inflation.
>
> This change will affect all working beneficiaries, starting in 2012, including those who took up their CPP pension in 2011 or before. This will ensure that all working beneficiaries are treated consistently with respect to CPP contributions and pensions.

Here's what it boils down to: if you are under sixty-five and are drawing the CPP, you are required by law to start making contributions again in 2012 at the same rate as everyone else. Depending on your income and whether you are self-employed, that could be as much as about $4,500 a year. Once you turn sixty-five, further contributions are voluntary.

In return, you'll receive a small boost in your CPP payments. On its website, the CPP gives an example based on a fictional character named Jean-Philippe. He is sixty-five years old, takes his CPP pension, and continues working part time. He decides to voluntarily keep contributing.

The website says: "In 2012, he earns $24,800 and makes a CPP contribution of $1,054 (his employer also contributes $1,054). Because of that contribution, his annual pension amount will increase by an estimated annual Post-Retirement Benefit of $164 beginning in 2013. This increased annual pension amount will then grow with the cost of living, as measured by the Consumer Price Index."

Using this example, the extra $164 would be the equivalent of an annualized return of 7.8 percent based on the total CPP contribution for that year. Of course, as the Finance Department points out, these figures would be adjusted for earnings and age, but they offer a guideline as to what we might expect.

That 7.8 percent return looks pretty good until you consider that almost thirteen years will pass before Jean-Philippe is paid back all the money he and his employer contributed. By then, he'll be seventy-eight years old.

What can you do if you have already started to draw CPP benefits and you're under sixty-five? It's not well publicized, but you can actually withdraw from the plan if you act within six months of starting to receive payments. You'll have to send a formal letter to Service Canada (I suggest by registered mail). State your desire to stop receiving benefits and provide your full name, address, and social insurance number. You will have to repay all the benefits you have received to date, but no penalty or interest will be charged.

Remember that even if you opt out of the CPP, you'll still have to make mandatory contributions until you reach sixty-five if you keep working. The difference is that the retirement pension you eventually receive will be significantly higher.

Other CPP Benefits

Apart from the retirement pension, there are several other benefits available from the CPP. They include the following:

DISABILITY BENEFIT. This is available to people who have a "severe" and "prolonged" handicap that makes them incapable of holding any kind of job. That's a very severe test and the CPP is notorious for rejecting applications, even from extremely ill people, on the grounds that they should be able to work at *something*. In fact, if you can't prove that you're dying you probably shouldn't apply, and even in that unhappy circumstance there are no guarantees.

Even if you have been accepted as "disabled" by some

other government body (if, for example, you've been approved for the disability tax credit from the Canada Revenue Agency), the CPP won't necessarily go along. You must be cleared by the organization's own medical adjudicators, and that is not easy. I know of one family that spent thousands of dollars on in-depth medical and mental evaluations and legal fees and was still turned down in the end.

If you *are* approved, the maximum monthly payment in 2011 was $1,153.37, or $13,840.44 a year. The average was $822.32 a month, or just $9,867.84 a year.

CHILDREN OF DISABLED CONTRIBUTOR'S BENEFIT. If a person is declared eligible for the disability benefit, his or her dependent children will also receive a monthly payment of $218.50 each (2011 rate). The children must be under eighteen or in full-time attendance at an educational institution.

DEATH BENEFIT. Unlike the disability benefit, there is no equivocation about this one. Either you are alive or you are dead. There's no need for anyone to adjudicate! If you die, your estate receives a lump-sum payment to a maximum of $2,500 in 2011. If there is no estate, the person responsible for the funeral expenses, the surviving spouse/partner, or the next of kin may be eligible, in that order.

SURVIVOR BENEFIT. The spouse/partner and dependent children of a deceased CPP contributor are eligible for monthly benefits from the plan. For a surviving spouse/partner, the amount will depend on several factors, including age, whether he/she is receiving CPP retirement or disability benefits, how much the contributor paid into the plan, and for how long (at least three years are needed to qualify). The maximum survivor benefit in 2011 was $576 a month, or $6,912 a year, for someone sixty-five or older. Younger people received a maximum of $529.09 a month, or $6,349.08 a year.

The survivor's children's benefit is paid to "a dependent natural or adopted child of the deceased contributor, or a child in the care and control of the deceased contributor at the time of death. The child must be either under age 18, or between the ages of 18 and 25 and in full-time attendance at a school or university," according to the CPP website. It was worth $218.50 a month, or $2,622 a year (in 2011).

Old Age Security (OAS)

Old Age Security as we know it today came into force in 1952, with a maximum benefit of $40 a month. It replaced a program of provincially run old age benefits that were means tested, a term that has long since vanished from the bureaucratic lexicon (we now refer to it as "income tested"). It was originally a contributory plan, similar to Social Security in the U.S., but that was later dropped and the program is now financed out of general revenues.

Everyone who has been a resident of Canada for at least ten years is eligible to collect OAS starting at age sixty-five. Normally, you qualify for the full amount only if you have been a resident for at least forty years, but there are some exceptions. See the OAS section of the Service Canada website for details.

OAS payments are indexed to inflation and are adjusted quarterly. For the third quarter of 2011, the maximum monthly payment was $533.70, or $6,404.40 a year.

The Clawback

Old Age Security was originally intended to be a universal program, providing an income safety net to all Canadian seniors. But in 1989, the Conservative government led by Brian Mulroney changed the rules of the game by introducing what it called the "social benefits repayment tax"— now better known as the "clawback." The rationale behind this move was that "rich" people should repay some or all of their OAS benefits at a rate of fifteen cents for every dollar received if a person's net income exceeded a certain level—called the "threshold."

The income threshold is indexed, so it increases annually. For 2011, the clawback applied to anyone whose net income exceeded $67,668. Beyond that, the surtax kicked in. As a result, a Manitoba resident who had net income of $75,000 and received OAS was effectively paying tax at a rate of 54.5 percent on $7,332 of OAS money (a regular marginal tax rate of 39.4 percent plus the surtax). No wonder many OAS recipients are angry! (If your net income is over the threshold, you can check out exactly how much the clawback will cost you by using the online calculator at retirementadvisor.ca.)

To make matters worse, any dividend income received outside a registered plan artificially adds to net income because of the gross-up calculation. See the chapter titled "The Tax System Is Stacked Against Us!" for more details.

GIS/ALLOWANCE

The Guaranteed Income Supplement (GIS) is available to anyone who receives Old Age Security and whose income falls below a certain level. In the third quarter of 2011, the maximum allowable income to receive a benefit was $16,176 for a single person or $21,360 for a couple who both qualified for OAS.

The maximum monthly payment for a single person at that time was $723.65, or $8,683.80 a year. Like OAS, the GIS is indexed to inflation and the payments are adjusted quarterly. For a couple who are both drawing OAS, the maximum monthly GIS payment was $1,203.49, or $14,441.88 a year.

As well, the government introduced a top-up payment for the poorest seniors, which took effect on July 1, 2011. This is worth an additional $600 a year for single people with an annual income of less than $4,400 (not including OAS and a $3,500 exemption for other income). A couple earning less than $7,360 can receive up to $840 a year in top-up payments.

But here's the catch: for every dollar of income over $3,500, you lose fifty cents' worth of GIS benefits. Income in this case includes CPP, OAS, annuities, pension plan payments, RRIF and RRSP withdrawals, investment income, rental property income, employment income, etc.

The major exception is TFSA withdrawals—they do not count as income for GIS purposes. This is why low-income people are encouraged to use TFSAs rather than RRSPs for retirement savings.

The Allowance is designed for low-income people between sixty and sixty-four who have a spouse eligible for OAS. To qualify, you must have lived in Canada for at least ten years after the age of eighteen. The maximum monthly benefit in the third quarter of 2011 was $391.72.

PRIVATE PENSION PLANS

There are basically two types of pension plans: defined benefit (DB) and defined contribution (DC). If you are a member of a pension plan and don't know which type it is, find out before you read any further in this chapter.

Defined Benefit Plans

As discussed in an earlier chapter, DB plans were long considered to be the gold standard of the pension world, but they are becoming increasingly rare in the private sector because of the huge financial burden they can impose on a company. They are still the norm in the public sector, but that may change in the future as governments struggle to cut expenses and balance budgets.

Writing in *The Globe and Mail* in July 2011, former Encana CEO Gwyn Morgan commented that there is "a strong and growing sense of unfairness among workers who don't work in the public sector, two-thirds of whom don't have any kind of company pension plan." He suggested that over the years, politicians had caved in to strong public-sector unions, granting pension demands in exchange for labour peace. Now all Canadians are paying the price for these expensive programs with their tax dollars. Something will have to give.

In a typical DB plan, employees contribute a percentage of their income (typically 4 to 6 percent) and the employer makes a matching contribution. The funds are invested by professional money managers. Members are guaranteed a specific income level at retirement, according to a formula that can vary from one plan to another. The formula may be based on the number of years of service plus an income factor. More generous plans define income as the average of your best three or five years of earnings. Others use your final three or five years (which may not necessarily be the peak earning years), while some base the pension on average career earnings. Obviously, the latter formula is the least desirable from the pensioner's point of view because the final payout will be based in part on your early years with the employer, when your salary was lower.

A typical formula for calculating a pension in a plan based on the best earnings years would be this:

(2% × years of service) × Average of best five years
of income = Annual pension income

If you had been with your employer for twenty-five years and your best five years averaged out to an annual income of $70,000, your pension entitlement would be this:

$$(2\% \times 25) \times \$70,000 = 50\% \times \$70,000 = \$35,000$$

That amount would be guaranteed, assuming the pension fund remained solvent. As we have seen in cases such as Nortel, that can no longer be taken for granted.

There are many variations on these basic approaches, so it's important to find out which one your plan employs. Ask for a calculation of your projected pension at retirement using different income hypotheses to see what you might expect. Of course, the closer you are to retiring, the more accurate the projection will be.

Defined Contribution Plans

If you work in the private sector and are fortunate enough to have any kind of a pension plan (only 25 percent of people do, according to Statistics Canada), it will likely be the DC type. This puts the onus on you to manage the money to your best advantage—unlike DB plans, you don't have the benefit of a professional money manager to help you. Unfortunately, many people have no idea how to make those tough decisions.

I occasionally lead seminars for DC plan members at which I explain how their plan works and how to use it to their best advantage. Most of the participants have no idea where to start. Many of them simply leave their contributions in a money market fund or put them into five-year

GICs. In both cases, the returns are well below the level needed to build a healthy retirement fund. For example, one plan I looked at in mid-2011 was paying less than 2 percent on a five-year GIC, while the one-year return on its money market fund was 0.96 percent. That's not good enough.

If you belong to a DC plan, you need to take control. Otherwise, you are going to be sadly disappointed when you discover how little income you'll receive when you retire. Here are some things you should do:

KNOW THE INVESTMENT OPTIONS. A typical DC plan will present members with a smorgasbord of investment choices—one I looked at had twenty-nine options, including stand-alone funds, portfolio funds, and GICs. Understandably, many people are overwhelmed when presented with such a complex menu. It's no wonder they fall back to the familiar world of GICs.

There are no easy shortcuts. You have to make the time to study the choices carefully or use a financial profes-sional to do it for you. Over the years, you'll be contrib-uting tens of thousands of dollars to the plan; in fact, it is probably the largest single investment you will ever make apart from your home.

DECIDE ON ASSET ALLOCATION. Before you make any commit-ment, decide on your asset allocation: the percentages of cash, bonds, and stocks you want to hold in your plan. The less able you are to handle risk, the greater should be your emphasis on cash and bonds. Younger, more aggres-sive pension plan members may give greater weighting to equity funds to maximize returns, but be sure to scale back the risk level as you get older.

MAKE CHANGES AS NEEDED. Your first selections are not locked in. Except for non-redeemable GICs, you should be able to make changes in your portfolio whenever you wish. So check the performance of your plan, and of the individual holdings, periodically—at least twice a year. Replace funds that are underachieving with better performers— you should receive regular updates from the company that administers the plan.

Also, review the asset allocation at least once a year. If one of the components does exceptionally well, the added value will skew your weightings and you'll need to rebalance. For example, if you have a target weight of 60 percent equity funds, and stocks have a great year as they did in 2009, you'll probably find the weighting at year-end has ballooned to 65 percent. At that point, switch some of the equity funds to bond or money market funds to get back to your original target.

MAXIMIZE YOUR CONTRIBUTIONS. Some defined contribution plans allow you to decide how much of your pay you want to contribute—usually it's between 4 percent and 6 percent. Choosing the highest level will pay off big time in the long run, especially if the employer is matching your contribution.

Let's say your income is $50,000 annually and you have thirty years remaining until retirement. You can choose a contribution level of 4 percent, 5 percent, or 6 percent, which the company will match. Assuming an average annual compound rate of return of 6 percent, the value of the plan after thirty years will be just over $316,000 if you choose the lowest contribution level. If you put in 5 percent of your pay, that increases to $395,000. But if you choose the highest level of 6 percent, the plan will be worth $474,000 when it comes time to stop work. The end difference between the lowest and highest contribution levels is $158,000 more in retirement savings! But that $158,000 will cost you only $1,000 year to achieve.

As you can see, there's a lot of money involved. That's why it is so important to take the time to properly manage your DC pension plan. It may not be the best plan around, but if that's the type you have, make the most of it.

Questions to Ask

No matter which type of plan you have, it is essential that you understand it thoroughly and have a good idea of how much it will pay when you retire. The more information you have, the better position you'll be in to plan your retirement. Here are some questions to ask your plan's administrator:

WHAT IS OUR BENEFITS FORMULA? DB plan members must understand exactly how their pension will be calculated when the time comes to stop work. If career average is used, probe more deeply. Some employers will upgrade career earnings to reflect inflation. The answer you'd prefer, however, is a formula based on your best three years of earnings.

WHEN AM I VESTED IN THE PLAN? Once you are vested in a DB plan, you are entitled to receive any benefits you accrue while you are a member. If you leave the plan before your retirement date, you'll usually be offered a deferred pension or a lump-sum buyout. Generally, the deferred pension is the better choice, especially if you have been in the plan for many years.

In the case of DC plans, vesting means you gain entitlement to the contributions the employer has made on your behalf. If you change jobs before you're vested, all you're likely to receive is a refund of your own premiums plus some modest interest. In most provinces, a pension plan is considered to be vested after two years.

If you leave your job, you may be entitled to a pension adjustment reversal (PAR). This is a way of restoring lost RRSP contribution room to people who lose pension or deferred profit-sharing plan benefits because they leave their employment before they become vested. If you think you may be eligible for a PAR, get hold of a copy of the Canada Revenue Agency booklet titled *Pension Adjustment Reversal Guide* (document number RC4137). You can obtain it from your local taxation office or download it from the CRA website.

WHAT IS MY PLAN INVESTED IN AND WHAT RETURN IS IT EARNING? This is a "nice to know" piece of information if you're in a DB plan. It's essential information if you're required to make decisions on what type of securities your pension money is invested in, as is the case with DC plans and group RRSPs. If the returns are not meeting your expectations, find out why and consider alternatives.

IS THE PLAN FULLY FUNDED? If you belong to a DB plan, it's reassuring to know it has adequate resources to meet its obligations. If it doesn't, ask for an explanation. It may be perfectly valid, but on the other hand, it may not. We have already seen many examples of DB plans trying to cope with financial shortfalls. In some cases, plan members have had no option but to accept reduced benefits and/or higher contribution levels to solve a serious problem. Ontario teachers found themselves in precisely that predicament in 2011 as their pension plan faced a projected $17.2 billion shortfall. After lengthy negotiations, they finally agreed to pay an extra 1.1 percent of their salaries in contributions and to accept a reduction in their inflation protection. Paying more and getting less may be a model for other plans in the future.

IS MY PLAN INTEGRATED WITH THE CPP? This means that the benefits paid by the plan will be adjusted to reflect payments you receive under the Canada Pension Plan. The argument is that the employer also contributed to the CPP and this should be recognized in the payments made to you. Most DB pension plans are integrated with the CPP.

WHEN CAN I RETIRE? Some plans allow for retirement after a certain number of years of service; with others, you must reach a specific age. A formula now being used more often involves adding age to years of service; if the total is equal to or greater than a target number (for example, ninety), you may retire with full benefits.

CAN I RETIRE EARLY? Find out if the plan has a set formula for early retirement, and if so, how it works. Ask especially about bridging arrangements, which provide for extra benefits until your CPP and OAS payments kick in.

WHAT HAPPENS IF I DIE? You should know what benefits your spouse and children can expect to receive from your pension plan if you're not around to collect. Make sure you understand the difference between survivor benefits if you die before retirement and the amounts payable after you begin drawing a pension.

AM I ALLOWED TO MAKE PAST SERVICE CONTRIBUTIONS, AND IF I DO, WHAT EFFECT WILL THEY HAVE ON MY PENSION? If you're allowed to make contributions for previous years of service (for example, you were with the employer but hadn't joined the pension plan), it may be in your interest to do so if it is a DB plan. But find out how much your benefits will increase as a result. Also, the government has tightened up on the tax-deductibility of past service contributions, so find out what you're allowed to claim before going ahead. For a full explanation of the current rules, obtain a copy of the current edition of the CRA guide titled *RRSPs and Other Registered Plans for Retirement*.

ARE BENEFITS INDEXED, AND IF SO, ARE THERE ANY LIMITS? If you have a DB plan, this is one of the most important questions you can ask. An unindexed pension plan (which is what most of them are) can put you in a vulnerable financial position as you grow older and the buying power of your pension cheque erodes. It's better to find out the bad news up front and plan accordingly rather than be hit with it at retirement. If the plan is indexed, count yourself lucky; very few Canadian pension plans offer this desirable but very expensive feature, and those that do are mainly in the public sector.

WHO PAYS WHAT? The employee contribution to the pension plan is usually clearly defined. The employer's may be more ambiguous, particularly with DB plans. Find out whether the company is on the hook for a certain percentage of salaries each year, or whether the only obligation is to contribute just enough to bring the plan's assets into line with the anticipated future benefits.

WHAT KIND OF REPORTS DO I GET? At least once a year, a well-managed DB pension plan will provide a benefits report that will detail your current status and outline your entitlements. A DC plan should give you statements at least semi-annually (quarterly is better) showing how much money has been credited to you, where it is invested, and the returns on your investments. If you're not receiving regular reports, ask why.

The more you know about your pension plan, the better you'll be able to assess how much income to expect from it. This will make it easier to determine how much additional income you'll need from other sources, such as RRSPs, TFSAs, and non-registered investments.

Group RRSPs

As an alternative to DC pension plans, or sometimes as a supplement to them, employers offer group RRSPs. As with DC pension plans, the end value will depend on a combination of contributions and growth rate, and the actual pension that will be paid cannot be predicted with accuracy until you're close to retirement.

There are some important differences between a DC pension plan and a group RRSP. In fact, technically, there is no such thing as a group RRSP. Every RRSP is registered in the name of a single individual. A group plan simply involves bundling many individual plans together under the same set of rules and with the same investment options.

In some ways, the group RRSP is a better choice than a DC plan because it provides greater flexibility. For example, a group RRSP allows you to open a RRIF (which has fewer constraints than a LIF), buy an annuity, or even take the money in a lump-sum payment if you prefer. The downside is that the employer may not contribute to a group RRSP.

Employers tend to prefer a group RRSP because it doesn't fall under the pension regulations, which means they aren't obliged to file all sorts of returns. Less paperwork means more efficiency.

Pooled Retirement Pension Plans (PRPPs)

In his 2011 budget, Finance Minister Jim Flaherty stated that the federal government plans to move forward with its proposal to create a new type of retirement savings vehicle, called Pooled Registered Pension Plans (PRPPs).

PRPPs are pooled defined contribution plans that can be used by employers, employees, the self-employed, and individuals to supplement their current retirement savings program. Participation will be voluntary. Because of their size, PRPPs will presumably be more cost-efficient than RRSPs. The investments will be administered by money managers from the private sector. Benefits will be portable, so that employees who change jobs will not lose any contributions made on their behalf. Funds could also be transferred tax-free to a new PRPP or to other types of registered plans.

Potentially, this could be a huge program with billions of dollars under administration within a few years. It is intended to appeal to small business owners who cannot afford to offer a traditional pension plan, as well as to independent workers. Some people may prefer the PRPP to an RRSP because of the lower costs and the professional money management.

At the time of writing, the Finance Department was seeking input from interested parties on a range of issues, including the minimum size for a PRPP, contribution rules, and limitations on investments. Since the government is currently in a majority position, it seems likely the concept will go ahead, but at the time this book was written, it was not possible to assess how useful and cost-effective PRPPs will be.

The Saskatchewan Pension Plan

Canadians who want to augment their pension savings should take a look at the Saskatchewan Pension Plan

(SPP). It is open to everyone and is run by two of the best boutique money management houses in Canada.

The SPP was set up in 1986 by the Saskatchewan government, so technically it is a public plan. However, I have included it with the private-sector plans because it is not a mandatory program and it operates in much the same way as a large DC pension plan.

Despite the fact that it is not marketed outside Saskatchewan, the SPP has grown into the twenty-sixth-largest defined contribution plan in Canada, with $282 million in assets and about thirty-two thousand members as of the end of 2010. It's a voluntary, fully portable plan and contributions can be made any time during the year, as long as you have available RRSP room. The maximum annual contribution is $2,500 (raised from $600 in December 2010), which is tax-deductible. You can also transfer up to $10,000 a year from existing RRSPs into the SPP. The plan's investment portfolio is well diversified and includes Canadian, U.S., and international blue-chip stocks, a pooled real estate fund, bonds, mortgages, and cash. The management expense ratio is slightly more than 1 percent.

Because the SPP is a DC plan, your retirement pension is not guaranteed but will be determined by the plan's returns during the time your money is invested. Members may choose to receive benefits as early as age fifty-five and no later than the year they turn seventy-one. It is important to note that your money must stay in the plan until you are at least fifty-five; you do not have the flexibility to make a withdrawal at any time.

When you retire, you can choose between receiving an SPP annuity or transferring your assets to a personal locked-in account such as a LIRA or LIF at any financial institution, or a combination of both. There are three types of SPP annuities: life only (all payments stop when you die), joint survivor (payments continue until the last spouse dies), and refund life (the balance in your account is paid to a beneficiary when you die). The amount of the monthly payment will vary depending on which type of annuity you select.

The SPP is open to anyone between eighteen and seventy-one. You can enrol online and make contributions by credit card if you wish.

IN SUMMARY

There are a wide range of pension options available, both public and private. It's important to understand how they work and what income you are likely to receive from them, as these will form the basis of most retirement plans. Once you have a reasonably clear idea of what to expect, you'll be in a better position to plan add-ons, such as TFSAs and RRSPs, which I'll discuss in the next chapter.

SOLUTION 4
BUILD AN RRSP

While researching this book, I came across a fascinating article written by Peter Shawn Taylor for the February 2007 issue of *Maclean's* magazine. The occasion was the fiftieth anniversary of the introduction of RRSPs, and Taylor had delved into the history of how this powerful savings tool came to be.

Flash back to early 1957. The Liberal government of Prime Minister Louis St. Laurent, which had ruled the country since 1948, was teetering. The raucous Pipeline Debate of the previous year, led by the pugnacious C.D. Howe, had divided the country and left a bitter taste in the mouths of Canadians. Progressive Conservative leader John Diefenbaker, an old-school grassroots Prairie politician, was quick to take advantage, branding the Liberals as arrogant and out of touch.

In an attempt to soften the government's image and woo back voters, the finance minister of the day, Walter Harris, made the removal of an unpopular 10 percent tax on candy, gum, and soft drinks the centrepiece of his March 1957 budget speech. After all, who wouldn't vote for a party that took the tax off sweets for little kids?

Almost ignored at the time, Taylor tells us, was a plan

to introduce what the finance minister described as a "registered retirement annuity." The St. Laurent government survived just long enough to pass its budget before being defeated by Diefenbaker's Progressive Conservatives in June. The registered retirement annuity, now known as the Registered Retirement Savings Plan, was born.

More than half a century later, the candy tax has long been forgotten. But the RRSP remains as one of the keystones of our retirement-planning program and the last hurrah of the St. Laurent administration. In the context of the time, it was a truly revolutionary change. Prior to its introduction, those who did not belong to an employer-sponsored pension plan had no tax incentive to save for retirement. Now all Canadians had a mechanism to put money aside for the future and could claim a tax deduction for doing so. Initially, the contribution limits were modest, but over the years successive governments expanded the program to the point that in 2012 you are allowed to put as much as $22,970 a year into your plan.

Some people have described RRSPs as the most powerful savings tool ever created for individual Canadians. Until the introduction of Tax-Free Savings Accounts in 2009, that was indisputably true. In some ways, TFSAs are even more advantageous in certain situations, but the RRSP remains the cornerstone of personal retirement planning for most people.

But if that's the case, why aren't more people using these plans? Over the years, the percentage of Canadians making RRSP contributions has been discouragingly low. In 2009, for example, interim statistics published by the

Canada Revenue Agency show that almost 24.5 million Canadians filed income tax returns. Of those, about 6 million claimed an RRSP deduction. That's less than one-quarter of all filers! Not surprisingly, the higher the income, the more likely a person was to contribute to an RRSP. But even among taxpayers earning over $50,000, the take-up rate was only 54 percent.

This was not an unusual year. I've observed the same pattern for decades. We are simply not making the most of a great opportunity to save taxes now while building a financial nest egg for the future.

There are all kinds of excuses for procrastinating, and I have written about them in the past. But the coming retirement crunch as the baby boomers hit their sixties is bringing a new sense of urgency. RRSPs are a big part of the solution to the harsh new realities facing soon-to-be retirees. The time has come to put this legacy from Louis St. Laurent to good use.

THE BASIC RULES

Whether or not you have an RRSP now, you need to know the basic rules. I receive a surprising number of questions from people who haven't taken the time to review the fundamentals and make expensive mistakes as a result. So while this may seem like boring stuff, take a few minutes to read through this section. It may pay off down the road.

ELIGIBILITY. Everyone age seventy-one or less may contribute to an RRSP, as long as they have earned income. There is some confusion about this because the cut-off age had been sixty-nine for several years before Finance Minister Jim Flaherty raised it in his 2007 budget. An RRSP must be cashed in or converted to a RRIF or an annuity by December 31 of the year you turn seventy-one.

There is no minimum age for setting up an RRSP. Even a child may have a plan, provided he or she has earned income.

CONTRIBUTION LIMITS. You can contribute up to 18 percent of the previous year's earned income. The maximum allowable contribution rises each year because of indexing. For 2012, it is $22,970. You would need to earn income of $127,611 to contribute that much. Note that members of registered pension plans and deferred profit-sharing plans have to deduct their pension adjustment (PA) from the amount they're allowed to contribute to an RRSP. Your employer will supply that number.

DEADLINE. The last day for contributions for the previous tax year is sixty days from January 1. That usually makes the deadline March 1, except in the case of a leap year or when that date falls on a Sunday.

CARRY-FORWARDS. If you don't make your full contribution, you can carry forward any unused portion to a future date. The CRA will track this for you and update your RRSP status each year on your notice of assessment.

TAX DEDUCTIONS. You may deduct the full amount of your RRSP contributions from your income. That makes them worth a lot more than a tax credit if your federal tax bracket is higher than 15 percent. It's important to remember that you are not required to claim a deduction immediately. If you wish, you can carry it forward to a year when you will be in a higher bracket. This can be very useful for students who earn money over the summer but have a low overall annual income.

ELIGIBLE INVESTMENTS. You can invest your RRSP money in almost anything you can think of, including guaranteed investment certificates (GICs), term deposits, treasury bills, Canada Savings Bonds and Premium Bonds, debt securities such as bonds and debentures, savings certificates, Canadian and foreign stocks listed on recognized exchanges, over-the-counter stocks traded on the NASDAQ and the Canadian Dealing Network (CDN), some limited partnership units, units in retail venture capital funds, shares of small businesses, mutual funds, ETFs, mortgages (including your own), call options, warrants and rights issued by companies listed on Canadian exchanges, bankers' acceptances, Canadian cash, and gold and silver bullion. Major exclusions from RRSPs include real property and collectibles.

FOREIGN PROPERTY. There is no longer any limit on the amount you can invest in foreign securities.

NUMBER OF PLANS. You can open as many RRSPs as you like, in any number of financial institutions. This allows maximum flexibility, but it can also create problems. Too many plans may be difficult to track. Also, they can be expensive, depending on what type you set up. So even though there's no official limit on the number of RRSPs you can have, use some common sense.

CLAIMING DEDUCTIONS. You must file an official receipt with your tax return to claim an RRSP deduction. If you've lost it, ask the financial institution to issue a duplicate.

SPOUSAL PLANS. You may set up an RRSP for your spouse and contribute to it as long as he or she is within the RRSP age limit. The total contributions you make to your own plan and the spousal plan may not exceed your personal limit. Common-law couples are also allowed to use spousal plans. Note that if you are over seventy-one and still have carry-forward room, you are allowed to contribute to a younger spouse's RRSP as long as he or she is still eligible for a plan.

TRANSFERS. You may transfer funds from one RRSP to another without penalty. Simply complete form T2033, which you can obtain from the Canada Revenue Agency or the financial institution to which you're transferring the money. You cannot, however, transfer money from your RRSP to someone else's (e.g., your spouse) or to a TFSA.

WITHDRAWALS. Any withdrawals from an RRSP are taxable at your marginal rate, unless they are made under the Home Buyers' Plan or the Lifelong Learning Plan. You are allowed to withdraw part of the assets from a plan without having the whole plan deregistered. A withholding tax may apply for each withdrawal.

CHOOSE THE RIGHT PLAN

The type of RRSP you choose can make a huge difference in the amount of money that will be available to you at retirement. Many people don't realize that an RRSP is not an investment in itself. They talk about "buying" an RRSP when in fact all they are really doing is opening a shell that can be used to hold any type of qualified investment.

Some RRSPs are more restrictive than others. If you choose the wrong type, it could mean a difference of tens or even hundreds of thousands of dollars in the amount of money that will be available to you at retirement. There are five basic types of RRSPs. Here's a summary:

SAVINGS PLANS. RRSP savings accounts used to be quite common; today they're rare—and with good reason. Interest rates have been so low that the growth in these plans would be painfully slow. The best rate I could find on a high-interest savings account in mid-2011 was 2.2 percent. That was less than the rate of inflation at the time, which meant that your money was effectively generating a negative return. This may change in the future, but as long as interest rates remain low, RRSP savings accounts should be avoided. The only advantages they offer is that they're simple to understand and are protected by deposit insurance up to $100,000. You can do better.

GIC PLANS. This is the type of plan that you're likely to get if you walk into a financial institution, plunk your money on the counter, and ask to open an RRSP. Your money will be invested in a guaranteed investment certificate for the period you select (usually one to five years) and automatically rolled over when it matures (unless you give other instructions). These plans are popular with risk-averse investors, particularly those who lost money in the stock market crash of 2008. But you won't see much growth, again because of those low interest rates. Small financial institutions were offering a maximum of 3.5 percent on five-year GICs in mid-2011, but as long as interest rates are low, I advise against locking in for an extended period.

One other GIC comment: some banks offer "no-risk" GICs that are linked to stock market returns. Avoid them. Usually, they have a relatively low cap on the amount of money you can earn. If you're going to invest in the market, you should fully benefit if it rises. If you must have a GIC, stay with the basic type that guarantees a return and protects your capital.

THE CANADA RSP. Several years ago, the federal government created a no-fee RRSP, called the Canada RSP. The price is right, but it is very restrictive: you can only hold Canada Savings Bonds and Canada Premium Bonds in this account, and in recent years the interest rates offered have been very low.

MUTUAL FUND PLANS. These RRSPs invest your contributions in mutual funds of your choice. They can range from ultra-conservative money market and mortgage funds to higher-risk stock funds, or any mix thereof. Most financial institutions offer these plans, but before you choose, ask about flexibility. Some plans limit you to the institution's own funds, while others offer more options.

Insurance companies offer a version of this type of plan using their own segregated funds. These are similar to mutual funds but come with more features (e.g., capital protection guarantees) and are more expensive.

SELF-DIRECTED PLANS. These RRSP plans allow you to invest in anything you want, as long as it's considered an eligible investment. A self-directed plan can be as conservatively or aggressively managed as you wish; you're in full control. The rate of return will vary depending on what you put into your plan, as will the risk level. You can open this type of plan only with a brokerage firm, and you should have some investing experience before you do.

I recommend novice investors start with a plan that offers the flexibility to invest in a variety of mutual funds. Begin with a single Canadian balanced fund and build from there. The average Canadian neutral balanced fund returned 6.8 percent annually over the twenty years to mid-2011, which is a lot more than you'll earn from a GIC or a savings plan.

MAKING YOUR CONTRIBUTION

If you don't put money into your RRSP, everything else becomes academic. The majority of Canadians don't bother. As I mentioned at the start of this chapter, fewer than 25 percent of Canadians put any money into a plan in 2009. Few of those who contributed put in the maximum allowable amount.

What's the problem? Actually, there are several, including lack of available cash as the post-Christmas credit card bills roll in; the desire to spend the money elsewhere, perhaps on a winter vacation in the south; or a *mañana* mentality—we'll do it next year. That kind of thinking can cost you tens of thousands of dollars by the time retirement comes around.

The short-term way to deal with a cash shortage is to take out an RRSP loan. All the banks promote them, and the terms are very advantageous. Interest rates are often at prime or even below. Your payoff is immediate—an Ontario resident with a taxable income of $50,000 in 2011 received almost one-third of his or her contribution back in the form of a refund (31.15 percent, to be exact). Someone in the highest bracket (taxable income of $128,800 and up) got a refund of 46.41 percent. You can use the refund to reduce the loan principal and pay off the balance within a year. Do not make the mistake of stretching the loan repayment beyond that. I know of people who have gotten into deep financial doo-doo that way.

The long-term solution is to set up an automatic contribution program at your financial institution. Estimate how much you want to contribute to your plan for the current tax year and have one-twelfth of that amount deducted monthly. By this time next year, the money will already be in the RRSP and you won't have to worry about it.

YOUR RRSP STRATEGY

Before you make a single investment, you need to understand exactly what you are trying to achieve with your RRSP. This is your personal pension plan, and it may be the only one you'll ever have. That means you need to think like a professional pension plan manager when making your decisions.

You have two goals. The first is to protect your capital from cataclysmic losses. You can't avoid risk entirely, but it must be kept to a minimum. As a wise broker told me many years ago: "If you want to gamble, go to Vegas. Don't do it in your RRSP."

The second objective is to generate returns that are better than a GIC would offer. Aim for what I call modest growth—an average annual return of between 5 and 6 percent is a reasonable target. Many people have a tendency to overreach, taking on far more risk than is appropriate for an RRSP. I am especially concerned when I see younger people doing this. They are the ones who are most likely to become discouraged if they experience big losses early on, and they may stop contributing as a result.

You can avoid this trap by deciding on your asset allocation in advance. This is the single most important investment decision you will make for your RRSP—getting the asset mix right will count for more in determining the return on your investments than the individual securities you pick. (Note that this applies only to mutual fund and self-directed plans; there are no asset allocation decisions in the three other types of RRSPs, since they invest only in cash or fixed-income securities like GICs and Canada Savings Bonds.)

There are four basic asset groups: cash, fixed income, variable income, and growth. Here is a quick look at each.

CASH. This consists of currency and highly liquid cash-equivalent securities such as treasury bills, money market funds, and Canada Savings Bonds. Any asset that can quickly be converted to cash for its full face value will qualify.

FIXED INCOME. These securities pay a specified (fixed) rate of return and have a maturity date, at which time your principal is returned. If they are sold or cashed in before that date, the result may be a loss or a penalty to the investor. Bonds, mortgages, some fixed-rate preferred shares, and GICs fall into this asset class.

VARIABLE INCOME. In the past, this was not considered a separate asset class, but times and markets change. A variable-income security offers cash flow on a predictable basis (usually monthly or quarterly), but the amount of the payment is not guaranteed and may vary considerably. These securities may or may not have maturity dates. Examples of variable-income securities include floating-rate preferred shares, monthly income mutual funds, and income trusts/limited partnerships (there are still a few left).

GROWTH. Assets in the growth category add value mainly through capital gains (although some may pay dividends as well). Stocks and equity mutual funds are the most common examples.

Now you have to decide how much of each asset class you want to hold in your RRSP. There are several factors to consider, including your age, your time horizon, the economic climate, your risk tolerance, etc. Generally, the higher the percentage of cash and fixed-income securities, the less risky your RRSP will be. However, the trade-off is that your profit potential will be reduced as well. The more variable-income and growth securities you have, the greater your chances of achieving above-average returns. But you will also expose yourself to greater losses during periods when the stock market is in decline or when interest rates are moving sharply higher. This is what makes the decision difficult. You have to weigh these considerations and decide where you want to place your portfolio on the scale. If you choose to be ultra-conservative, you need to reconcile yourself to the fact that it will probably take quite a bit longer to build a retirement portfolio with the value you require. If you decide in favour of growth, you must be ready to accept the ups and downs of volatile stock markets.

I recommend you start from the position that you will include all four asset classes in your portfolio. I have heard ultra-aggressive investors say: "To heck with that. Stocks are where the action is, and I'm going to put all my money there." The danger in adopting that approach at the outset is psychological as well as financial. Suppose you had made a decision in early 2008 to load up with stocks or equity funds. By the time the market crash of 2008–2009 was over, the S&P/TSX Composite Index was down about 50 percent. Very few people can deal with that level of psychological trauma. Not only will it take a long time to recover from such a heavy loss, but you may be left with mental scars that will never heal. I once had a friend who, having lost heavily in the stock market collapse of the 1970s, never invested again in equities for the rest of his life. That's not a healthy, or wise, approach.

So use all the asset classes. No zeros for any of the four. Rather, it's a matter of deciding how the distribution will be made.

Cash is normally allocated the smallest percentage in an investment portfolio because of the low return it generates. But there are two reasons for holding some. First, cash is the safest asset you can possess in difficult times. Second, a cash reserve allows you to take advantage of opportunities in the stock and bond markets. If you don't have any cash, you'll be forced to sell something else, which you may not want to do at that moment. The minimum cash holding in your RRSP should be 5 percent. The maximum should be 25 percent, and that would be reached only under very unusual circumstances, such as during a period when short-term interest rates are high and the stock and bond markets are slumping. These conditions do occur from time to time, but rarely.

The percentage of fixed-income assets will be governed by two main considerations: your risk-tolerance level and the outlook for interest rates. Under normal conditions, fixed-income securities carry much less risk than growth securities. So a portfolio that is weighted towards bonds and GICs will be less volatile than one that holds only a small percentage of such assets. In fact, certain types of fixed-income securities, particularly bonds, have the potential to generate above-average returns during periods when interest rates are falling, so this can be another factor in your allocation decision. The proportion of fixed-income securities in an RRSP can vary from as low as 25 percent to as high as 75 percent, depending on the circumstances. The closer you are to retirement, the higher your fixed-income allocation should be.

Variable-income securities are trickier. These are most often used to generate cash flow after retirement, but there is a place for them in a younger person's RRSP as well. The weighting should gradually increase as you grow older.

Growth securities should receive the largest allocation share when you're young and gradually diminish as you approach retirement. The minimum allocation should be 20 percent, and you would be at that level only during full-blown bear markets or if you are approaching, or past, retirement. The maximum weighting for growth securities is 70 percent.

The following table shows model weightings for asset allocation based on age:

	20–25	26–49	50–59	60–65	66+
Cash	5%	5%	10%	10%	15%
Fixed income	30%	20%	30%	40%	50%
Variable income	10%	10%	10%	15%	15%
Growth	55%	65%	50%	35%	20%

You'll see that for those in the first age group, the fixed-income recommendation is higher than for those in the second group, while the growth component is smaller. I believe that younger people who are just starting out should take a more balanced approach to investing until they have learned more about how securities perform and better understand the ins and outs of RRSP management. There is a danger—and I have seen it happen—that young people will be somewhat aggressive with their initial investments. It's a risk I would advise you to avoid.

As a person becomes more comfortable with investing—and the ages shown here are only a broad guideline—the percentage of higher-risk variable-income and growth securities in the plan can be increased. People in their late twenties or thirties, and even in their forties, can take a long-term view of the markets and not be overly concerned by temporary setbacks. However, I recommend that a portion of all portfolios be kept in fixed-income securities, both to mitigate risk and to take advantage of those occasions when bonds outperform stocks.

As you approach your retirement years, you should gradually reduce the risk in your portfolio, since the time left to ride out any severe stock market setback is running short. Build your cash and income components, which will be needed when the time comes to convert your savings to a revenue stream. However, I suggest you always retain a portion of your portfolio in growth securities as a protection against even modest rates of inflation. You don't want to outlive your money!

CHOOSE THE RIGHT SECURITIES

Don't treat your RRSP money carelessly. Give careful thought to what you want to put into the plan. The performance of the securities you select will have a profound impact on your standard of living in the final twenty or thirty years of your life.

There are many possible choices available for your RRSP—so many, in fact, that the whole process may seem daunting. The following are some of the investments I feel are suitable for an RRSP. I have chosen only those that are easy to acquire. Note that some of these can be held only in mutual fund or self-directed plans.

Cash-Type Securities

These investments can be easily converted to cash at full face value within a short period of time. There are four main kinds of cash-type securities.

MONEY MARKET MUTUAL FUNDS. These are the core cash holding for most RRSP investors. These funds may own treasury bills, short-term corporate notes, and bankers' acceptances. They are conservatively managed, and the net asset value (NAV) is fixed, usually at $10. However, when interest rates are down, as they have been in recent years, returns are very low.

HIGH-INTEREST SAVINGS ACCOUNTS. When interest rates are low, these can sometimes be better parking places for cash than money market funds.

SHORT-TERM DEPOSITS. Offered by financial institutions, these deposits are guaranteed and may pay a higher return than money market funds. However, a high-interest savings account offers more flexibility because you can take out your money at any time and the interest rate may be comparable.

CANADA SAVINGS BONDS. Technically, these are misnamed. These aren't real bonds at all, but short-term savings certificates issued by the federal government. The interest rate reflects current short-term rates, and CSBs can be cashed any time for full face value. Note, however, that the companion Canada Premium Bonds (CPBs) have restrictions on when they can be redeemed, so they don't really qualify as "cash."

Fixed-Income Securities

This type of security guarantees to make payments (interest or dividends) at a set rate on specific dates, and it has a fixed maturity date. I have also listed several types of fixed-income funds below because they invest in these types of securities. However, the funds themselves do not have a maturity date and the payments are not guaranteed, so it could be argued that they more rightly belong in the variable-income category.

GUARANTEED INVESTMENT CERTIFICATES (GICS). For many Canadians, these were the backbone of their RRSPs for years. The classic GIC has a term of one to five years, during which time you are guaranteed a specific rate of return.

Your principal is locked in for that period. There are also index-linked GICs available, but I do not recommend them for registered plans because their returns are unpredictable.

MORTGAGE-BACKED SECURITIES. These are a useful investment for those who are looking for steady income with very little risk. They are actually much better suited for retirees in RRIF accounts because they combine safety with cash flow, but you should be aware of them because they provide a conservative RRSP option.

MORTGAGE MUTUAL FUNDS. These funds invest in residential first mortgages and mortgage-backed securities, and their safety record is first rate. Even in recessionary times, Canadians are very conscientious about their mortgage payments, which means that defaults are minimal. These funds hardly ever lose money over a calendar year. There will be some movement in unit price as interest rates rise and fall. But it won't be as dramatic as with a bond fund, because the average term to maturity of the holdings in a mortgage fund is shorter (typically around three years). You can ignore these shifts or take advantage of them to add more units at a reduced price.

Don't go into mortgage funds looking for big gains. When interest rates are low, so are the returns. But you'll usually earn somewhat more than you will from a money market fund, with only slightly higher risk.

SHORT-TERM BOND FUNDS. If rates are on the rise, short-term bonds are one of the safest types of fixed-income securities to own. The term to maturity is no longer than five years, which means the market price of the bonds held by the funds is more stable. That doesn't mean they can't lose value, but it does mean that any decline will be small compared to medium- and long-term bonds.

There are many short-term bond mutual funds, as well as several exchange-traded funds (ETFs) that invest in these securities. The ETFs usually have the lowest management expense ratios (MERs); however, you will have to pay a sales commission to buy or sell your units.

UNIVERSE BOND FUNDS. These invest in a broad range of bond maturities, short, medium, and long. Some of them track the performance of the DEX Universe Bond Index, which includes both government and corporate issues. Again, you can choose between mutual funds and ETFs.

HIGH-YIELD BOND FUNDS. These invest in lower-grade securities, so they can be more risky than other types of bond funds—but also potentially more profitable. Some portfolios are made up entirely of so-called junk bonds; I suggest avoiding those in your RRSP. Instead, choose a more conservatively managed high-yield fund, such as the one offered by the Vancouver-based firm of Phillips, Hager & North.

STRIPPED BONDS. Some investors use stripped bonds as the backbone of their self-directed RRSPs. Strips, as they're called, have been available in Canada since the mid-1980s. The concept was imported from the U.S., where zero coupon bonds, as they're known in that country, had already been popular for many years.

With strips, there are no surprises. If you're planning to retire in fifteen years, you simply buy fifteen-year strips when interest rates are high, tuck them away in your RRSP, and forget them. The money will be there when you need it. And since financial dealers normally select only the highest-quality bonds to strip, the chance of the issuer defaulting is very low.

However, strips are not covered by deposit insurance, and they are much more volatile than regular bonds. They can experience some significant price swings as interest rates move up or down. If you intend to hold them for the long term, that's not a problem. But if you think you might sell before maturity, it's something to consider.

I do not advise buying strips when interest rates are very low. If you do, you'll be locking in an inferior return for many years.

FIXED-RATE PREFERRED SHARES. There are two types of preferred shares: fixed rate and floating rate. The fixed-rate type pays a set dividend that never varies, so I am including it with the fixed-income securities. Floating-rate preferred shares are quite different, and I'll discuss them in the variable-income section.

A preferred share is a type of debt security issued by a corporation. Investors receive dividends, and the shares may be redeemable after a certain time or at stated intervals (although some are perpetual). Preferred shares rank behind bonds in terms of priority in the event a company runs into trouble, so they can be higher risk. One of their main attractions is the eligibility of their payments for the dividend tax credit, but that benefit is lost inside an RRSP.

Variable-Income Securities

These differ from fixed-income securities in that the payment is not guaranteed and may vary according to a number of conditions. For example, in some cases the payment will rise or fall in line with changes in the Bank of Canada's key lending rate or the prime rate.

FLOATING-RATE PREFERRED SHARES. This type of preferred share offers protection against rising interest rates. The dividend is adjusted periodically according to a specific formula, which is usually tied to the prime rate. Otherwise, floating-rate preferreds have the same characteristics as straight preferreds. Preferred shares can be purchased on the Toronto Stock Exchange.

PREFERRED SHARE FUNDS. There are a few mutual funds and ETFs that specialize in preferred shares. If you want a diversified portfolio of these securities, they are a better choice than buying individual issues. Most of these funds pay distributions monthly or quarterly, although the amount may vary from one payment to another.

INCOME TRUSTS/LIMITED PARTNERSHIPS. Income trusts and limited partnerships (LPs) were extremely popular with investors until Finance Minister Jim Flaherty effectively shut them down by imposing a new tax, which took effect on January 1, 2011. But there are still a few left, such as Brookfield Renewable Energy Partners LP and Inter

Pipeline Fund, which can be purchased through brokers for self-directed RRSPs.

If you invest in one of these securities, remember that the higher the yield, the less suitable it is likely to be for a retirement savings account. The reason is simple: yield equates with risk. Nobody gives away something for nothing in the investment world, so if an income trust or LP is offering a big payout, there's a reason. Since one of the priorities of RRSP management is to keep risk within reasonable limits, my advice is to focus on those that are at the lower end of the yield range.

Also, avoid highly volatile sectors, such as oil. A worldwide recession, such as we experienced in 2008, will knock back oil prices, and the market value of these securities will suffer accordingly. A retirement plan is not the right environment for that kind of risk. Stick with more stable businesses, such as pipelines and utilities.

REAL ESTATE INVESTMENT TRUSTS (REITS). These are the only trusts that were not affected by the new tax, with a few exceptions. Most REITs invest in residential, commercial, and industrial properties (e.g., shopping malls, office buildings, apartments), while a few specialize in health care facilities such as nursing homes. REITs typically pay monthly distributions, so they offer good cash flow. Some have a long history of steady distribution increases, but payments can be cut in tough economic times. Because some of their distributions are tax-advantaged, they are better held in a non-registered account, but they can certainly be considered for RRSPs.

INCOME FUNDS. There are many mutual funds, ETFs, and closed-end funds that are designed to produce steady cash flow. This can be from interest, dividends, capital gains, or any combination of these. Some of these funds have a track record of steady performance with relatively low risk, and they should be at the top of your RRSP list.

Growth Securities

These assets add value to a portfolio mainly through capital gains. They include the following:

STOCKS. These are the classic growth securities. If you have a self-directed RRSP, you may invest directly in Canadian, American, or international stock markets. This can be good or bad, depending on your stock-picking skills and your timing. Generally, I suggest that only seasoned investors go this route with their RRSP.

EQUITY MUTUAL FUNDS. For most people, equity (stock) mutual funds are the entry point to growth securities. That's because they're readily available, affordable, and offer professional money management. Canadian equity funds are the most common type sold in this country, for three reasons: they are the most familiar; they have been good performers in recent years; and the strong loonie has made U.S. and foreign funds less attractive.

ETFS. Exchange-traded funds have become a popular way of investing in stocks (and other types of securities), both domestic and foreign. The typical ETF tracks the performance of a specific index, such as the S&P/TSX

Composite Index or the Dow Jones Industrial Average. Several companies now offer ETFs in Canada, including BlackRock (the iShares group), Claymore, BMO, Invesco (PowerShares), Royal Bank, and Horizons BetaPro.

RRSPS AND THE STOCK MARKET

There are many theories about the best way to invest RRSP money. Over the years, I have personally tried them all. Each strategy has its advantages and its drawbacks. In the end, the decision on which to choose depends on several factors, including your age, the number of years that remain until your planned retirement, your risk tolerance, and the amount of time you are willing to devote to managing your plan.

I believe that stocks have a place in your RRSP if you have the investment knowledge to choose wisely. But the risk has to be managed carefully. Over time, I have obtained the best results in my RRSP (and later in my RRIF) by using a mix of stocks and fixed-income securities. Investment purists may be shocked at this approach. Conventional wisdom is that equities should be held in non-registered accounts because of the favourable tax treatment of dividends and capital gains. But that assumes a person has enough investable assets to run parallel registered and non-registered plans.

In my case, and I believe many readers will be in a similar situation, most of my investable savings were accumulated inside RRSPs. By maximizing my contributions to obtain the greatest tax benefit, I ended up in a situation where the total value of my registered assets far exceeded that of my non-registered portfolio.

For a short time, I followed the "expert" advice and put most of my RRSP money into fixed-income securities such as GICs and bond funds. But the returns were well below my targets and were unlikely to improve. At that point, I began to look more closely at what professional pension managers were doing, and I saw that they were investing in the stock market. The potential gains clearly outweighed the loss of tax advantages in their estimation.

That's when I made a strategic switch in one of my RRSPs (I had as many as four at one point in time). I decided to allocate 60 percent of the RRSP to stocks and began to redeploy the money accordingly. Although I did not use any hard-and-fast rules for stock selec-tion—other than avoiding speculative issues—I focused on large-cap equities that offered above-average profit potential with minimal risk. Not every pick was a winner, of course, but the overall return over time was several percentage points higher than my fixed-income approach had produced.

This strategy can be very rewarding, but it requires a lot of attention and the willingness to trade in and out of stocks according to the circumstances. It is also more expensive than any other type of RRSP investing because of the trading commissions (although these can be minimized by using a discount broker) and the higher fees for a self-directed plan.

In practical terms, you'll need enough money in your

RRSP to provide proper diversification. If the plan is worth less than $50,000, use the mutual fund strategy, which I'll describe next.

RRSPS AND MUTUAL FUNDS

I was looking through statistics about RRSP contributors in the 2010 *Canada Year Book* (published by StatsCan) and I came across a disturbing pattern: the percentage of Canadians who use RRSPs appears to be in gradual but steady decline. In 2002, 27.3 percent of tax filers claimed an RRSP contribution. By 2005, that number had dropped by a full percentage point, to 26.3 percent. In 2008, it fell again, to 25.7 percent.

There is no obvious reason why we are seeing these patterns, although I can speculate that the prolonged period of low interest rates and two stock market crashes in the first decade of this century discouraged people from saving and investing. What is clear, however, is that if these trends continue, we are heading for some serious social problems down the road as hundreds of thousands of baby boomers reach retirement age with inadequate financial resources. The decline of defined benefit pension plans is exacerbating the situation.

There's a lot in all this of the old proverb "You can lead a horse to water, but you can't make him drink." Over the years, the federal government has put into place two of the most attractive personal savings programs that you'll find anywhere: RRSPs and Tax-Free Savings Accounts. We don't have any meaningful data for TFSAs yet, but based on what we're seeing it appears that RRSPs are gradually falling out of favour.

I think we might see a reversal of that trend if RRSP returns begin to improve. I know from the emails I receive that many people are frustrated by the weak profits they are earning from traditional RRSP securities such as GICs. But they are afraid to venture into anything more "risky" after seeing what happened during the financial meltdown of 2008–2009. These people wouldn't even consider building their retirement plans around stocks or exchange-traded funds.

My advice in such cases is to create an RRSP based on conservative mutual funds. Yes, there is more risk to capital than you'd get simply socking the money into a GIC, but over time the rewards will be greater. Some of the companies that offer relatively low-risk funds are Beutel Goodman, Phillips, Hager & North, Mawer Investment Management, Leith Wheeler Investment Counsel, and Steadyhand Investment Funds. All have the added advantage of low MERs.

RRSP DOS AND DON'TS

According to a recent poll conducted by TD Waterhouse, 61 percent of baby boomers say they will use RRSPs to help fund their retirement plans. Surprisingly, that was slightly higher than the number who cited CPP/OAS as an important factor in their planning. If RRSPs are that central to the financial mix, it stands to reason that we had better get them right. So to end this chapter, I have compiled a list of RRSP dos and don'ts that sum up the main points I want to leave you with.

1. *Don't ask friends for advice.* There are a lot of misconceptions about RRSPs out there, so don't assume that what someone tells you over lunch is necessarily right. Go to a reliable source. There are numerous books on the subject, as well as magazine and newspaper articles. The Canada Revenue Agency has a page that is a useful gateway to a wealth of RRSP information, and a Google search will turn up many more references.

2. *Do choose the right plan.* I have not seen any precise numbers, but it's a safe bet that billions of dollars of RRSP money is tied up in guaranteed investment certificates. The banks love GICs and promote them aggressively. Why not? They get to use your money for many years (five-year maturities are standard), loaning it out to others at higher rates and making a nice profit in the process. Meantime, your RRSP grows at a snail's pace.

   My advice is to open a self-directed RRSP that gives you the maximum possible investment flexibility. Yes, it will cost you—the annual fee will probably be in the $100 to $150 range. But you should more than make up for that with much higher long-term returns. As mentioned earlier, an average annual gain of between 5 percent and 6 percent, which is realistic in a conservatively managed plan, will keep you ahead of inflation and build genuine value in your RRSP.

3. *Don't speculate.* Never forget that your RRSP is just a mini pension plan. That means you must think like a pension fund manager—protecting capital, avoiding unnecessary risk, and aiming for a reasonable return on investment. While all investments carry some degree of risk, there's a wide chasm between prudent risk and speculation. Your RRSP is not the place to gamble. Keep it conservative, even dull.

4. *Do contribute regularly.* I know you've heard this a million times. Well, now it's a million and one. The easiest, most painless way to build an RRSP is to have automatic contributions deducted from your account each month. People who wait until RRSP season comes around often end up without any money to invest. They vow to do it next year but usually don't.

5. *Don't blow the refund.* The tax refund generated by an RRSP contribution is windfall money. It's like winning the lottery—it is all yours to keep, with no tax to pay on it. Depending on how much you contributed, we could be talking about thousands of dollars. The temptation, especially with younger people, is to spend it. I can suggest several better ideas that will build your personal wealth in the process. Pay down credit card debt. Pay down the mortgage. Contribute it to a TFSA. Put it back into the RRSP as the first contribution for the next tax

year. Add it to your non-registered investment account. Just don't blow it!

6. *Do borrow, but carefully.* If an RRSP loan is paid off quickly, preferably within a year, the math is compellingly in favour of going that route if the cash for a contribution is not immediately available.

Let's look at the case of someone who has a 35 percent marginal tax rate and needs $5,000 to make an RRSP contribution. We'll assume interest of 4 percent on the loan. Using our assumptions, a $5,000 loan will generate a tax refund of $1,750. If the invested money earns 5 percent this year, the RRSP will grow by $250 in twelve months. The total gain (investment income plus tax savings) is $2,000, which is a 40 percent return on investment. If the loan is repaid over twelve months at a rate of $425.75 per month (principal and interest), the total interest expense will be only $108.99. That can be reduced further by applying the tax refund against the loan principal. In sum, it has cost slightly more than $100 to generate a cash benefit in the first year of $2,000. And the invested $5,000 keeps on giving. With an average annual compound rate of return of 5 percent, it will grow to almost $17,000 over twenty-five years.

So by all means, borrow for an RRSP as long as the loan can be repaid within a year, or two at the most. But avoid getting locked in to a long-term loan, even if the interest rate is attractive. The returns diminish for each year that you are paying it off, especially since the interest is not tax-deductible.

7. *Don't contribute if you expect your income to be low.* RRSPs are great savings vehicles, but they aren't right for everyone. In particular, older people who expect to have low incomes after retirement should avoid them. Any money available for savings should be put into a TFSA instead. This is because RRSP/RRIF withdrawals are taxable income and will affect your eligibility for income-tested government benefits and tax credits, including the Guaranteed Income Supplement (you lose fifty cents for every dollar in income over $3,500), the GST tax credit, and the age credit. TFSA withdrawals, on the other hand, are not considered income for any of these calculations.

8. *Do pay off high-interest loans first.* I have always regarded RRSPs as one of the pillars of wealth building, but that doesn't mean they should always take top priority. Anyone carrying high-interest, non-deductible debt, such as a credit card balance, should pay that off first before even considering an RRSP contribution.

And finally, do open an RRSP and contribute to it regularly. In future years, you'll be happy you did.

SOLUTION 5
OPEN A TFSA

When Finance Minister Jim Flaherty stood up to give his budget speech in the House of Commons at 4 p.m. on February 26, 2008, no one expected very much. All the tax cuts and other goodies had been announced in a mini-budget the previous fall, in anticipation of a general election that never happened. As a result, the pundits and the public anticipated little more than a housekeeping budget.

So it came as a surprise when, early in the speech, the minister made this announcement: "The Government will unveil the single most important personal savings vehicle since the introduction of the RRSP: the Tax-Free Savings Account. This flexible, registered, general-purpose account will allow Canadians to watch their savings grow, tax-free. It's the first account of its kind in Canadian history."

For once, this was not political hyperbole. The TFSA is indeed the most powerful savings tool since the creation of RRSPs. In fact, in some ways it is even better.

The decision to introduce the plan was a well-kept secret. The Liberals had said they would study the idea when they were in office, but they did nothing to follow up on a brief mention in the 2004 budget plan. Perhaps that was because the Conservatives had incorporated it into their 2004 campaign platform in a one-line sentence that read, "Introduce a new Registered Lifetime Savings Plan that will allow Canadians to withdraw their money tax-free."

After the Tories lost that campaign to Paul Martin's Liberals, the idea languished in limbo for almost four years. Then, faced with the prospect of a ho-hum budget in what would likely be an election year (and was, as it turned out), the minister and his staff started casting around for ideas. In pre-budget consultations with a range of business-people, academics, and special-interest groups, Finance officials kept returning to two key themes: demographics and retirement. As a subtext, the minister was very aware of the lingering anger of many seniors over his decision to impose a tax on income trusts, which was announced October 31, 2006.

In its "shadow budget" brief to the government prior to the 2008 budget, the C.D. Howe Institute returned to the theme of Tax-Free Savings Accounts, which it had been promoting since 2001. However, TFSAs rated only six lines in a thirteen-page report—it was almost as if the institute had given up. Whether it was that reference or something else that was the trigger, the minister seized on the idea. It was a good ideological fit, even though the promise of 2004 had not been repeated in the 2006 Conservative Party platform.

The enabling legislation was subsequently passed, and TFSAs were formally introduced to the Canadian public on January 1, 2009.

THE BASIC RULES

RRSPs have been around for more than half a century, but even now many people don't understand some of the most basic rules—I can say that with certainty because of all the questions I receive on the subject. Since TFSAs have been with us for only a few years, it's hardly surprising that they are still something of a mystery to many people.

Not understanding the rules can get you into a lot of trouble, as tens of thousands of people discovered in the summer of 2010. The Canada Revenue Agency began sending out notices of reassessment demanding hundreds or even thousands of dollars from TFSA owners because they had unintentionally violated the overcontribution rules in 2009. In many cases, they had withdrawn the money from one account and used it to open another. You can't do that—at least not in the same year. When the CRA's computers sniffed out what was happening, red flags went up everywhere. Fortunately, the issue was resolved in the end by what amounted to a government amnesty.

Much the same thing happened in the summer of 2011. Despite the publicity the previous year, many people made the same mistake in 2010. Again, the CRA said it would forgive genuine mistakes. But don't expect the tax collectors to be so lenient forever. Pay close attention to the rules and you'll be fine. Here they are:

ELIGIBILITY. You must be a resident of Canada to open a TFSA. You'll have to provide your social insurance number (SIN) and date of birth when you set up a plan.

AGE LIMIT. In theory, anyone eighteen or older can open a TFSA. That's what the federal legislation says. However, in some provinces and territories, the age of majority is nineteen. This means that contracts entered into by eighteen-year-olds—who are legally minors in those jurisdictions—can be voided by the courts if challenged. However, accumulation of contribution room will start at eighteen for everyone, even if a plan cannot legally be opened for another year.

There is no maximum age for holding a TFSA—unlike RRSPs, where seventy-one is the cut-off.

CONTRIBUTION LIMIT. The initial annual contribution limit was set at $5,000 per person, and that maximum applied for all the years from 2009 to 2011.

INDEXING. The contribution limit is indexed to inflation and, theoretically at least, adjusted annually. But for TFSAs, the Department of Finance introduced a new type of indexing that is done in increments of $500, using a rounding-up or -down calculation. The effect is to delay any increase in the TFSA contribution limit until the cumulative inflation factor has reached at least $250 since the time of the last hike.

CONTRIBUTIONS IN KIND. You don't need to have cash to make a TFSA contribution. You can also build a plan through what are known as contributions in kind. This allows you to deposit securities you already own directly into a TFSA.

However, if you make a contribution in kind, the Canada Revenue Agency treats the transaction as if you sold the security on the day it went into the plan. This means that if you have a capital gain, that gain is triggered and must be declared on your income tax return for that year.

Although you will have to pay tax on any capital gains created by contributing a security to a TFSA, you may not claim a capital loss. So you should never contribute a money-losing security directly to a TFSA. Sell it first—thereby creating a deductible capital loss—and then put the cash from the sale into the plan.

SWAPS. Swaps involve exchanging cash or securities from outside a TFSA for assets of equal value inside the plan. They were initially permitted, but the government changed the rules in late 2009 after receiving evidence that the practice was being abused. Now they are prohibited.

OVERCONTRIBUTIONS. The penalties for overcontributions are draconian, so be very careful about this. Any profits from intentional overcontributions will be taxed at a rate of 100 percent! If you make an overcontribution by mistake, withdraw the money from the plan as soon as you discover the error.

DEDUCTIONS. None. You do not receive any tax deduction for a TFSA contribution. Any money that goes into a plan is contributed on an after-tax basis. This is a major difference between TFSAs and RRSPs.

CARRY-FORWARDS. The carry-forward rules are similar to those for RRSPs, in that any unused contribution room may be carried forward indefinitely. For example, if you contributed only $2,000 to a new TFSA in 2010, your limit in 2011 was $13,000 ($5,000 for 2009 plus the $3,000 carried forward from 2010 and $5,000 in new contribution room for 2011).

You do not have to file a tax return to accumulate carry-forward room. But if you don't, the Canada Revenue Agency will not be able to keep track of the amount you are allowed to put into a TFSA. You will need to do that yourself.

TFSA YEAR-END. For purposes of contributions and carry-forwards, TFSAs operate on a calendar-year basis, so the annual cut-off date is December 31. RRSP contributions, by contrast, may be made up to sixty days after the end of the calendar year to qualify for a tax deduction in the previous year.

NUMBER OF PLANS. There is no limit on the number of TFSAs you can open. But common sense suggests that you limit yourself to one plan for ease of administration. If you decide to open a second TFSA, make sure you have a good reason for doing so.

WITHDRAWALS. You can take money out of a TFSA at any time, with no tax consequences. You don't even have to declare it on your income tax return—it is like withdrawing money from your bank savings account.

RECONTRIBUTING. Any withdrawal will be added back to your contribution limit for the *next* calendar year. Don't make the mistake of recontributing it in the withdrawal year or you could be in overcontribution territory.

TAXES. All withdrawals from your TFSA are tax-free—unlike RRSPs, where withdrawals are taxed at your marginal taxation rate. The investment income earned within the plan is fully sheltered.

REPORTING. All reporting responsibility is in the hands of the financial institution that administers your plan. The institution files an annual information return that includes details of all contributions, withdrawals, and transfers made during the year, as well as the value of the plan's assets at the beginning and end of the year. Your annual CRA notice of assessment contains a section advising you of the status of your TFSA and your available contribution room.

INCOME TESTING. TFSA withdrawals don't compromise your eligibility for income-tested tax credits such as the age credit, the Canada Child Tax Benefit, the Working Income Tax Benefit, or the GST tax credit. You can also withdraw money from TFSAs without affecting Employment Insurance benefits. For older Canadians, TFSA withdrawals don't affect their eligibility for programs such as the GIS and don't result in OAS clawbacks.

INVESTMENTS. TFSAs are highly flexible when it comes to the investments you can choose. The rules for qualified securities are the same as those applied to RRSPs. Almost anything is allowed: GICs, mutual funds, stocks (Canadian and foreign), bonds, gold, and cash. Even shares in a small business are eligible under certain conditions. The major exceptions are real estate and non-arm's-length investments, such as shares in a company you control. If you are uncertain whether an investment qualifies, get professional advice before going ahead, because the penalties for including non-eligible investments in a TFSA can be severe.

DEPOSIT INSURANCE. The Canada Deposit Insurance Corporation (CDIC) covers certain types of TFSA deposits up to $100,000, including cash, term deposits, and GICs. Securities such as stocks and mutual funds (including money market funds) are not protected.

INTEREST DEDUCTIBILITY. You may borrow money to invest in a TFSA, but you cannot claim the interest on the loan as a tax deduction. These rules are the same for RRSPs.

SPOUSAL PLANS. There are no spousal TFSAs. Also, there is no such thing as a joint TFSA. Each plan is the property of one individual. However, one spouse is permitted to give the other the money to open a TFSA.

INCOME SPLITTING. The usual income-attribution rules do not apply to TFSAs. This means that one spouse can provide the money for the other to open an account, with no penalty. So even if the other spouse has no income or savings, he or she can have a TFSA.

MARRIAGE BREAKDOWN. TFSA assets can be transferred from the account of one spouse or partner to the account of the other in the event of a marriage breakdown. The person from whom the money is transferred will not be given new contribution room to compensate, as this is not considered a withdrawal. Any such transfer will not count against the contribution room of the spouse or partner who receives the money.

TRANSFERS. You can transfer assets from one of your TFSAs to another one. This is called a "qualifying transfer." However, you *cannot* transfer money from an RRSP to a TFSA under any circumstances.

LOAN COLLATERAL. Unlike RRSPs, TFSAs can be used as collateral for loans. This could be useful if you suddenly need cash to deal with an emergency but the money in your TFSA is not accessible (perhaps because it has been invested in a locked-in GIC). If the lender is satisfied that the assets in the plan are sound, the TFSA can serve as collateral for a cash advance.

LIVING ABROAD. If you leave Canada after opening a TFSA, you can maintain the account and continue to make withdrawals. However, you will have to check whether such withdrawals would be regarded as tax-free by the country in which you are residing. You may not make any new contributions while you are out of the country, and no new contribution room will accrue.

PLAN TERMINATION. A TFSA ceases to exist when one of three things happens: the last account holder dies, the plan ceases to qualify for whatever reason, or the account is not being administered according to the law.

DEATH. When you die, the assets in your TFSA can be transferred to the plan of your spouse or common-law partner as the successor account holder. You'll need to sign forms to ensure this. When the last spouse or partner dies, all of the assets in a TFSA at the time of death can pass to the next generation tax-free.

CHOOSING A PLAN

There are five types of TFSAs: savings accounts, GIC plans, mutual fund plans, multiple-option plans, and self-directed plans. The terms and conditions for each type may vary considerably, even within the same company, and you may be able to select several investment options within a single plan. Make sure you fully understand what type of plan you are opening and all the associated costs. Investors may be caught off guard by some of the fees, such as a charge to transfer an account to another institution, which is standard for most companies.

Each type of TFSA is suitable for specific purposes. For example, a savings account plan will pay very little interest but give you easy access to your money. This type of TFSA is useful for holding the family emergency fund. GIC plans should never be used for this purpose because the money will be locked in for several years. But GICs are suitable for low-risk investors who want predictable long-term growth.

For a retirement savings TFSA, the best choice would be either a self-directed plan with a broker or a multiple-option plan that enables you to invest in GICs and mutual funds.

As a general rule, look for a plan that offers maximum

flexibility in your investment options at the lowest possible cost. This will require some shopping around, but it will be worth it.

WHAT MAKES THEM SO GOOD?

You've almost certainly heard about the magic of compound interest. It is sometimes referred to as the "eighth wonder of the world" because it is a simple route to wealth. The reason I like TFSAs so much is that they offer Canadians an investment vehicle that enables them to realize the full benefits of compounding. The income we earn in a TFSA is 100 percent ours to keep. No part of it will be taxed away. By contrast, all RRSP withdrawals are taxable, which eats up some of your profits.

Here's a table that illustrates what this means in terms of wealth building and shows the value of a TFSA at the end of various periods of time. I've assumed an average annual compound rate of return of 5 percent in all cases.

ANNUAL CONTRIBUTION	10 YEARS	20 YEARS	30 YEARS	40 YEARS
$1,000	$13,207	$34,719	$69,761	$126,840
$2,000	$26,414	$69,439	$139,522	$253,680
$3,000	$39,620	$104,158	$209,282	$380,519
$4,000	$52,827	$138,877	$279,043	$507,359
$5,000	$66,034	$173,596	$348,804	$634,199

Assumption: Contribution is made at start of year

After fifty years of $5,000 annual contributions, the value of the plan would surpass $1 million. With life expectancy increasing, readers who are twenty-five today have a realistic hope of achieving that $1 million.

There are two key points to take away from this table: start young and contribute as much as you can.

START YOUNG. Compounding is like a rolling snowball— it takes time to gather speed and mass. The more years a plan has to grow, the more impressive the returns will be. Look at the $1,000 line in the table. After one decade, the plan has added only $3,207 to your $10,000 in contributions. But after twenty years, the investment income earned within the plan has ballooned to $14,719 ($34,719 minus $20,000 in contributions). After forty years, the magic of compounding has given you a total tax-free profit of $86,840, on top of your own investment of $40,000.

So the sooner you begin, the more effectively a TFSA can work for you. Obviously, no one can turn back time. But whatever age you are today, the same basic rule applies: the earlier you start, the more effective your TFSA will be.

CONTRIBUTE AS MUCH AS YOU CAN. Slide your eyes down each column. You'll see that the greater the amount you contribute annually, the more profitable a TFSA will become over the years. If you double the annual contribution from $1,000 to $2,000, your profit from compounding will also double after the first decade, from $3,207 to $6,414. If you are able to contribute the initial maximum amount of $5,000 annually, your ten-year profit will increase to $16,034. (Of course, these figures assume no withdrawals are made along the way.)

The powerhouse effect of combining high contributions with many years of growth is apparent in the cell on the bottom right of the table. This shows you how much money will be in a plan after forty years of growth at 5 percent with an annual contribution of $5,000. The total is $634,199, which means that your tax-free profit after deducting all contributions is $434,199. That's a nice nest egg to draw on in retirement!

Suppose you do better than a 5 percent average annual return. The next table shows you the value of a TFSA if you are able to add one percentage point of annual return over the years, moving to 6 percent.

ANNUAL CONTRIBUTION	10 YEARS	20 YEARS	30 YEARS	40 YEARS
$1,000	$13,972	$38,993	$83,802	$164,048
$2,000	$27,943	$77,985	$167,603	$328,095
$3,000	$41,915	$116,978	$251,405	$492,143
$4,000	$55,887	$155,971	$335,207	$656,191
$5,000	$69,858	$194.964	$419,008	$820,238

Assumption: Contribution is made at start of year

After a decade, that extra return doesn't translate into a large profit gain—at the $1,000 level, the additional growth is only $765, which suggests that for older people the added risk involved may not be worth it. But look at what happens as the years pass and the magic of compounding takes hold.

At the end of the second decade, the $1,000 contributor has earned an additional $4,274. After forty years, this person is ahead by $37,208, simply because he or she invested the money wisely and earned one percentage point more.

Here again, the more you contribute, the greater the impact of the extra percentage point of return. An annual contribution of $5,000 that is invested to earn an average annual gain of 5 percent grows to $634,199 after forty years. But at 6 percent, the TFSA is worth $820,238 at that stage. The extra percentage point has given you an additional $186,039 to help fund your retirement. Now that's impressive!

TFSA OR RRSP?

So which is better for retirement savings: a TFSA or an RRSP?

There's no easy answer to this question. TFSAs provide a valuable option for retirement planning, but your situation will determine whether they should be used in preference to an RRSP.

For starters, you need to understand that TFSAs and RRSPs are two different creatures from both a tax and a savings perspective. In the jargon of economists, TFSAs are so-called TEE plans—taxed, exempt, exempt. That means the money going into the plan has already been taxed, but earnings within it are tax-exempt, as are all withdrawals.

In contrast, RRSPs are called EET plans—exempt, exempt, taxed. Contributions are tax-free because they generate an offsetting deduction. Investment income earned within an RRSP is also tax-free. But all the money that comes out is taxed at your marginal rate, regardless of its source. That means you'll pay more tax on capital gains and dividends earned within an RRSP than you would if those same profits were generated in a non-registered account.

There are groups of people for whom TFSAs will clearly be a better choice than RRSPs for retirement-planning purposes. Here are three of them:

1. *Pension plan members.* Anyone who belongs to a pension plan loses RRSP contribution room because of the pension adjustment (PA). This is a complex calculation that takes into account the amount contributed to a pension plan by you and your employer, as well as the retirement benefit you will eventually receive. The more generous the plan, the higher the PA will be.

   Anyone with a defined benefit pension plan (that is, one that provides guaranteed retirement income based on a combination of salary and years of service) is likely to have a high PA. People in higher income brackets may find they have little or no RRSP room left after the PA has been deducted.

   In this situation, TFSAs offer a valuable alternative for supplementing pension income. By making the maximum possible contribution each year, you can build a tax-paid nest egg that will provide extra income for travel, a home in the Sunbelt, helping your kids buy a first home, a grandchild's post-secondary education, or anything else you may want to do after you stop work.

2. *Modest-income Canadians.* In a report prepared for the C.D. Howe Institute a few years ago, Dr. Richard Shillington described Canadians with less than $100,000 in retirement assets as "futile savers" because they will probably need financial support from governments after they stop work. Those benefits will be reduced or even eliminated if there is any income from RRSPs and RRIFs. (Remember, every dollar in income from one of those plans reduces the GIS benefit by fifty cents once the $3,500 general exemption is exceeded.)

    Using a TFSA instead of an RRSP eliminates that problem. TFSA withdrawals are not treated as income, nor are they taken into account when the government calculates eligibility for GIS, tax credits, Employment Insurance, and so forth. This means that anyone with a modest income should favour TFSAs over RRSPs for retirement savings purposes, even when the amounts being put aside are small.

3. *Canadians with no earned income.* You cannot make an RRSP contribution unless you have what the government calls "earned income." Mostly, this is money earned from employment, but some other types of income, such as rents and alimony, also qualify. Investment income does not count as earned income, nor do pension payments, whether from the government or from a private plan.

If you don't have any earned income, or if the amount is small, TFSAs become your retirement savings vehicle by default. That's because you don't need any earned income to make a TFSA contribution.

There are also some people for whom an RRSP is a better option than a TFSA—in fact, it may be the only choice for some. One example is a child or teenager with earned income. You must be eighteen or older to open a TFSA, but there is no age limit for RRSPs. As long you have earned income, you can have an RRSP account.

Also, you should contribute to an RRSP *before* a TFSA if you expect to be taxed at a lower rate after retirement. That's because the tax deduction you can claim now will be worth more than the tax you have to pay when the time comes to withdraw that money from the plan. If you expect your tax rate to be higher when you retire, a TFSA is the better choice.

A PENSION PLAN TFSA

TFSAs can be used to achieve a variety of investment goals. But this book is about saving for retirement, so we'll focus on that aspect here.

Although the annual contribution limits are much lower in dollar terms than those for RRSPs, TFSAs have built up some financial heft now that they have been around for a few years. As of the beginning of 2012, every Canadian resident who was eighteen or older in 2009 and was not a recent immigrant had $20,000 in TFSA contribution room, so $40,000 for a couple. (This assumes no indexing increase in 2012, which was not known at the time of writing.) That's a good start for any retirement fund. The issue is using that money to best effect.

Before we get to that, let me emphasize one point: with the exceptions noted earlier, RRSPs are the best place for most people to start because of the immediate tax refund they generate. TFSAs should be used only after the RRSP contribution has been maximized.

When a TFSA is used for retirement savings, the same general rules apply: aim for reasonable growth while keeping risk to a minimum. Consider your TFSA a personal pension plan, then remember what I said in the previous chapter about how professional money managers handle pension accounts. They are very conservative, and with good reason. These men and women have been entrusted with the retirement savings of all the contributors to the plan, and those people are depending on them to ensure that the money will be there when it comes time to draw on it. So the last thing they can afford is to take big risks that might result in heavy losses. Your TFSA should be handled the same way. Keep risk to a minimum and choose your securities with care.

Over the years, I have seen people throw caution to the wind in their RRSP accounts and suffer the consequences for their recklessness. I believe there are two reasons for this. One is the fact that retirement seems a long way off, especially to anyone under forty. As a result, the assets in an RRSP take on the aura of Monopoly money and taking chances doesn't seem like a big deal. If things don't work out, there will be no immediate impact on the person's lifestyle, so why not roll the dice?

Rolling the dice is fine for TFSAs, in which the main goal is to maximize tax-free profits. But that is not the objective in a retirement plan. What you want in this situation is steady long-term growth, with minimal losses along the way. So never invest carelessly. Always keep the twin objectives of modest growth and capital preservation at the front of your mind. If a security doesn't fit this mould, pass on it.

During the stock market collapse of 2008, many people were bewailing the losses they suffered and complaining that they had been forced to put their retirement plans on hold as a result. If you are counting on your TFSA to help you maintain your lifestyle when you stop work, don't make that mistake.

Suitable securities for a retirement savings TFSA include money market funds, bonds, bond funds, GICs, preferred shares, balanced funds, conservatively managed large-cap equity funds, and carefully selected low-risk stocks such as utilities and telecoms. Avoid speculative stocks, ETFs, and high-volatility mutual funds.

POST-RETIREMENT INCOME

TFSAs have opened up a whole new world of investing opportunities for older people. Until they were introduced, there was no cheap and effective way to tax-shelter investment income after age seventy-one, the year when

RRSPs must be terminated. But there is no age limit for contributing to a TFSA, so Canadians who have passed the RRSP cut-off and have some money to invest should take advantage of these plans.

Most people in this age group will have one of two goals: either they will see a TFSA as a way to provide a tax-sheltered estate for their heirs, or they will want to make periodic withdrawals from the plan to supplement their retirement income. If generating tax-free income is the main objective, you should focus on low- to medium-risk securities that provide decent cash flow. Examples include high-grade corporate bonds (rated BBB or better), good-quality preferred shares, conservative dividend-paying stocks (e.g., utilities), some REITs, monthly income mutual funds, and low-risk ETFs. A self-directed TFSA is the best suited for this purpose.

If possible, don't make withdrawals from the TFSA for a few years to allow the capital to build to a respectable level. Once you begin drawing income, try to limit the annual amount to no more than the cash flow generated within the plan over the previous twelve months. That way, your capital will remain intact.

A READER'S TFSA STRATEGY

Because TFSAs are still relatively new, people are continuing to devise ideas about how to use them effectively. Here's one strategy that was sent to me by a newsletter reader in Kingston, Ontario:

We have developed a strategy to (partially) address the problem of grossed-up dividends artificially inflating income such that OAS is clawed back.

We are in our early sixties, retired, and both receive CPP, OAS, and some pension income. We use our unregistered assets to produce additional dividend and interest income. We each have a TFSA account and started depositing $5,000 respectively in early 2009. Assume that each TFSA account earned $250 (5 percent) of income in 2009. Here's what happened:

1. In December 2009, $250 was withdrawn from each TFSA and was not included in 2009 taxable income. Similarly, the $250 withdrawal was not counted as income towards the 2009 OAS clawback.

2. Because $250 was withdrawn in 2009, the January 2010 contribution room increased to $5,250. We each made a $5,250 contribution in January 2010; there is now $10,250 in each account.

3. Assume that each TFSA continued to earn 5 percent, i.e., $513, in 2010. That $513 was withdrawn tax-free in December 2010, with the consequence that contribution room in January 2011 is increased to $5,513.

This pattern continues each year. Gradually, we shift taxable income from unregistered investments into the TFSA. If we continue this process of contribution and withdrawal (and the 5 percent assumption holds), we could be receiving nearly $6,300 of tax-free annual income ($3,144 each) within a decade. Not huge, but not to be ignored, and none of it affects our clawback limits. If we had been able to start this process when we were in our fifties, our tax-free retirement income would have been much more significant.

Accordingly, we are loading our TFSAs with blue-chip dividend-producing shares, which hopefully will also generate non-taxable capital gains. When one of us dies, the surviving spouse (we are our respective sole beneficiaries) continues to receive the combined tax-free income from both TFSAs for as long as they survive, again without affecting the clawback.

As you can see, there are many ways to use a TFSA for retirement planning. I recommend that if at all possible you make full use of this great new savings tool.

SOLUTION 6
EDUCATE YOURSELF

If this comment offends some readers I'm sorry, but it needs to be said: when it comes to finances, many of us are woefully ignorant. Millions of Canadians have no understanding of the most basic concepts needed to function in today's world, from budgeting to handling debt. The federal government's Task Force on Financial Literacy was more diplomatic in its language, but that was the essence of its message to the government and the Canadian people. The challenge is made even more difficult by the fact that 42 percent of adult Canadians have problems reading, and almost 50 percent "struggle with simple tasks involving math and numbers," according to the 2003 International Adult Literacy and Skills Survey, which was included in a Statistics Canada submission to the task force.

More recent polls confirm that the level of financial knowledge among Canadians is discouragingly low. For example, in June 2011 the non-profit Investor Education Fund, which is funded by the Ontario Securities Commission (OSC), released a study reporting that the average score for respondents who were asked twenty-three questions about personal finance was only 50 percent. With 60 percent a passing grade, only 29 percent of Ontarians scored well. The survey found that knowledge of financial planning and goal setting was extremely low.

"As a matter of note, every question was answered correctly more often by people who are putting away money for retirement now than by those who are not," the report said. "This echoes a finding in many other studies that people are more likely to get informed when they are personally involved and need to make decisions." In other words, people aren't going to take the time to learn about money out of academic interest. There has to be a tangible, real-life benefit involved to motivate them.

Surprisingly, even saving money on income tax is not enough of a motivation for younger people. The study found that those under thirty-five have very little under-standing of the tax advantages of putting money into an RRSP. "Educating this age group about the tax benefits might spur earlier investment or retirement savings," the report concluded.

Ignorance and/or indifference costs Canadians billions of dollars every year—that's right, billions! Here are some almost unbelievable numbers from the findings of the Task Force on Financial Literacy:

- Roughly 160,000 eligible seniors are not receiving the Old Age Security benefit (representing almost $1 billion in pre-tax benefits).
- About 150,000 eligible seniors are not receiving the Guaranteed Income Supplement.
- Approximately 55,000 eligible Canadians are not receiving Canada Pension Plan benefits.

- The take-up rate for the Canada Education Savings Grant is just 40 percent.
- The median RRSP contribution represents only 6 percent of the total eligible room available.

Although much of the problem is due to a lack of education, some of the blame can be laid at the feet of governments that make applying for benefits too complicated, the task force said. "Several factors impede the take-up of benefits: some eligibility criteria and application processes are unnecessarily complicated, and many Canadians are unaware of the level of benefits to which they are entitled, or even that a specific program exists for them," the report concluded.

"To better connect Canadians to their financial benefits, we believe that policy-makers should be sensitive to the need for simplicity in program structure and documentation. A study commissioned by the Task Force suggests that the uptake and impact of public benefits could be improved through measures to simplify application processes."

As might be expected, the task force called for more financial education, for both young people and adults. That's clearly necessary, but in what I regard as a very pertinent comment, the report also zeroed in on the issue of motivation. All the courses and books in the world won't help if people aren't willing to allocate time to learn.

"Research shows that people are most interested in financial learning when it is associated with real money or a real financial decision," the report states. "Those 'teachable moments' include when workers join a pension plan or workplace retirement savings scheme; when consumers are seeking financial advice or considering the purchase of a financial product or service; [and] when individuals apply or check their eligibility for, or obtain benefits from, government programs."

Taking advantage of "teachable moments" is directionally a good suggestion, but it is too limited. Those moments may come any time. They aren't limited to joining a pension plan or applying for a government program. It's a "teachable moment" when you prepare your tax return, apply for a credit card, consider buying a house, take out a student loan, make an RRSP contribution, or work on the family budget. Anything that involves a financial decision offers an opportunity to learn about good money management.

I believe that the real key to improving financial literacy is to provide people with easy access to tools that will help them solve their immediate problem and educate them in the process. One of the recommendations in the report was on target in this regard: the task force called on the federal government to "create, maintain, continuously upgrade and promote a single source website for financial literacy, in an effort to increase public awareness about, and ease of access to, information."

That is certainly something Ottawa can and should do. In fact, it's surprising that action hasn't been taken already. Ontario's Investor Education Fund website (see appendix 4), which would be an excellent model for the federal government to build on, has been in existence for several years.

But while I support the idea of a government website, I think the best answers to the financial literacy crisis lie in an area the task force did not address in any meaningful way: new technology. Not long after the report came out, it was announced that the very first app created for Research In Motion's new tablet computer, called PlayBook, was designed to help people enrol in company pension plans. The idea is to make it easier and less stressful to complete the paperwork necessary to sign up. Not surprisingly, the app was created by Sun Life Financial, which administers many corporate plans in this country.

Sun Life's senior vice-president of senior retirement services, Thomas Reid, described the app as "a real catalyst for changing behaviour." He added: "We actually are quite convinced it's going to be very powerful in getting higher enrolment rates." Obviously, a higher enrolment rate would be good for Sun Life's business. But it would also be good for the financial future of the people who sign up, some of whom might not have done so had the process been more difficult.

This may be where some of the best solutions to financial illiteracy ultimately lie: in the creation of a wide range of user-friendly apps for popular devices like the iPhone and iPad, the BlackBerry, the Samsung Galaxy, and all the other new electronic gizmos that are appearing. If we can invent apps that tell people how long it will be before the next bus arrives, we can certainly create them for preparing budgets, managing investments, building retirement plans, and all the other financial details that we confront in our daily lives.

In fact, there are already many sources of action-able financial information using new technologies. The problem is finding them and choosing those that are best suited to your needs. Here are some suggestions to help.

USEFUL SOFTWARE

There are many financial software programs available. However, because of the differences between our tax laws and those of the U.S., only those that have Canadian versions should be used in most cases. You should also avoid programs that are highly complex. Start with a couple of inexpensive basic programs, learn how to use them effectively, and then move on from there.

Tax-Preparation Programs

I can't stress this strongly enough: if you aren't using software to complete your income tax return, do so! Not only will you significantly reduce the chances of making a mistake, but you'll learn a lot about your taxes and how to save money by responding to the various queries the program will ask. As a bonus, you may save hundreds of dollars because the software will optimize calculations for medical expenses, charitable expenses, RRSP contribu-tions, and pension income splitting.

"But I have my taxes done by a professional," you may say. My answer is that unless you are spending top dollar for the services of a professional who is familiar with your family situation, it will be cheaper to do it yourself with the help of a good software program. You may also get a larger refund, because no one cares about saving tax dollars as much as you do. Perhaps most important, you'll come away with a better understanding of the tax system, which may help you save more money in the future.

The best-selling tax software in Canada is TurboTax, which used to be known as QuickTax. It is produced by Intuit Canada, a subsidiary of the big U.S. software maker of the same name. If you visit the company's website (see appendix 4), you'll find a basic refund calculator you may want to try.

TurboTax comes in several versions, with varying degrees of sophistication and cost. For most people, the Standard version is adequate. I have used the program for several years and it does a good job. One of the advantages is that you can immediately see the result on the bottom line for both you and your spouse/partner every time you make or change an entry. So if, for example, you switch the medical expense claim from one person to the other, you will know right away if that saved you any money.

But while TurboTax is useful, it is not perfect. Some of my newsletter readers have complained that the font is too small for aging eyes. The program does not contain an easy copy/paste feature, which means re-entering the same data several times, such as the name of the family dentist when completing the medical claim form.

There are several other tax programs on the market, including one from H&R Block, the leader in the tax-preparation business. Presumably, the folks in their offices are using a version of this same software, so why not save a few dollars and enter the data yourself? I have also received some complimentary reviews about Tax Chopper, an online program that was described by one reader as being "pretty straightforward, has Help functions, and suggests optimum pension-splitting amounts." And I was especially interested in this part: "They will even talk to you to help with your return if you need it." I haven't tried it myself, but it sounds like it is worth a look.

Cash Management Programs

Everyone needs a budget. Yes, it's a hassle to prepare one, much less try to live within it. But the alternative is to go down that same road to ruin that many others, including governments, have taken: spending more than you earn. That only leads to big trouble.

Budgeting will be a lot easier if you use a good software program to help you. I have been using Quicken, another Intuit product, for that purpose for a long time, and I highly recommend it. Quicken can be as simple or as sophisticated as you wish. At the most basic level, you can use it to track all your expenses—cheques, electronic fund transfers (EFTs), debit card payments, cash withdrawals, etc. Every time you make a new entry, you'll immediately see your current bank balance.

By entering in advance all known payments and income—such as property tax payments, mortgage payments, utility bills, and salary—you can get an accurate picture of how your finances will look at the end of the month, or over any other time frame you wish. If you wish, you can categorize every expenditure for easy reference. Quicken has a pop-up menu that allows you to select from a range of personal or business expenses, from auto to travel. Other features allow you to manage bills, track your net worth, review how your money is spent, link to your bank account, and more.

This is a very useful program, and it makes budgeting much easier. It's not cheap, but it is worth the money.

Financial Apps

There are dozens of financial apps already available and more on the way. One example is Account Tracker, made for Apple products. It was chosen App of the Month by *Zoomer Magazine* in May 2011. In its review, the magazine described it as easy to use and said it can "turn any account and budgeting nightmare into a manageable situation."

Some other iPhone financial apps that were being offered at the time of writing included Tomorrow's Gas Price for Canadians, Canada Sales Tax Calculator, Canada Income Tax Calculator, HMP Canadian Mortgage Calculation, ATM Locator Canada, AM Canadian Mortgage Advisor, iTip Calculator Canada, Tax Man RRSP, and Canadian Taxes Discounts and Tips. Several financial institutions also offer their own apps, usually at no cost.

Not all iPhone apps are available for the iPad, even though both are Apple products, and the choices for tablets in general were very limited at the time of writing. A search of the Apple App Store turned up only one specifically for Canadians: the TurboTax Refund Calculator. A search for general money apps produced more than forty hits, however, at prices ranging from $0.99 to $29.99.

I have not reviewed any apps here because the field is evolving so quickly that by the time you read this, the technology will have moved on to the next level. Also, apps are often created specifically for one manufacturer and sometimes for just one product.

My advice is to check out what is available for your specific device, specifying "Canada" or "Canadian" in your search parameters. Then do an online search to see if you can find any reviews of the product, especially if it is relatively expensive. I did a Google search for "reviews of iPad financial apps" and got 65 million hits. When I added the word "Canadian," the number dropped to 17.5 million. I think that's enough to work with!

VALUABLE WEBSITES

Finding good financial websites is much easier than locating the best apps. For starters, websites are accessible to anyone with an Internet-enabled device. Also, they're usually free—you don't have to shell out good money only to discover that the program doesn't meet your needs or hasn't been adapted for Canada. Here are some of the best websites, both public and private.

Investor Education Fund

I mentioned the Investor Education Fund earlier. It is a non-profit organization established by the Ontario s Commission (OSC) to provide unbiased, dent financial information. The fund's website is a gold mine of useful information and offers eleven helpful calculators (at the time of writing), half a dozen worksheets, and numerous articles and tips.

Young people and their parents will find the University Cost and Debt Calculator especially valuable. Among other features, it tells you approximately how much it will cost to earn a degree in various disciplines at almost every university in Canada. (Although the site is funded by the OSC, it does not restrict itself to Ontario only.) I learned that a four-year engineering degree at the University of Alberta will cost approximately $17,000 a year, including tuition, books, room and board, entertainment, and transportation. The same degree at McGill will cost about $15,100 a year, while at the University of New Brunswick it will set you back over $19,000 annually. If cost is an issue, you have to pick your school carefully! The same calculator also allows you to figure out how to finance a college education and how much it will cost to pay off the loans after graduation.

Of course, if the parents start early by using an RESP, the financial strain of sending a child to university can be eased immensely. I did a test run using a middle-income Ontario family with two children, Joe (born in 2011) and Sally (born in 2009). I assumed both would start college at eighteen, take four years to earn a degree, and live at home for the duration. The program calculated that the parents would need to contribute $1,963 to an RESP annually, invested to earn 6 percent, to pay for the full cost of their schooling. That figure included an annual inflation adjustment of 4.4 percent—education costs are rising faster than most other expenses.

If both children decided to live elsewhere while they attended college, the amount the parents would have to save each year skyrocketed to—hold on for this one—$5,463! That's a daunting number, but it's better to discover the unpleasant truth while the children are still young.

Other calculators on this site will tell you whether it is better to pay off debt or invest, how long it will take to retire a credit card balance, and how quickly an RRSP will grow. Some of the calculators are also available in French.

Financial Consumer Agency of Canada (FCAC)

The Financial Consumer Agency of Canada is the federal government body primarily charged with providing financial literacy programs. Although the agency's website (see appendix 4) is nowhere near as comprehensive as some of the others described here, you'll find some interesting and potentially useful tools.

One that I did not see anywhere else is the Credit Card Selector Tool. Using a database that is regularly updated, this tool enables you to identify which cards best meet your requirements. Step one asks you to choose your province of residence. The next five steps require you to indicate what kind of card you want (regular or specialized), how it will primarily be used (purchases, cash advances, balance transfers), what your payment habits are (carry a balance or pay in full each month), whether you are willing to pay an annual fee, and what kind of rewards/ benefits programs you want. One key point that is missing is a screen for low interest rates, but the final result will be useful in narrowing down the possibilities.

British Columbia Securities Commission

If you're prepared to devote some time to learning about the basics of personal finance, this site is worth a stop. It's really designed to help teachers deliver financial education programs to students and to give parents some tips on how they can support the process. But anyone who doesn't know a lot about money can benefit, and the worksheets provided are very practical. If you have a teenager in your family, have him or her complete the Freedom 18 Budget and then discuss it with you. It could be a very illuminating conversation.

Canada Revenue Agency (CRA)

The CRA actually offers tips to save money on your taxes, but they aren't well organized, so you have to spend time exploring the site to find them. You can find tips on Tax-Free Savings Accounts by selecting "Newsroom" on the left-hand menu and then clicking on "Tax Tips." There are also menus directing you to information on a variety of topics, from pension income splitting to claiming credits for disabilities.

Ernst & Young

Want to know your marginal tax rate? Interested in finding out whether dividends or capital gains are more tax-effective? Use the Tax Calculator offered by Ernst & Young Canada (see appendix 4)—in my experience, it's the best of its kind.

By playing around with the numbers, you'll discover that many Canadians can receive $35,000 a year in dividend income and pay no tax at all if they have no other income. You'll also find that British Columbia, Alberta, and Newfoundland and Labrador are the best places, tax-wise, for a low-income person to live. High-income Canadians should avoid Nova Scotia (50 percent marginal tax rate) and flee to Alberta (39 percent).

Franklin Templeton Retirement Calculator

This one is a real eye-opener. Don't use it unless you are prepared for a wake-up call. You only need to fill in a few fields to get an idea of whether your current savings plan will achieve your retirement goals.

I ran a few scenarios to see what results were generated. The first was for a twenty-five-year-old Alberta man who wants to retire at sixty-five with 80 percent of his current $50,000 annual income. He has no employer pension plan but expects to receive $11,200 a year from CPP. He wants enough money to sustain him in retirement for twenty-five years. He has just opened an RRSP and is investing $100 a month. I assumed an average annual compound rate of return of 6 percent both before and after retirement. I plugged in inflation at 2 percent and used the same figure for increases in his salary and CPP benefits. The calculator assumes that the tax refund generated by the RRSP contribution is always reinvested. That's highly unlikely in real life, however.

The results show that by age sixty-five, the man will have accumulated $285,346 in his RRSP. But to meet his objectives, he needs $1,014,828! To achieve that, he would need to increase his monthly contribution to $356. And for every year he delays, that figure will go up.

Next, I looked at the situation of a thirty-five-year-old Ontario woman who makes $65,000 a year and contributes $200 a month to her newly opened RRSP. She is fortunate enough to have a pension plan that she expects will pay her $25,000 a year on top of her CPP. All the other assumptions are the same.

You'd think that someone in her situation would be just fine, but that is not the case. The results show a shortfall of almost $173,000 in the amount she will need at retirement to obtain 80 percent of her current income. She will have to add $122 a month to her savings to make up the difference.

Finally, I looked at a fifty-year-old Nova Scotia man with an annual income of $100,000. He has a very good pension plan that he expects will pay him $55,000 a year after retirement at sixty-five, on top of his CPP. He has already built up $25,000 in an RRSP and is contributing $5,000 a year to the plan. He must be in great shape, right?

No! He will need an additional $45,263 in his RRSP when he retires. That means he must add $1,184 to his annual contribution, bringing it to $6,184. Alternatively, he can reduce his income target to 77 percent of his salary.

If the RRSP refund is not reinvested, all these scenarios look much worse. The fifty-year-old Nova Scotian would need to more than double his annual RRSP contribution, to $10,160. The thirty-five-year-old Ontario woman would need to increase her monthly contribution from $200 to $455. As for our twenty-five-year-old in Alberta, his monthly contributions would have to more than quintuple, from $100 to $510!

Of course, the only scenario that really matters is your own, so try the calculator yourself. Just be prepared for a shock.

Fiscal Agents

You'll find a smorgasbord of financial tools at this website. The company, which is based in Oakville, Ontario, provides a range of financial services, but you don't have to be a customer to make use of the calculators, tables, and worksheets they offer online.

The site has something for everyone. If you're in the market for a new vehicle, print off a copy of their Shopping for a New Car Worksheet and take it with you to the showroom. If you want to know how large a mortgage you can afford, the Qualifying for a Mortgage Calculator is what you need. If you're interested in knowing how much risk you should take with your investments, try the Investment Philosophy Score Card—a fascinating exercise in self-analysis. Wondering whether you have adequate home insurance? The Contents Insurance Checklist will provide the answers.

I've only scratched the surface here. There are many more useful tools on this site. It's worth checking out.

Dinkytown.net

Don't be put off by the name. This is not a children's website. It's an international site that claims to offer more financial calculators than any other on the Internet, and after scanning through the lengthy menu, I believe them. (Note that you will need the latest version of Java installed on your computer to use them.) Many of the calculators have been specifically adapted for Canadians, so there is a wealth of financial information here just waiting for you to tap into it.

The Rent vs. Buy Calculator will be of special interest to anyone who is trying to decide whether to become a first-time homeowner, or someone contemplating selling an existing home and moving into a rental unit. Playing around with some numbers, I was intrigued to discover that an Ontario resident with $25,000 in available cash could buy a resale home for $250,000 but could not afford a new house. The reason? The province's 13 percent HST.

The Auto Loan Calculator will tell you quickly whether you can afford the car of your dreams. By entering a minimal amount of data, I found that financing a $35,000 auto will cost you $779.45 a month over four years, assuming a $7,000 trade-in, a loan interest rate of 7 percent, and HST of 13 percent.

Want to know when you'll be a millionaire? Try the Cool Million Calculator. It generates a graph that shows exactly how long it will take to accumulate that first million bucks. A twenty-five-year-old with no previous savings will hit the magic number at age sixty-six if she saves $500 a month and earns an average annual return of 6 percent. But if she saves only $250 a month, she won't get there until she is seventy-seven.

There's so much more on this site it would almost take a full book to provide the details. Better you see for yourself.

MoneySense

MoneySense magazine has a website offering a range of financial articles on planning, saving, investing, home buying, retirement, education, and more. There are also a few calculators, although the selection is much more limited than you'll find at Fiscal Agents or Dinkytown.

You might want to try the Life Expectancy Calculator. It projects how long you are likely to live based on several lifestyle and biological considerations (smoking habits, parents' health) and allows you to change your responses to see if some adjustments in the way you live might extend your life. I discovered that reducing my wine consumption at dinner might add one-tenth of a year to my life. I decided the wine was worth it!

Knowing your life expectancy isn't just an academic exercise, however. While we can't predict with certainty how long we'll be around, this kind of estimate can be helpful in putting together a realistic retirement plan.

The site also claims to have a Portfolio Tracker service, but I was unable to get it to load.

Globeinvestor

There are twenty calculators on this site, some of which will be of special interest to stock market investors. They are grouped under the heading "Calculators," and they are especially valuable for working out an appropriate asset allocation for your portfolio.

The Diversification and Bear Markets Calculator allows you to see at a glance how the value of a portfolio can be protected by adjusting the mix of stocks, bonds, and cash during a bear market. Using the 2008 market plunge as an example, an all-stock portfolio would have lost 43.3 percent of its value from the peak to the trough. However, one that was equally divided among stocks, bonds, and cash would have dropped only 11.6 percent. If the equity mix were lowered to 20 percent, bonds raised to 70 percent, and cash reduced to 10 percent, the overall loss would have been only 3.5 percent. A portfolio that was entirely in bonds would have actually *gained* 7.2 percent during the worst bear market since the Second World War.

Another calculator enables you to see how various asset mixes would have performed over a complete bear–bull cycle. I looked at the results from August 2000, which was the start of the high-tech market collapse, to May 2008, which marked the end of the rebound that followed. Interestingly, the value of a $100,000 all-stock portfolio at the end of the period was $152,284, only about $2,600 more than a portfolio that was evenly divided between stocks, bonds, and cash. The diversified portfolio did not do as well during the bull market period, but nor did it sustain the heavy losses incurred by the stock portfolio when the market tanked. And this is the most fascinating part: an all-bond portfolio would have done best of all. Instead of losing value during the bear market, it would have gained $19,500, meaning it did not have to play catch-up during the bull market years. Its final value would have been $168,069.

Other useful calculators on the site allow you to compare the value of investing money in a TFSA instead of a non-registered account, track your income and expenses (a great budgeting aid), and estimate how much life insurance you need.

MoneyVille

The *Toronto Star*'s MoneyVille.ca website is a good source for current financial information and tips. It also has several calculators; these can be found by clicking on various tabs. For example, under Budgeting you'll find a Second Income Calculator, an Emergency Fund Calculator, a Cash Flow Calculator, and more. Clicking on the Saving tab reveals a GIC Rate Comparison that shows the current rates being offered by a range of financial institutions. The Retirement tab offers a tool that compares returns between RRSP investments and those held outside a registered plan, as well as a Retirement Age Calculator that helps you figure out when you will be financially independent enough to stop work.

Keep Searching

I have only scratched the surface here. There are many more websites that offer valuable financial information and tools. A Google search will uncover them for you. Just be specific in your terminology and be sure to specify that you want Canadian information.

The point I want to leave you with is that the information you need is out there and is readily accessible. So you don't have to make a major time commitment to become financially educated in the areas of special importance to you. Just use your computer mouse or touchpad. It's that easy.

SOLUTION 7
FIND DEPENDABLE ADVISORS

In an earlier chapter ("Harsh Reality 5: We Don't Know What We're Doing"), I mentioned an email I'd received from a frustrated reader. He'd been told that because he was sixty-seven, he could no longer continue contributing to an RRSP. That email made me angry. Whoever had told this gentleman that he couldn't contribute to an RRSP because he was too old obviously knew nothing about the rules.

The message got me thinking, though, about how people get financial guidance. In this gentleman's case, I could only assume the erroneous information came from a well-meaning but ignorant friend. Even the most poorly trained financial advisor would know something as basic as the RRSP cut-off age.

The problem, of course, is that not enough people are seeking professional advice when it comes to handling money. There are a number of reasons for this, including reluctance to discuss personal finances with a stranger, concern about the expense, lack of knowledge about how to find an advisor, a preference for a do-it-yourself approach, and a lack of trust.

I receive comments and complaints about the trust issue quite often. Here's an example: "We believe we need a really impartial financial planner and have now discovered that we really don't know how to find one we can trust. And upon asking our friends and family for suggestions, we now know that many of them are in exactly the same position.

"Our banks tend to want to sell us their products. Ditto insurance companies and most other 'financial advisors' that we know. So how do you advise seniors about finding impartial financial advisors?"

It begins by understanding the semantics of the money management industry. The terms "financial advisor" and "investment advisor" have come to refer to anyone who provides guidance and/or sells securities to individuals. However, there are degrees of competence, as well as potential conflicts of interest, that investors need to understand.

These were well summarized in comments sent to me by Roy E. Adam, the vice-president and Calgary branch manager of Assante Capital Management, after I wrote an article in one of my newsletters about a couple who had been persuaded to borrow against their home to invest and ended up losing a lot of money.

"The investment industry has undergone a sea change in the past 30+ years whereby professionals giving technically knowledgeable and prudent advice are now outnumbered by those who may know just 10 percent more than their client, but are enthusiastic marketers of mutual funds and 'managed money,'" Adam wrote. "They are purveyors of a portfolio manager's investment competency, with little knowledge of their own, and thus [the term] 'salesperson' is more correct than 'investment advisor'...

"There are still many who are competent; however, we face an uphill battle against those who are less so, but are much better salespeople. The mutual fund companies do nothing to dispel this, as they are the primary beneficiaries."

Adam went on to say that investors should ask about the professional qualifications of anyone they are considering doing business with. He pointed out that those who have successfully completed the Chartered Financial Analyst (CFA) and/or Certified Investment Manager (CIM) programs have much greater knowledge of the markets than those who have taken only the Canadian Securities Course.

"Good financial planning is very helpful," he said. "Over the past couple of years the comfort in knowing that a long-term plan is in place is very reassuring to many current or soon-to-be retirees. This would have to include reasonable rate-of-return assumptions when projecting retirement income (we use 6% pre-retirement and 5% post retirement)."

The key, of course, is finding someone who will provide that "good" planning and not simply sell you a lot of high-priced products.

A CAUTIONARY TALE

Before I explain how to find a good advisor, let me tell you how I went wrong on my first attempt.

Many years ago, when I was just beginning to dabble in the stock market, I was introduced to a young broker who, I was told, was one of the rising stars in his company. "Invest your money with him and he'll make you rich," a mutual acquaintance told me.

I met with him at his office a few days later. It was impressive—a stately oak desk, a view over Lake Ontario, an oriental rug on the floor, original paintings on the wall. For someone who I guessed was in his early thirties, he seemed to be doing very well.

He ordered coffee—those were the days when a secretary would serve it on a tray, complete with biscuits—then we talked for about an hour. Or to be more precise, he talked and I listened.

There were no questions about my objectives or risk tolerance, or any of the other key information brokers are required to elicit now. Instead, he entertained me with fascinating stories about what for me was the new and exciting world of investing. He told me how he had discovered an unknown micro-cap company that was developing an exciting new technology that would revolutionize its industry. I can't even remember what that industry was, but I do clearly recall him telling me that the stock had gone from pennies to over ten dollars a share within a year. He put all his clients into it, and they made a fortune!

He regaled me with anecdotes about some of the best-known personalities on Bay Street. He talked about new IPOs—or initial public offerings—a term I had never heard before, and said he would tip me off to the best ones if I decided to work with him. He described how I could double or triple my profits by buying on margin. He assured me that he would be in regular contact with me and would be available any time I called.

By the time the meeting was over, I was convinced this was the right person to look after my money. We shook hands, and the next day I sent a cheque for about $10,000—all our savings at the time—to open a trading account. (Fortunately, as it turned out, I decided against opening a margin account as well.)

The broker was as good as his word when it came to the communications side of things. Initially, I would receive about one phone call a week. They always began with the same line: "Have I got one for you!" He would then excitedly describe his latest stock discovery in vivid detail.

The stories were intriguing. A Montreal company had patented a technique for making body armour out of spider silk that was even stronger than Kevlar. The U.S. government was interested. The stock was about to take off. I bought some.

A Calgary firm had acquired a massive oil field in some remote Asian country for a ridiculously low price and was going to make a fortune selling the output to China. It went into my portfolio.

A Toronto outfit had developed a new type of outdoor advertising and was about to sign a huge contract with the city. Get the shares while they're still cheap, he urged. I did.

And on it went—one great story after another. There was never any suggestion to buy shares in Bell (now BCE), Royal Bank, Canadian Pacific, or any other blue-chip company. They were for the plodders. He wanted his clients to be where the action was.

Well, there was action all right—mostly of the wrong kind. The stocks in my portfolio turned out to be extremely volatile. At the time, I knew little about liquidity and how thin volumes could result in big price swings, both up and down. All I knew was that my stomach would churn every morning when I looked at the market reports.

Not all his picks were losers, of course, but over time the value of my portfolio steadily declined. Coincidentally, the phone calls became less frequent. When he did call, it was usually to suggest that I inject more money into the account to take advantage of the "great new opportunities" that were coming.

It took several months for me to accept the fact that I had made a huge mistake. This guy wasn't a broker—he was a storyteller! A charming, highly articulate storyteller, but a storyteller nonetheless. The problem was that a good story doesn't necessarily translate into profits when it comes to stock picking. Much of the time, the good stories are nothing more than hype.

It was an expensive lesson. By the time I had the good sense to move my money elsewhere, the account was worth less than half the amount I had invested. My wife pointedly noted that I would have been better off paying down the mortgage. I couldn't argue.

I still like hearing good stock stories, but I rarely invest money based on them. If I do, it is only after extensive research into the company, with special attention to revenue growth, profitability, and the balance sheet.

Over the years, I have learned that the safest and most profitable way to invest in the stock market is to buy top-quality, dividend-paying companies and stay with them. TD Bank, Enbridge, Suncor, Fortis, Rogers Communications, Transcanada, Tim Hortons, and yes, BCE are all mainstays in my portfolio.

FINDING THE RIGHT ADVISOR

Despite my initial bad experience, there is no doubt in my mind that a financial advisor whose primary goal is to help you preserve and add to your wealth can make a huge difference in your life. But finding that advisor—someone who is on the same wavelength, will spend time helping you, and will not sell you securities that are inappropriate to your needs—is a challenge. You will have to devote some time, perhaps a lot of it, to research and interviewing, and there is likely to be some trial and error involved.

The best way to begin your search is to talk to family and friends. If some people in your circle already have advisors they have confidence in and are willing to recommend, you're more than halfway there. Otherwise, you will have to do some scouting around. As I mentioned in an earlier chapter, there's a search feature on the website of the Financial Planning Standards Council (FPSC) that, while flawed, may be a useful starting point.

First, enter your postal code, then use the Advanced Search Option feature to narrow the parameters of your search. Start with your language of choice. There are twenty-two options, from Arabic to Urdu. Then select your preferred compensation method: commission, fee-only, salary-only, etc. Finally, you can specify an area of specialization, and there are many from which to choose. Hit Enter and a list of names, with addresses, phone numbers, and a profile link, will appear.

The major problem with this tool is that it doesn't limit the results to professionals in your area—unless you happen to believe that Edmonton is in proximity to North Toronto. The results appear to sweep up every advisor who fits the parameters you entered, no matter where they are located. Fortunately, those closest to your area code appear at the top of the list, so you can ignore the rest.

Once you have decided on a list of four or five names, you have to begin the interview process. You are hiring someone to work on your behalf in one of the most important roles you can entrust to an outsider. So you *must* make an effort to meet with the candidates personally and interview each in depth. Those who won't take the time to meet with you should be crossed off the list; if they won't spend an hour with you to earn your business, they certainly won't go out of their way to see you after they have it.

Prepare yourself thoroughly before each interview. The following are some questions to ask:

- Are you registered with a securities regulator? If an advisor is not registered it probably means he or she does not have the appropriate qualifications.

- Have you ever been disciplined by a securities regulator or a professional organization? If the answer is yes, you can ask why but you'd be smarter just to thank the person for his or her time and leave.
- What are your professional credentials? As Roy Adam mentioned, a CFA or CIM certificate is desirable, although it's not absolutely essential if you are satisfied with the person's overall qualifications, experience, and apparent competence.
- How long have you worked with this firm? Where were you before and why did you leave? The second question should be asked only if the person has been with the company a short time. You're looking for someone who will work with you over the long term.
- Do you specialize in certain areas? What are they? This is very important. If you need estate-planning advice, for example, make sure the person is qualified in that field.
- What products and services do you offer? If you are planning to invest, you want an advisor who can supply you with a complete range of products: stocks, mutual funds, bonds, ETFs, etc. Someone who is licensed only to sell mutual funds may not be the best choice.
- What is your investment philosophy? If you're a conservative, risk-averse individual (most Canadians are), make that clear to the prospective advisor. If there seems to be a philosophical mismatch, go elsewhere.
- Will you provide me with references? Good advisors have satisfied clients who should be willing to write a letter or talk to you about the service they receive.

- How would you handle my investments? If you are looking for investment advice, bring a copy of your current portfolio and ask the person what changes he or she would recommend.
- Will you show me a sample report? You should receive a monthly report from the advisor that provides details of your account status, trades made during the month, income received, expenses deducted, changes from the previous month, etc. Review it carefully.
- Will I be dealing with you directly or with an assistant? Some advisors run big offices with two or three "associates" who handle day-to-day transactions with all but the wealthiest clients.
- How often will we communicate? The advisor should take your phone calls promptly, contact you if account changes are warranted, and arrange for a sit-down meeting at least once a year.
- How are you paid? This is a critical question. You need to understand exactly how the advisor is compensated because, one way or another, you're picking up the tab.
- What is your position on leveraging? Some advisors actively encourage clients to borrow to invest— called leveraging—by using margin accounts. This is a highly risky strategy that should be used only by knowledgeable investors.

The bottom line is that you should interview several possible advisors before making a choice. Yes, that's time-consuming and requires homework on your part, but look at it this way: would you test drive only one vehicle before buying a new car? Or inspect just one house before submitting an offer? Is choosing someone to handle your money any less important?

IF YOU'RE OLDER

For older people, one of the most important qualifications for a financial advisor to have is experience with income-oriented portfolios. Many advisors focus their business on growth portfolios—stocks and equity mutual funds, in particular. There's a good reason for that: they command higher compensation. In the mutual fund business, trailer fees (annual payments based on the market value of funds held by clients) have become the gold standard. The trailer fees on equity funds are much higher than those on fixed-income and money market funds, so it is no surprise that's where advisors look first.

If you find an advisor who has a considerable number of clients with income-oriented portfolios, you are on the right track. It's an indication that he or she is likely putting the customers' needs first. That's good business because it usually generates referrals, but not everyone recognizes that.

As mentioned above, you should look for an advisor who is philosophically on the same page as you. If you're a conservative investor who is interested in capital preservation and cash flow, but all the advisor wants to talk about is the stock market, move on. A good test is to ask a prospective advisor what asset mix he or she would recommend after you've outlined your investment goals. See how well it meshes with what you had in mind going in.

SPLIT THE BUSINESS

An alternative approach is to separate the advisory and implementation functions. Hire a fee-for-service financial planner who does not sell any securities. It will cost money, but you'll get an unbiased plan that is tailored to your needs. See "Harsh Reality 8: We Don't Know Who to Trust" for tips on how to do that.

Once you have a plan, take it to a broker or mutual fund salesperson and instruct him or her to implement it exactly as laid out. This eliminates any potential conflict of interest and ensures that your plan will be structured with your best interests in mind.

Despite the potential conflict-of-interest issues and the occasional bad apple who scams clients, I strongly believe in the value of good financial advice. And all the surveys I have seen support that view. For example, the 2011 Canadians and Retirement Report from TD Waterhouse found that poll respondents who worked with an advisor were far more likely to have a financial plan (52 percent) than those who had no help (7 percent). That's a huge discrepancy, especially since a financial plan is a fundamental first step in the whole money management process.

So make the effort to find the right person. The rewards will follow.

SOLUTION 8
MINIMIZE TAXES

In the first section of this book, I wrote about the many ways the income tax system is stacked against older Canadians. But that doesn't mean the situation is hopeless. Despite the inequities, there are still many ways to reduce the amount of tax you have to pay. But you need to understand the rules of the tax game and how to use them to your advantage. That's what this chapter is all about.

TIPS FOR YOUNGER PEOPLE

We'll begin with some tips for younger people. The goal here is to free up some of those tax dollars so that they can be used for building a retirement savings plan instead of going to the government.

MAKE AN RRSP CONTRIBUTION. It doesn't get easier than this. Your RRSP contribution will produce a tax refund and go to work for you in a tax-sheltered program. You'll get even more bang for your RRSP buck if you use the refund to top up the RRSP (assuming you have not used all your contribution room) or to build your Tax-Free Savings Account.

CLAIM A SPOUSE/PARTNER TAX CREDIT. If you supported a spouse or partner who had an income of less than $10,527 (all figures are for the 2011 tax year and are indexed to inflation), you can claim a credit on your return at line 303. The amount allowed is reduced for every dollar your spouse or partner reports as net income. So if his or her net income is higher than $10,527, there is no claim. Your federal tax reduction will be 15 percent of the amount claimed (this is the actual value of most tax credits in terms of the amount of money you save on your federal government return). You'll receive a provincial tax credit as well.

CLAIM A CHILDREN'S TAX CREDIT. You may claim an amount of $2,131 for every child under eighteen who is living with you.

APPLY FOR THE CANADA CHILD TAX BENEFIT (CCTB). These tax-free monthly payments are available to families with children, but some parents don't claim them because there is a widespread impression that they are only for lower-income people. That's not the case; many middle-income families are eligible to receive payments that could amount to $114 a month or more, depending on the number and age of their youngsters. But to obtain the CCTB, you must do the following two things:

1. Both parents must file a tax return every year, even if one has no income at all.

2. You must submit a formal application. You can apply online if you set up an account with the Canada Revenue Agency. For information on how to do that, go to the CRA website and click on My Account.

Don't wait to apply. Retroactive CCTB benefits are available for only eleven months. Also, several provinces offer their own child benefit programs to supplement the CCTB. Check with your provincial government for details.

At the start of 2011, the annual basic CCTB was $1,367 per child. If you have more than two children, there is a supplement of $95 each per year. Benefits are reduced for families with a net income in excess of $41,544. These numbers are readjusted every July 1 for inflation.

CHILDCARE EXPENSES. If you pay someone to look after your kids while you work, you can claim childcare expenses when you file your return. You will need to include form T778. There are a lot of rules governing this claim; for example, you cannot submit for expenses paid to a parent, other supporting person (such as a grandparent), or a relative under age eighteen.

You must have receipts to claim childcare expenses, and this can be a sticking point. If the child is being looked after by an individual, that person must also include his or her social insurance number on the receipt. Of course, many people balk at that—they want to be paid in cash, with no written record of the transaction, for reasons that are obvious. If you go along with this tax dodge, you're the one who will suffer, because the CRA will disallow your childcare expense claim. So take the time to find a qualified childcare provider who will give you the documentation that you require.

GST CREDIT. The GST credit is available to all families. Each qualifying adult is eligible to receive up to $253 a year, while children under nineteen get $133. The payments are made quarterly and are adjusted every July to account for inflation. There is an income test involved. To see if you qualify, complete the worksheet on the CRA website.

The GST tax credit is often overlooked by older children, particularly students. They often fail to make a claim because they have little or no income, and therefore don't bother to file a tax return. They could be missing out on more than $250 a year!

TIPS FOR OLDER PEOPLE

The following tips will apply mainly to older Canadians:

SPLIT PENSION INCOME. Pension income splitting offers the potential to save hundreds or even thousands of dollars in tax, depending on your situation. For those sixty-five or older, most types of pension income qualify, with the main exceptions being government payments and cash withdrawals from RRSPs.

The problem is figuring out the optimum split. It is almost impossible to do so without the aid of a software program. This is because transferring income from one spouse or partner to another may trigger undesirable side effects. These may include increasing one person's income to the point that the OAS clawback is triggered (net income exceeds $67,668 for 2011) and/or eligibility to claim the age tax credit is reduced or eliminated, the spousal tax credit is affected, provincial tax credits are lost, etc. The benefits of splitting income will more than offset the negatives in many cases, but only a sophisticated tax program or a knowledgeable tax advisor can tell you that with certainty. If you don't want to purchase a program, try using the free online tax calculator at taxtips.ca. It includes a separate pension-splitting box.

It would be helpful if the CRA offered calculators of this type on its website (it has already set the precedent with a payroll deduction calculator), but so far there has been no move in that direction. However, the CRA site does offer a lot of general information about pension splitting that may be useful. Go there to find out more.

USE THE PENSION CREDIT. One beneficial side effect of pension splitting is that it may allow both spouses or partners to make use of the $2,000 pension income amount (only one might have been able to use it before this rule came into effect). Also, any unused pension credit can be transferred to a supporting person.

MAXIMIZE THE MEDICAL CREDIT. Although we have medicare, there is no escaping the fact that the older we get, the more likely we will have to cover some health care expenses ourselves—sometimes very costly ones. You can get some of that money back (although not enough, in my opinion) by making full use of the medical tax credit. But you need to understand the rules.

Most people know that out-of-pocket expenses for such things as dental care, glasses, and hearing aids are eligible for this credit. However, there are many other health-related costs that qualify but may be overlooked. They include the cost of supplementary health insurance, travel medical insurance, and fees paid to a family doctor to cover uninsured medical services. (Note that these must be medical in nature; the CRA may disallow a claim that covers the cost of non-medical services such as filling in forms.)

But there's a lot more that can be claimed under this category, including many things you might not even consider. The list of allowable medical expenses includes up to $500 for installing an air conditioner for someone with a chronic respiratory ailment, elevators or lifts for disabled people, hair transplant surgery, home care services, moving expenses (to a maximum limit) for relocating a disabled person to more accessible housing, renovating costs, diapers for illness-related incontinence, talking textbooks, a scooter used in place of a wheelchair, and much more.

There's a complete list of eligible medical expenses on the CRA website, but don't treat it as the last word on the subject. If you think you have a legitimate medical claim that's not on the list, include it anyway. All the CRA can do is say no, and if the claim is sound, they will usually accept it. Remember, you can make a claim for any twelve-month period ending in the tax year for which you are filing the return, as long as you don't include expenses claimed in previous years.

While we're on the subject, I have two major complaints about the medical tax credit. First, you have to foot the bill for any expenses up to 3 percent of net income, to a maximum of $2,052. For this reason, the lower-income spouse should normally make the claim. Three percent of, say, $20,000 means the ineligible amount is only $600. If your net income exceeds about $66,000, you'll be on the hook for the full deductible.

Second, the federal credit is worth only 15 percent of the eligible expenses (provincial credits increase this). But no one incurs medical expenses for the fun of it. Families should be allowed to include *all* qualified expenses, and the credit should be for a much higher percentage. Even charitable donations over $200 get a 29 percent federal credit.

CLAIM THE AGE CREDIT. Anyone age sixty-five or older is eligible for this credit, but the higher your income, the less you'll receive. The basic amount was $6,537 for the 2011 tax year, but that starts being reduced when your net income exceeds $32,961. There's a federal government worksheet you can use to determine eligibility in the income tax package.

LOOK CLOSELY AT THE DISABILITY CREDIT. This has been described as the most underutilized but widely available tax credit. Tax expert Alan Rowell, speaking recently at a conference of financial advisors in Orlando, Florida, said that Canadians lose out on millions of dollars in tax savings every year because they don't consider themselves "disabled," even though they actually are (at least according to the Income Tax Act and government guidelines). As the population ages, the situation is only going to get worse.

The disability amount for an adult for the 2011 tax year was $7,341, which translates into about $1,100 in actual tax saved at the federal level, plus a reduction in provincial tax. The amount is indexed to inflation.

Rowell, who has more than thirty years of experience in tax practice and is president of the Accounting Place in Stoney Creek, Ontario, said that one of the reasons people miss out on the disability credit is that they refuse to acknowledge developing physical and/or mental limitations as they grow older. Often these changes happen so gradually that people don't even realize they have crossed the impairment threshold—hearing loss is a prime example. Rowell told the audience that he frequently encountered clients who had qualified for the credit for years but never claimed it. Fortunately, there is a ten-year carry-back rule that he uses to claim thousands of dollars in tax overpayments for these people.

The other reason people don't claim the credit is the intimidating application form. To illustrate, Rowell asked a volunteer from the audience who was more than six feet tall to hold a stapled copy of the whole form over his head and let the pages drop. They reached all the way to the floor—some eight and a half feet. If you don't believe me, you can see for yourself. You can download the twelve-page form at the Canada Revenue Agency website.

So how do you know if you or someone in your family is a potential candidate for the disability credit? You can start by taking a short self-test on the CRA site—click on "Information for persons with disabilities" in the column on the left-hand side of the homepage. That will take you to a screen with several links, one of which reads "Are you eligible for the disability tax credit (DTC)?" Click on that and answer "Yes" to the first question. A list of eligible disabilities will appear. If one applies to you, click on it and you'll be taken to a definition of that particular condition. For example, someone who takes an "inordinate amount of time" to understand another person in a quiet setting, even with the use of hearing aids, would qualify for the credit. "Inordinate" means it takes a person significantly longer to comprehend what is being said than would be the case for someone with normal hearing.

Other physical limitations that qualify include difficulties with speaking, walking, dressing, feeding, and waste elimination. People who are on what is called "life-sustaining therapy" are also eligible. Kidney dialysis is an example.

The impairment does not have to be physical. Someone with significant mental limitations—for example, from Alzheimer's disease—would qualify. Unfortunately, as the population ages, this affliction is becoming more prevalent. If someone in your family is suffering from it, make sure that whoever prepares his or her return applies for the credit.

If the disabled person does not have enough income to take full advantage of the credit, it can be transferred to a family member who can make use of it. The list of eligible people who can claim the credit is surprisingly long, ranging all the way from a spouse to a great-aunt or great-uncle. So even someone with very low income who qualifies should apply for a disability tax credit certificate.

Of course, that involves tackling the twelve-page form, which is known as T2201. However, it is not as daunting as it appears at first glance. The applicant, or a representative, only has to fill out one page. A qualified medical practitioner handles the rest. This can be your family doctor or a specialized practitioner, such as an occupational therapist for feeding, dressing, or walking or an audiologist for hearing loss. All sections of the form that don't apply can be ticked as "not applicable."

The doctor or practitioner does not have the last word. That's the prerogative of the CRA, which will review the application and determine whether the certificate will be issued and if it will have any limitations. For example, the certificate may have a time limit, after which you will need to reapply.

Aging Canadians aren't the only people who are missing out, Rowell said. He cited the case of a young couple whose taxes he prepares every year. They told him about the birth of their child three years earlier, so he dutifully claimed the appropriate credits. What the couple had *not* told him was that the youngster was disabled. They had been missing out on hundreds of dollars' worth of tax savings as a result. Rowell quickly took the appropriate steps to recover the lost money.

Disabled children under eighteen receive an extra credit to a maximum of $4,282, bringing their total disability amount to $11,623. Since the child probably won't have any income, that amount may be transferred to a supporting person, such as a parent.

That's not all. Any dependant under eighteen who qualifies for the disability tax credit is also eligible to receive the Child Disability Benefit (CDB). It's a tax-free payment that was worth up to $2,504 a year in 2011. This benefit is income-tested and starts to phase out when the family's net income surpasses $41,544 (2011 level). Disabled children also benefit from an additional $500 for the children's fitness tax credit.

The bottom line is that if you or anyone in your family appears to be eligible for this tax break, you should discuss the situation with your doctor. If he or she agrees, download the form from the CRA site and submit it. And remember that if the condition has existed for some time, you can go back as far as ten years. There may be several thousand dollars just waiting for you or a loved one to claim. Don't miss out!

TIPS FOR INVESTORS

Investing decisions are never easy. There are several factors that need to be taken into account, but the expected rate of return, which is the first thing most people look at, is actually one of the least important.

One of the key points to consider is taxes. All that really counts in the end is how much you keep in your pocket after the Canada Revenue Agency and its provincial counterparts are through with you. That calculation can be very complex. I was reminded of this when I received a question from a reader in Comox, British Columbia. He wrote as follows:

"We are retired and live off our investments from the sale of a small business. One of us receives OAS and some CPP. Eventually we will tap into [our] RRSP and RRIF funds. It seems the most difficult investment task at present is finding ways to invest our taxable funds. It would be very beneficial for us not to generate too much in the way of dividends, as well as interest. Since we are in British Columbia, the gross-up on dividends adversely affects our 'income' as used to determine the amount we must pay for provincial health care coverage and drugs— anything that is means-tested really. Any suggestions?"

The reader is absolutely right about the complicated dividend gross-up formula. As I discussed in "Harsh Reality 7: The Tax System Is Stacked Against Us," this calculation has the effect of inflating a taxpayer's net income by adding money that never existed to the total. This can result in people being hit with the clawback tax on Old Age Security, losing part or all of the federal age tax credit and/or the GST/HST credit, being stripped of provincial benefits as the reader describes, and more.

As a result, you need to look carefully at the tax implications of every potential investment before making a final decision. Basically, there are four types of investment income—interest, dividends, capital gains, and return of capital—and each is treated differently for tax purposes if the security is in a non-registered account. Let's look at each type in more detail.

INTEREST. All interest income is taxed at your marginal rate—that is, the rate that applies on the last dollar you earn. So if your combined federal/provincial marginal rate is, say, 35 percent, you will keep only sixty-five cents out of every dollar you receive in interest. At the time of writing, major banks were offering rates of about 2.2 percent on five-year GICs, but the true after-tax return for someone in a 35 percent bracket was only 1.43 percent, less than the rate of inflation.

DIVIDENDS. The dividend tax credit (DTC) reduces the amount of money you will have to pay the government, sometimes dramatically. It is especially effective for lower-income people; in Ontario, anyone with taxable income of less than $37,750 will pay no tax on "eligible" dividends (that is, those from large Canadian companies), according to the 2011 online calculator of Ernst & Young.

However, as we have seen, the DTC gross-up calculation is a potential tax trap that can end up costing you in several ways. Check out all the implications before committing to dividend-paying securities.

CAPITAL GAINS. Half of any taxable capital gain is yours to keep, but the rest will be assessed at your marginal rate. Generally, the effective tax rate on capital gains is higher than that on dividends but less than you'll pay on interest income.

RETURN OF CAPITAL. This can be a very tax-effective way to receive investment income, but the calculations are complex. In theory return of capital (ROC) suggests that your own money is being paid back to you, but in practice that is often not the case. For instance, some real estate investment trusts (REITs) pay a portion of their distributions in the form of ROC that reflects depreciation claimed on properties owned by the trust. In 2010, RioCan REIT, Canada's largest, paid a total of $1.38 per unit in distributions, of which about fifty-eight cents was treated as return of capital.

ROC amounts are not taxable in the year they are received. However, that does not mean they are tax-free. All such payments must be deducted from the original price you paid for a security to arrive at what is known as the adjusted cost base (ACB). This is the figure on which capital gains will be calculated when you sell your shares.

To illustrate, let's say you purchased units of RioCan at a price of $20 each and received the full 2010 distribution. You would subtract fifty-eight cents from the purchase price to arrive at your ACB, which would be $19.42. This process is repeated each year you receive ROC distributions.

Let's assume that after a few years, your ACB is down to $17.50 and you sell your units at $20, the same price you paid originally. You may think that no capital gains tax is payable—since you sold at your original price—but you'd be wrong. As far as the government is concerned, you have made a profit of $2.50 per share ($20 − $17.50), of which half ($1.25) is subject to tax.

If your ACB falls to zero, all ROC income received after that will be taxed at the capital gains rate. When you sell, the entire proceeds from the sale, less any commissions and expenses, will be taxable as a capital gain.

Registered Plans

If your investments are in registered plans (RRSPs, etc.), you may think that you don't have to worry about taxes.

If it's a TFSA, you're right. But if the securities are in an RRSP, a RRIF, a LIF, or something similar, you need to consider what will happen when the money eventually comes out.

Any investment income paid into an RRSP or a RRIF will be received tax-free at the time. But you will pay tax at your marginal rate when you make a withdrawal. In the case of interest income, it doesn't matter because your tax rate will be the same whether the money was received directly or through the registered plan. But dividends, capital gains, and return of capital will all end up being taxed at a higher rate when they are taken as RRSP/RRIF withdrawals than they would if they had been paid to you directly.

That makes Tax-Free Savings Accounts the best solution if you want to avoid paying any tax on your investment income. Withdrawals are not taxable, and they are not treated as income for purposes of calculating government benefits and tax credits.

The bottom line is that Canada has a very convoluted tax system, with both advantages and disadvantages. There are ways to save money, perhaps a lot of it, but you need to work through all the numbers carefully or have a financial professional do so on your behalf.

SOLUTION 9
REVIEW ALL YOUR RETIREMENT OPTIONS

Where is the money going to come from after you retire? Surprisingly, considering the relatively low number of Canadians who make contributions every year, 90 percent of pre-retirees interviewed for the 2011 RBC Retirement Myths and Realities Poll named RRSPs and RRIFs as one of their top income sources after stopping work.

Government pension plans such as the CPP came next at 84 percent, followed by Old Age Security at 66 percent. About 56 percent said they plan to draw on the equity in their homes to sustain their lifestyle—a potentially dangerous idea because it assumes that Canada won't experience a housing depression along the lines of the one that decimated home prices in the U.S. Only 58 percent said they expected an employer pension plan to be a major contributor to their retirement income. That was down markedly from 65 percent in 2010 and appears to be yet another indicator of the diminishing role of pension plans in the workplace.

One of the most striking aspects of the survey was the relatively small number of pre-retirees who listed TFSAs, annuities, and non-registered investments as important income sources. In fact, more respondents (26 percent) cited a potential inheritance as an important income source than those who mentioned annuities (15 percent).

I believe it is essential to look carefully at all your income options when preparing a retirement plan. The take-up rate on RRSP contributions suggests that many people who expect to draw significant income from this source are dreaming. I don't say this to discourage you from contributing—quite the contrary. But unless you start early and commit a significant portion of your annual income to the plan, odds are you will end up with a relatively modest amount of capital. Consider this: an RRSP valued at $100,000 will generate $7,000 a year in pre-tax income at a withdrawal rate of 7 percent. That's nice to have, but even when combined with CPP and OAS, it won't be enough for most people to live on comfortably.

That's why you need to review all your retirement options, not just the most obvious ones. Unless you have a gilt-edged pension, your retirement plan will include income from a variety of different sources. They may include some of the following:

- CPP or QPP benefits
- Old Age Security
- RRSP/RRIF withdrawals
- TFSA withdrawals
- employer pension plan payments
- non-registered investment income
- annuities
- insurance policy payouts

- Guaranteed Income Supplement (low-income people only)
- post-retirement employment income
- rental income

You'll see that I have not included home equity on the list. Some respondents to the RBC poll said they would consider borrowing against their home to partially finance their retirement, but I think that's a bad idea. A home equity loan or conventional mortgage has to be repaid, and the interest will eat into any income that is generated. In some circumstances, a reverse mortgage could be considered, because with it, no payments are needed until the home is sold or the last surviving spouse dies. But the accrued interest on such loans will mount up quite quickly, which is an important consideration if leaving an estate for the children is a priority.

The fact that only a small percentage of those polled mentioned annuities was worrisome (15 percent of pre-retirees and 19 percent of actual retirees). Annuities were once regarded as an important source of retirement income, but they have been pushed into the background in recent years, in large part because of the low interest rates we've experienced. But as life expectancy continues to increase, I believe they will stage a comeback. Let me explain why.

INCOME FOR LIFE—HOWEVER LONG THAT IS!

Like many people, I wouldn't mind living to a hundred as long as I can have two wishes. My first wish is that my health, both physical and mental, stays reasonably good. My second is that my money lasts as long as I do, so that I can continue to enjoy the lifestyle to which I'm accustomed.

In other books, you'll find advice on staying healthy to one hundred and beyond. But how can you be sure you won't run out of money? No one wants to spend their final years depending on their children or the charity of others to survive.

Unless you're a multi-millionaire or win the lottery, there is only one way to ensure that you will have enough income to live comfortably for as long as you're around. That is to use some of your retirement savings to purchase a life annuity.

Annuities can come with all sorts of bells and whistles. But when you strip those away, a life annuity is simply a contract between you and a life insurance company under which they agree to pay you regular income for as long as you live, however long that may be. The insurance companies employ teams of high-powered actuaries to figure out to the month how long people in various age groups are likely to survive, and they base their rates on those projections. If you die early or on schedule, the insurance company wins. If you live well beyond your normal life expectancy, you win. In a sense, it's something of a gamble. The constant that makes it worth taking is the fact that you'll continue to receive regular payments no matter how long you live. You should never have to worry about where the next cheque is coming from.

Annuities have fallen out of favour in recent years

because of two factors: low interest rates, which reduce the income you'll receive for your capital, and the desire of seniors to retain control of their assets and leave something for their children when they go. Despite this, I suggest that retirees who don't have the certainty of pension plan benefits consider buying an annuity when they reach their eighties. The reason is simple: under current minimum withdrawal rules, the capital in your RRIFs and LIFs will be depleted rapidly after that. At age eighty, you are required to withdraw 8.75 percent of a RRIF's annual opening value. By eighty-five, the minimum is up to 10.33 percent; by ninety it has reached 13.62 percent, and after ninety-four it is 20 percent a year. As a result, the capital in a RRIF will be depleted at an accelerating rate as you grow older.

You can stop the financial bleeding by purchasing a life annuity while you are in your eighties. I suggest waiting that long because the older you are when you enter into a contract, the higher your payments will be. The amount of the payment will vary depending on your age and five other factors: the amount of money you invest, your sex (men get more than women because they tend to die sooner), the interest rates when you make the purchase (the higher the better), the type of annuity you choose, and the life insurance company you deal with.

When you shop for an annuity, you'll need to keep your wits about you. Like most insurance products, annuities tend to be much more complicated than necessary, and apples-to-apples comparisons between companies can be difficult. There are three basic types of life annuities: single male, single female, and joint. The latter continues to make payments to the last surviving spouse until death.

But that's just the beginning. You will be offered guaranteed annuities (payments will be made for the guarantee period even if you die), indexed annuities (payments increase with inflation), impaired annuities (when you have a health condition that makes it probable you will die sooner than normal), and more. Except in the case of impaired annuities, the more options you choose, the less cash you will receive each month.

Globeinvestor.com has a feature that enables you to check current prices for various types of basic annuities. I visited the site at the time of writing to check on quotes for buying an annuity using money from a registered plan. All were based on an investment of $100,000. I found that the best payout for a single male with no guarantee was from Desjardins Financial Security. If someone bought the annuity at age seventy, the monthly cheque would be $741.05. Waiting until eighty increased the monthly payout to $1,129.26. That was $131.15 a month more than the second-best quote, which was from Standard Life.

If a single male opted for a ten-year guarantee, meaning payments would continue to his heirs if he died during those ten years, the monthly cheques from Desjardins would be reduced to $672.10 for a seventy-year-old and $823.04 for an eighty-year-old. The longer the guarantee period, the lower the monthly payment.

A single female with no guarantee would do slightly better with Empire Life, which was quoting $638.58 a month for a seventy-year-old. But Empire did not post a quote for an eighty-year-old. Among the companies that did, Desjardins was best, at $931.38 a month.

For a joint annuity with no guarantee, BMO Insurance was the best at age seventy, with monthly payments of $558.79. At eighty, Desjardins was back on top, at $774 a month.

As you can see, careful shopping pays off, so be sure to do your homework before deciding which company to deal with. And don't lose sight of the fact that there are downsides to annuities. For starters, you surrender your capital to buy one. Once you hand over your $100,000 (or whatever amount you've settled on), it's gone. You no longer have it to invest or to pass on as part of an inheritance—which is why many people choose guarantees, even though they reduce the monthly payment.

Also—and this is a recent concern—there is a possibility that your annuity could be affected if the insurance company you deal with runs into financial problems. An industry-run organization called Assuris provides protection of up to a maximum of $2,000 a month if the annuity provider fails, but any amounts beyond that are at risk. You'll find more details on the organization's website (see appendix 4).

Despite these negatives, annuities offer a solution to the problem of outliving your money, a concern many people have. Just make sure you stay healthy enough to enjoy the benefits.

INVESTING FOR INCOME

The other finding from the RBC survey that especially concerned me was the dramatic decline in the number of people who expect to receive a significant amount of retirement income from non-registered investments. Only 47 percent of pre-retirees mentioned this source in 2011, down from 58 percent in 2010. Among those already retired, the percentage dropped from a respectable 63 percent in 2010 to 54 percent in 2011.

The sharp drop-off is puzzling. The best explanation I could come up with is that it was a consequence of ultra-low interest rates. Older people are more conservative by nature, and they tend to favour low-risk, fixed-income securities as a result. GICs, bonds, and money market funds provide a sense of security that stocks can never offer. But with interest rates at their lowest levels since the Great Depression, the returns on these securities were depressed. The average Canadian money market fund generated a gain of only 0.49 percent in the first half of 2011. The average annual compound rate of return for the three years to that point was just 0.53 percent. No one can live on that!

In late July 2011, five-year Government of Canada bonds were yielding 2.75 percent. Five-year GICs from smaller financial institutions were a little more generous, paying as much as 3.5 percent, but even that was well below what investors were accustomed to receiving in the past. The major banks were offering only 2.2 percent on five-year terms. For people with money in non-registered accounts, the situation was made even worse by the fact that interest payments are taxed at their marginal rate. So the after-tax returns on these securities were negligible.

This doesn't mean you should never consider fixed-income securities for a non-registered investment portfolio. However, they should not be the only type of security you hold if you want to generate respectable tax-advantaged cash flow from your assets. Here are some other ideas that will work effectively.

Preferred Shares

When we think of the stock market, we think of common shares. Preferred shares are a different type of security. Think of them as bonds that pay dividends instead of interest. It's not quite that simple, but it gives you the idea.

As I explained in the previous chapter, the advantage of dividends is that they get you a tax break. The rationale for this is that corporations pay dividends to shareholders out of after-tax earnings (that is, money that has already been taxed). The dividend tax credit is supposed to eliminate double taxation.

The magnitude of this tax advantage cannot be overstated. A top-bracket Ontario taxpayer paid a rate of 46.41 percent on interest income received in 2011, but if the money had been received as eligible dividends instead, the rate would have been only 28.19 percent. That's a tax savings of $182.20 on every $1,000 of dividend income. Lower-bracket taxpayers fare even better.

Preferred shares—or preference shares, as they are

more correctly known—are actually something of a cross between a common stock and a bond. Like bond interest, the dividend is usually (but not always) fixed. Payments are normally made quarterly. Preferreds rank ahead of common stocks in the financial pecking order, which means that a company must pay all its preferred dividends first, including any that are overdue, before owners of common stock get a cent. In the event a firm is wound up, preferred shareholders rank ahead of common stock owners but behind bondholders in terms of asset distribution. Normally, preferred shareholders have no voting rights in a company, whereas common stockholders do.

Although the price of preferreds will usually not vary as greatly as that of the common stock of the same company, these shares tend to rise in value if interest rates decline and fall in value if rates rise, in the same manner as bonds. Fixed-rate preferreds, which pay exactly the same dividend at all times, will be the most affected by interest rate changes. So in times of rising rates, choose floating-rate preferreds to reduce risk. The dividend on these shares is tied to prime or some other key rate, so it will rise or fall with the general movement of rates. If you expect interest rates to fall, an investment in good-quality fixed-rate preferreds could pay off handsomely, for exactly the same reason that bonds will do well in that situation.

Blue-Chip Stocks

They're riskier than preferreds, but dividend-paying blue-chip stocks can give a big boost to returns from a non-registered portfolio. The dividends are eligible for the tax credit and only half of any capital gain is taxed, so the after-tax return is very attractive.

However, capital gains should be viewed as a bonus. Your main priority is to generate good cash flow at reasonable risk. To do that, you should focus on industry leaders with a long business history and a track record of steadily increasing dividends. Banks, utilities, and telecommunications companies are all logical choices.

Don't succumb to the siren call of unrealistically high dividends. If a stock is yielding significantly more than its peers, it's an indication that the market believes it carries a greater degree of risk. Often, a very high yield is a warning signal that a dividend cut is imminent.

The following are a few tips to help you choose the best blue-chip stocks for a portfolio:

- *Stick with your priorities.* Your number-one goal is to earn good tax-advantaged cash flow with reasonable risk. Period! Keep that in the front of your mind every time you consider buying a security. Don't let the fact that your broker recommends it, or that it's a "hot" stock, affect your judgment. Some investors made a fortune on Apple shares when they more than quadrupled in value between March 2009 and August 2011. But the shares pay no dividends. On that count alone, they do not belong in this kind of portfolio.
- *Diversify.* Make sure your portfolio is properly balanced. This means you should not put all your money in one or two stocks. You need to spread your investments across several companies and industry sectors.

- *Make sure it's tax-efficient.* Only dividends from Canadian companies are eligible for the dividend tax credit. So even if you find a U.S. stock with an attractive yield, it won't be as valuable to you after the tax folks take their cut.
- *Never speculate.* The stock market is not a casino, although some people tend to see it that way. It's serious business, and a careful, well-informed investor can do very well by sticking with good-quality companies. You don't have to speculate in penny stocks to reap big rewards, and they don't fit this portfolio model anyway. I've seen many blue-chip stocks double and triple in just a few short years. For example, in my *Internet Wealth Builder* newsletter I recommended shares in BCE Inc. in December 2008, when they were trading at $21.30. BCE is about as blue chip as a stock gets in Canada. On July 1, 2011, the shares were trading at $38.14, and for each one, we had received dividends totalling $4.80. That represented a gain of 101 percent in a little over two and a half years! Clearly, you don't have to speculate in juniors to do well, nor do you have to spend hours in front of your computer indulging in day trading.
- *Take advantage of buying opportunities.* One of the brokers with whom I do business has a good sense of humour and the ability to maintain his perspective, no matter what happens. When I called him in the midst of a recent market sell-off, his first words were "Have you heard we're having a sale?" When the markets go into a slump, that's how you should look at stocks—

as if they're on sale. It may be a long time before you can pick up such valuable merchandise at knock-down prices like these. We saw a classic example of that in early 2009, when the world was in panic mode over the financial meltdown. Canadian banks, which emerged as the strongest in the world, saw their shares dragged down like everyone else's. It was the bargain of the generation, truly. Within a year, most of the banks had doubled in value. Not a single one cut its dividend.

• *Never panic.* The worst investment decisions are made at times of high emotional stress. People who rushed to sell during the crash of 2008 regretted it later as prices rallied strongly. If you are prone to overreact to stock market movements, let someone else make the decisions—an investment counsellor or a mutual fund manager. Remember, all market corrections end up looking like small blips in retrospect.

REITs

Real estate investment trusts offer another good source of tax-efficient income. This was the only sector to be exempted from Ottawa's 2006 decision to impose a new tax on high-yielding income trusts. REITs invest in a variety of rental properties, including office buildings, shopping malls, industrial complexes, hotels, apartments, and nursing homes. They typically pay monthly distributions, so the cash flow is steady. The money is received as return of capital, capital gains, and occasionally, dividends, so you are taxed at an advantageous rate on those amounts.

REITs can be quite volatile in their share price movement—sometimes even more so than blue-chip stocks. Recessionary periods and times of high interest rates are especially dangerous, so keep your REIT holdings relatively low (no more than 20 percent of your non-registered portfolio).

ETFs

The popularity of exchange-traded funds (ETFs) just keeps growing. Canadians have invested $40 billion in these relatively new products since they were created, and more new money pours in every day. ETFs are still a long way behind traditional mutual funds in terms of market share, but the gap is gradually closing.

Many ETFs are designed to generate steady cash flow for investors and are well worth a look. The iShares group offers several funds based on fixed-income securities, such as the iShares DEX Universe Bond Index Fund (which trades on the Toronto Exchange as XBB) and the iShares DEX Short Term Bond Index Fund (which trades as XSB). Although bond funds do not offer any tax advantage, ETFs such as these are worth including in your income portfolio for the stability and predictability they provide.

Almost all the major ETF players in Canada—BMO, Claymore, iShares, Invesco, and RBC—have in their lineup equity-based funds that generate good cash flow. Some examples follow. I'm not suggesting that you run out and buy these, though; I'm simply giving you some idea of what's available.

- *Claymore Equal Weight Banc & Lifeco ETF (TSX: CEW).* This ETF holds an equally weighted portfolio of shares of the largest Canadian banks and life insurance companies. There are no surprises here— top positions are held by Scotiabank, National Bank, CIBC, TD, and Great-West Life. The fund has been operating since early 2008. Based on net asset value, the three-year average annual compound rate of return to June 30, 2011, was 8.1 percent, while the most recent twelve-month gain was 18.2 percent. Monthly distributions were running at $0.021 per unit ($0.252 annually) in mid-2011. In 2010, the entire payout was tax-advantaged, with slightly less than 50 percent received as return of capital and the rest as dividends and capital gains.

- *BMO Covered Call Canadian Banks ETF (TSX: ZWB).* This is a newcomer to the growing BMO lineup, having been launched in January 2011. It invests in a portfolio of Canadian banking stocks, with about half the assets in the BMO S&P/TSX Equal Weight Banks Index ETF. What differentiates it from most other income ETFs is the use of covered call options to generate additional cash flow. (Covered calls are options that guarantee the buyer the right to purchase shares you own at a specific price by a certain date.) This involves active management, so you pay a little more than normal for this fund (MER is 0.65 percent). But if the strategy works properly, you should recover that through extra income.

- *iShares Diversified Monthly Income Fund (TSX: XTR).* This is a portfolio fund that invests in units of nine iShares ETFs. About 54 percent is in equity-related funds (including REITs and preferred shares), while the rest is in bond index funds. So the portfolio offers a good balance for investors who don't want too much exposure to the stock market. BlackRock Asset Management, which owns the iShares funds, uses a strategic asset allocation approach in deciding the weighting of each ETF. Rebalancing is done at least quarterly, and more frequently if market conditions warrant. The monthly distribution in mid-2011 was $0.06 per unit, a small portion of which is tax-advantaged.

Income Mutual Funds

There are many mutual funds that are specifically designed for income-seeking investors. Some of these can be useful additions to a non-registered portfolio, but you need to choose carefully. The following are some guidelines that may help:

• *Look at the long-term track record.* Income-oriented funds should not be expected to generate big gains. What you want is consistency, a reasonable return, and relative safety. Finding all three in a single fund can be a challenge. For example, the National Bank Mortgage Fund has never lost money over a twelve-month period since it was launched in 1991, and it pays a regular monthly distribution. But the average annual compound rate of return over the five years to June 30, 2011, was only 3.4 percent, almost all of which was fully taxable. Most people would want to earn a little more. The 6.5 percent average annual gain reported by the Fidelity Monthly Income Fund, Series B units over the same period looks a lot better, but the risk is higher because about half the portfolio is invested in the stock market. You have to decide if that higher return is worth the extra risk.

- *Check the distribution history.* Ideally, you want a fund with a long history of consistent distributions, as long as the net asset value has been maintained or has increased. The RBC Monthly Income Fund, which tends to be equally divided between stocks and bonds, meets those criteria quite nicely.

- *Review previous tax history.* This isn't always easy. Unlike ETFs, most mutual fund companies don't publish a tax breakdown of their distributions on their websites. You may have to ask your financial advisor to get the information for you, or you can try contacting the company directly. Since the money is going into a non-registered account, and the income is therefore taxable, it's worth the effort. Also, there are some funds that are structured for maximum tax efficiency. They include the T series offered by several companies, and all the funds from NexGen Financial.

- *Examine the portfolio.* Make sure you understand how the money is invested before you make a decision. Some funds, such as the Mackenzie Sentinel Income Fund, focus on fixed-income securities and therefore carry less risk. Others are weighted to equities, such as the Mackenzie Maxxum Monthly Income Fund, which holds about three-quarters of its portfolio in stocks.

TAKE A MULTI-DIMENSIONAL APPROACH

The point I want to leave you with from this chapter is that you must take a multi-dimensional approach to your retirement planning. Don't put on blinkers and assume there are only a few possible sources of retirement income. There are many, and each can play a different role at various times in your life.

Use them strategically. In your early retirement years, focus on your employer pension plan, if you have one, and supplement it as needed with RRSP/RRIF withdrawals. When you're sixty-five, OAS will kick in. Delay your CPP/QPP application until age seventy if possible, so as to obtain the maximum benefit. As needed, draw from your TFSA and your non-registered investment account. When you reach your eighties, move some of the remaining RRIF assets into a life annuity.

In this way, you will continue to add to your retirement income as the years pass, thus compensating for inflation and ensuring you will have adequate income for the rest of your life—even if you live to 110!

IN CONCLUSION

Throughout this book, there has been a single under-lying theme: we must bear a much greater degree of responsibility for our financial well-being in retirement than in the past. Employers are abdicating what used to be a traditional role. Defined benefit pension plans are becoming increasingly rare outside the public service, and even that last bastion may begin to crumble under the weight of soaring government expenses. Defined contri-bution plans are better than nothing because the employer does kick in some money, but in the end, the value of the pension will depend on how successfully the contributions were invested—and that is being left to the discretion of the individual employee.

Governments are becoming increasingly reluctant to commit scarce resources to support a rapidly aging population. The main initiatives in recent years have cost Ottawa relatively little while encouraging more people to save on their own. Tax-Free Savings Accounts and Pooled Registered Pension Plans are just two examples. The $300-million boost to the GIS in the summer of 2011 may be the last such initiative we see for a long while.

With Big Brother playing a diminishing role in helping us prepare for retirement, we are left with no choice but to do the job ourselves. Fortunately, we have the tools to accomplish that: RRSPs, TFSAs, and the soon-to-come PRPPs, as well as basic Canada Pension Plan and Old Age Security benefits. Despite the sea change in the way our retirement system operates and the harsh new realities we face, we should be able to manage just fine.

But it will require time, commitment, and patience. This has to become one of your life's priorities, along with raising a family, paying off the mortgage, and succeeding in your chosen career. Retirement planning is not something you can kick down the road. If you wait until you're fifty, it's too late.

I haven't pulled any punches in explaining the problems you'll face. But I have tried to provide workable solutions to every one of those problems. I hope I have given you the motivation to make use of them.

As a long-time *Star Trek* fan, I leave you with the Vulcan blessing: "Live long and prosper."

YOUR RETIREMENT QUESTIONS

Every year I receive hundreds of questions relating to retirement planning. I have selected some of general interest for inclusion in this book.

ANNUITIES

GOOD IDEA FOR AN EIGHTY-SIX-YEAR-OLD?

Q – Is an annuity in a RRIF appropriate for an eighty-six-year-old? I understand this type of investment is not good when interest rates are low; however, this investment vehicle has been suggested. It is a large amount of money, and capital preservation is a must. I would really appreciate a reply.

A – I have never heard of an annuity being held within a RRIF. Typically, money is transferred from a RRIF, tax-free, to purchase a registered annuity from an insurance company. It is not necessary to use all the proceeds of the RRIF to do this—you can use any amount you wish.

I have long advised older people to use some of their RRIF money in this way to ensure they will always have income, no matter how long they live. Ideally, the annuity should be purchased when rates are high, but since you are already eighty-six, there is no point in waiting.

Your capital will not be preserved when you buy an annuity. Basically, you are paying it to the insurance company in exchange for a guaranteed income stream for the rest of your life. If you use all the money in the RRIF, the result will be zero remaining capital but the maximum possible income flow.

There are several different types of annuities, so be sure you understand exactly what you are getting. Also, do some price shopping—rates vary from one company to another, sometimes significantly. The income will be taxable in your hands, just as the RRIF income currently is.

WHAT ABOUT AGE SIXTY-FOUR?

Q – I am sixty-four years old, retired, and need guaranteed income. I have been exploring a single life annuity with no guarantee. I can get a single life annuity return of 8 percent on my $250,000 locked-in RRSP funds. However, the current wisdom appears to be that this is a poor time to lock in an annuity due to the record low long-term rates. I understand the theory but don't believe the advice is prudent in current market conditions.

This annuity would provide $20,000 per annum for as long as I live. I understand that if I die early, I forfeit the principal; however, I am single and retired, and if I had an equivalent defined benefit pension it ceases at death also, so I am prepared to take that risk due to good health.

I am a well-educated financial professional and I am

confused by the consensus opinion that this is a poor time to purchase an annuity. An 8 percent guaranteed return for life looks pretty good to me.

Many seniors are afraid to buy annuities based on this advice and end up invested in GICs, but I do not believe there is anywhere else an 8 percent guaranteed return for life is available. Any advice you could provide to me and thousands of seniors who want the safety of guaranteed income would be much appreciated.

A – Just so there is no confusion, you are not really getting an 8 percent return—you are receiving 8 percent cash flow, which is different. If you invest in, for example, a GIC at 3 percent, you keep your principal and receive payments of $7,500 a year on your $250,000 investment. When the GIC matures, your money is paid back to you. In the case of the annuity, you are left with no capital. A portion of the income you receive is actually your own money coming back to you.

A non-guaranteed annuity is a gamble, especially at your relatively young age. If you die within twelve years, the insurance company wins because you will not have received payments equalling your original investment. Also, don't lose sight of inflation. Even at relatively modest rates, increases in the consumer price index will gradually chip away at your purchasing power as the years go by. You may want to consider an indexed annuity to offset that.

ESTATE PLANNING

DEATH TAXES

Q – Is it true that upon my demise, my daughters will be taxed if they cash in my RRSP, TFSA, and investment portfolio? They are my beneficiaries in my will. Would that be like a death tax? Also, if they have their own RRSP accounts, could they transfer my funds without having to pay taxes?

A – Technically, your daughters won't pay any tax. Your estate will look after that before the assets are conveyed to the beneficiaries. But the net result is that they will get less. Your RRSP will be deemed to be cashed out when you die. The assets in the plan will form part of your income on your final tax return (the one that will be filed by your executor after you die). TFSA assets can be transferred to your daughters tax-free, although some rules apply. Assets in your non-registered investment account will be deemed to be sold on death, and any capital gains and accrued interest will be taxable. There is no tax on cash.

You cannot transfer RRSP assets into your daughters' accounts—that is prohibited by law. However, you can give them gifts of money from your non-registered account with no tax implications, assuming they are adults.

YOUNGER SPOUSE

Q – My situation is this: I am seventy-three and my spouse of thirty years is fifty-six. Presumably, I will predecease him. He will be the beneficiary of my RRIF and TFSA. What are the ramifications of his age re: the RRIF and the status of the TFSA (added to his own).

A – It's really quite simple. All the assets in the two plans will pass to your spouse tax-free. To make sure everything happens smoothly, name him as the beneficiary of your RRSP and as the successor account holder of your TFSA.

INVESTING STRATEGIES

FUND DISTRIBUTIONS

Q – I am very fond of income funds that pay a monthly distribution. However, advisors often tell me that most of these funds generate the majority of their yield by return of capital. As an example, there is a monthly income fund that has a current yield of 6 percent, but an advisor told me that two-thirds of that yield comes from a return of capital. The net asset value (NAV) on this particular fund has remained relatively stable over the past five years, so it does not appear that the distributions are affecting the NAV. As well, this fund has maintained the same monthly distribution of six cents on every unit for over seven years. My question is, If the fund does utilize a return of capital, how would this affect me if the fund is held within an RRSP and the distributions are reinvested on a monthly basis?

A – Since you do not name the fund, I can't verify that the return-of-capital portion is as high as you say. But I can tell you that the mix of dividends, interest, capital gains, and return of capital from distributions will vary from one fund to another and from year to year. Also, "return of capital" doesn't necessarily mean that the fund is paying back your own money and the NAV must decline accordingly. This is an accounting term, and there are several ways return of capital can be created in an investment fund.

If the units are inside an RRSP, there are no tax consequences to receiving part or all of the income as return of capital. In a non-registered account, that portion of the income would not be taxed in the year it is received, but the cost base of your units would be adjusted to reflect the payment. The result would be a higher taxable capital gain when you sell.

LIVING ABROAD

RRSP BLUES

Q – I moved to the U.S. in March 2003. I have RRSPs at the Royal Bank of Canada and the Bank of Montreal. What can I do to manage these investments to ensure diversification and try to get the best return? I also have a savings deposit in the RRSP account with Royal Bank, and I was told I could only purchase a GIC with the funds. I need to get as much information as possible on any and all options I have with my money invested in Canada. Any information you can provide will be greatly appreciated.

A – You're out of luck, I'm afraid. The U.S. tightened its rules on foreign accounts a few years ago, and now Canadian brokers have their hands tied and cannot take instructions from people in the U.S. You really have very few options now, beyond investing in GICs or cashing out.

LOCKED-IN ACCOUNTS

MORTGAGE IN A LIRA

Q – I have about $100,000 in a federally regulated LIRA (locked-in retirement account) and an $80,000 mortgage. I am a thirty-eight-year-old professional. Would I be able to buy my own mortgage and keep it within my LIRA?

A – Generally, the investing rules for a LIRA are the same as for an RRSP, but there are a few exceptions. Mortgages are legal for regular RRSPs, but only a few financial institutions actually allow clients to use them because of the administrative complexities.

Because LIRAs represent money from pension plans, they are regulated by the provinces and the federal government (depending on which jurisdiction had responsibility for the original pension). Federal LIRAs are governed by the Office of the Superintendent of Financial Institutions (OSFI). There is nothing on the OSFI website to provide guidance in this regard, so I sent an email to Rod Giles, the manager of communications and public affairs, requesting clarification. I received a prompt reply confirming that mortgages can be held in LIRAs, LIFs, and LRIFs under federal jurisdiction, as long as the plans are self-directed.

"This type of arrangement allows investment in a number of options not usually available under arrangements that are not self-directed," Giles wrote. "These options include Canada Savings Bonds, bonds, mutual funds, treasury bills, individual stocks, and home mortgages."

He also pointed out that Ontario takes a similar position for plans under its jurisdiction, and he included a detailed explanation of the rules from the website of the Financial Services Commission of Ontario, as follows: "Self-directed locked-in accounts that are designed to hold a personal mortgage must be administered at arms-length from the homeowner. The mortgage must be insured and set at rates generally available in the open market. If mortgage payments are in default, the administrator of the mortgage may foreclose. In such circumstances, the property can be sold and the outstanding loan amount paid back into the locked-in account."

One more point: although you can hold a mortgage in a self-directed LIRA, you cannot use locked-in accounts to take advantage of the Home Buyers' Plan.

BUYING A U.S. CONDO

Q – I would like to purchase a condo in the U.S. and I don't know what my options are to fund that purchase. Can I use the money in my LIRA to invest in a mortgage for myself? Can I somehow use my LIRA as a down payment toward the purchase of the condo?

Also, what is the best way for a Canadian to get a mortgage to buy a condo in the U.S.? Are there fees and taxes we need to be aware of?

A – Registered plans such as LIRAs cannot invest in real property. You can hold a mortgage in a LIRA, as explained above, but it must be insured. Unfortunately for you, only homes located in Canada are eligible for such insurance through the Canada Mortgage and Housing Corporation (CMHC).

American banks are notoriously reluctant to write mortgage loans against property owned by non-residents. You might have better luck with a Canadian-owned U.S. bank, such as TD.

Taxes vary depending on the state where the condo is located. Florida, for example, imposes extremely heavy taxes on non-residents. These have become a deterrent for some people considering Florida property.

PENSIONS

PENSION INCOME SPLITTING

Q – My husband is receiving his provincial government pension while he is still working for another company. He is fifty-eight, and I am fifty-five. We are hoping to split his pension income, as I have very little income to report. But I have been getting very confused answers regarding the age requirement to qualify for pension splitting. Please advise us if we can split my husband's pension.

A – Yes, you can split the pension income. Age is not an issue if the money is received as a regular payment from a registered pension plan. Nor is the fact that your husband is still working a problem.

ADVERSE EFFECTS OF SPLITTING

Q – I will be sixty-five soon and was wondering about the possible adverse effects of pension splitting. For example, what will be the effect on claiming a spousal credit on my return? She has only about $4,000 in income.

A – You would lose part or all of the spousal credit. However, transferring some taxable income to your spouse may still work out in your favour. The pension splitting calculation can be complicated, and there are many factors to take into account. My advice is to buy some high-quality tax-preparation software that includes a pension splitting optimizer. It will calculate the best formula for you.

RETIREMENT PLANNING

PAY MORTGAGE OR SAVE FOR RETIREMENT?

Q – I am twenty-five and have a thirty-year mortgage. I am currently making weekly payments and paying extra money every week as well. However, is it smarter for me to think about my retirement and put that extra money into mutual funds or RRSPs? Or should I continue doing what I am doing?

A – Actually, you can do both. Contribute the extra payments to an RRSP, which will generate a tax refund. Use the refund to make a lump-sum payment against the mortgage principal each year. This gives you more bang for your bucks.

RETIREMENT INCOME

Q – My wife is going to retire in about four years at age sixty. She has no pension. I would like to use my RRSP to withdraw money, about $10,000 a year. I will withdraw twice a year, $5,000 each time, so I do not have to pay 20 percent tax.

At the moment, my RRSP is mixed with mutual funds. Do you think I should remove the mutual funds from my RRSP and put the money into a redeemable GIC so I can withdraw my $10,000 each year with no penalty? Or should I put it in a RRIF?

A – There are several points to be dealt with here. First, the tax you pay on the $10,000 withdrawals will be calculated at your marginal rate. Tax is withheld at the time the money is taken out at a rate of 10 percent up to $5,000 and 20 percent on withdrawals between $5,001 and $15,000 (except in Quebec, where the withholding rates are higher). However, the withholding is simply a down payment. Your final tax will be assessed when you file your return.

Second, I do not advise switching to a RRIF until you are required to do so by law. Leaving the money in an RRSP gives you more flexibility—you are not required to take out a minimum amount each year, and you can continue to make contributions as long as you have earned income and/or carry-forward room. There is no advantage to moving to a RRIF prematurely.

RETIREMENT INCOME STRATEGY

Q – I have a defined benefit pension plan that I split with my wife. I have RRSPs in both names, and we are both fifty-six years old. Would it be wise to cash these out yearly, trying to keep the same tax rate until age sixty, when I plan to apply for CPP and my tax rate will increase?

A – I get this kind of question a lot, and there is no simple answer. It requires a detailed financial analysis that only a professional can perform for you. However, as a general rule my advice is to defer paying taxes for as long as possible. It will be fifteen years until you are required to begin making RRSP/RRIF withdrawals. During that time, the money already in the plans could be earning a lot of tax-sheltered income. For example, at an average annual return of 5 percent, the money now in the plans would more than double by the time you both turn seventy-one. That's a pretty strong incentive for staying the course.

RRIFS

RRSP CONVERSION

Q – My RRSPs have to be converted into another investment vehicle. Is a RRIF the best place to invest my money, or is there a better investment? As for taxes, will I pay taxes only on the amount I withdraw? And what is the minimum I can withdraw?

A – If you have to convert, it means you are turning seventy-one this year. You have three options: switching to a Registered Retirement Income Fund (RRIF), buying a life annuity, or cashing out the plan. Most people opt for a RRIF because it provides the greatest flexibility. I prefer a self-directed RRIF, which will allow you to invest in any type of security you wish. Ask your financial institution if they offer such a plan.

You pay tax only on the amount of money you withdraw from the RRIF each year. Your first withdrawal does not have to be until the year after the RRIF is opened, and the minimum is a percentage of the plan's value on January 1. For someone age seventy-one at the start of the year, the minimum withdrawal is 7.38 percent. So if your plan is worth, say, $50,000 on January 1, the minimum withdrawal will be $3,690. This can be taken in one lump sum or in instalments, whichever you prefer. Tax will be withheld at the time of each withdrawal.

MANAGING A RRIF

Q – My mom, age eighty-two, has a RRIF worth $140,000. She would like to know which the following two approaches would be in her best interest. She makes $45,000 in annual pensions and is quite comfortable. Should she cash in the RRIF now and pay the tax on it, or keep the RRIF as is and let her estate pay the taxes with whatever is left, depending on how much longer she lives?

As she ages, more has to be taken out annually, which she doesn't need, and this incurs higher taxes. In her words, which is the better way to preserve her $140,000?

A – She's not going to preserve the $140,000 no matter what she does. One way or the other, the government will grab a share of that in the form of taxes. The trick is to minimize the tax cost. Withdrawing the whole amount in a lump sum certainly will not achieve that. Taken on top of the $45,000 she receives in pensions, it would push her income for that tax year to $185,000. A portion of that will attract tax at the highest marginal rate in her province of residence.

The better course is to draw down the RRIF gradually, which will keep the tax rate relatively low. Let me give you an example. In Ontario, the top marginal tax rate is 46.41 percent. Your mother's actual marginal rate, based on her pension income, is likely in the 20 to 24 percent range. That moves up to 31.15 percent with a few thousand more in taxable income, and then stays at that level until just over $65,000. This means your mom can withdraw about $20,000 a year from the RRIF at the 31.15 percent marginal rate. She could then reinvest some of the after-tax money in a Tax-Free Savings Account and give the rest to her children, tax-free, if she doesn't need it to live on.

"TAX-FREE" RRIF MONEY?

Q – A friend suggested I consider withdrawing from a RRIF early in my future retirement because the first $2,000 withdrawn is tax-free. Here is her logic: *Starting at* *age sixty-five, the first $2,000 of pension income is tax-free. CPP doesn't count as pension income. Money coming out of a RRIF or an annuity is pension income for this tax credit, but money coming out of an RRSP is not. You can convert to a RRIF at any time (I think after fifty-five), and you don't have to convert all of your RRSPs at any particular time, until you reach seventy-one. You can convert just a portion.*

So as far as I can see, it would make sense to set up a RRIF for $20,000, and then draw out $2,000 per year. There is no minimum withdrawal amount before the age of seventy-two, and you can withdraw as much as you want. After six years (ages sixty-six to seventy-one), you've drawn out $12,000 tax-free. When it's drawn out, it could then be put into your non-RRSP investments (or spent on a trip to Florida).

Does this make sense, and is it legal? Could you start this before sixty-five if you retired earlier?

A – The strategy is basically correct, but some of your facts are wrong. For starters, the first $2,000 of RRIF income is not "tax-free," as you suggest. It qualifies for the pension income tax credit, which means it earns a 15 percent credit against your federal taxes (worth $300), plus whatever provincial/territorial credit applies. So the only people who would receive the money tax-free are those in the lowest bracket.

You also state that there is no required minimum withdrawal from a RRIF until age seventy-two. Again, this is not correct. The minimum becomes effective in the first year after a RRIF is set up, regardless of age. The formula for calculating it is different up to age seventy-one, however.

It is the value of the RRIF at the start of the year divided by ninety minus your age on January 1. So for a sixty-five-year-old with $20,000 in a RRIF, the minimum withdrawal that year would be $800. There is no maximum.

But those are technical points. The idea itself is valid and is used by many people. As you correctly point out, you don't need to convert all your RRSP assets, only enough to take advantage of the pension income credit.

To answer your last question: no, you cannot do this before age sixty-five, except in certain limited circumstances. Check the Canada Revenue Agency website for more on that.

IN-KIND WITHDRAWALS

Q – In CIBC Wood Gundy's Winter 2011 newsletter, there was an article that read in part as follows: "If you are required to make a RRIF withdrawal and do not need the liquid funds, you may wish to withdraw your legislative minimum annual payment which is not subject to withholding taxes by conducting an 'in kind' withdrawal. In the absence of withholding tax, you are effectively receiving an interest-free loan from the government, which can then be invested in the most tax-efficient way possible." What is your opinion of this strategy?

A – Well, it's an interesting idea. Of course, you are only deferring the tax, not avoiding it. The in-kind withdrawal must be treated as taxable income when you file your next tax return. But it could be more than a year between the time of the withdrawal and the tax-filing deadline. If you think you can invest the money profitably in the interim, why not?

RRSPS

SMART INVESTMENT?

Q – I've invested my RRSP in a TD Canada Trust three-year Security GIC Plus RSP, which means I cannot redeem any money from it until maturity. After three years, the interest I will earn could be as low as 0.662 percent or as high as 9 percent, depending on the level of the stock market the day it matures. I will turn seventy-one a couple of weeks before it matures. Was this a smart investment?

A – Well, you won't know until maturity, will you? I have not looked at this specific indexed GIC, but generally I have found that this type of security is a bad deal for investors. Everything depends on timing, so you need to be lucky. In almost all cases I have looked at, people end up earning much less than the maximum, and sometimes they get nothing. Had you asked me this question before you made the decision, my response would have been negative. But now you're in, so hope for the best.

RRSP CONFUSION

Q – I am uncertain what constitutes a good investment choice for inclusion in my RRSP. I recently added the Claymore Oil Sands Sector ETF, and now I have read in your newsletter that it is better held outside my RRSP. I also have Daylight Energy, Inter Pipeline, and RioCan. Are these suitable for an RRSP? If not, what should I use as a guideline for choosing an investment inside my RRSP?

A – This is really a case of theory versus practicality. Ideally, the least tax-efficient investments (anything that pays interest) should be held in registered plans. Securities that offer a tax advantage, such as the ones you mention, should be in the non-registered portfolio.

That makes sense, of course—why give away a tax break by tucking a security into an RRSP? But the theory assumes that investors have enough money to maintain two relatively equal portfolios. Most don't. If you are in that position, forget the theory and choose securities for your RRSP that are low-risk and offer reasonable return potential. The tax advantages would be nice to have, but if it doesn't work in your case, don't worry about it.

RRSP WORRIES

Q – Is it wise for single people to build up their RRSPs when they end up paying twice as much tax as when they worked? Plus their old age pension gets reduced.

A – I don't know where you got the idea that you'll end up paying twice as much tax on the RRSP money. You'll pay tax at your marginal rate when you make withdrawals. Most people have less income after retirement than they did when they were working, so their tax rate is lower.

I assume your reference to "old age pension" means Old Age Security (OAS). You will not lose any of your payment unless your net income exceeds a certain level, which was

$67,668 in 2011. That threshold is indexed, so it increases annually.

If you are still concerned, use a Tax-Free Savings Account to save for your retirement. The withdrawals are not considered income, but you do not get a tax deduction for your contributions.

CONFLICTING ADVICE

Q – I am a follower of your newsletter and have read your TFSA books with great interest. My wife and I are both nearly fifty years old and have approximately $200,000 to invest. I currently have $180,000 in my RRSP, and she has about $230,000 in her RRSP. We both have remaining RRSP contribution room, hers being about $40,000 and mine less than $10,000. We also have an emergency fund of $50,000, which is in a high-interest account should one of life's surprises present itself.

I have spoken to a number of financial advisors regarding potential investment options with minimal risk. Some tell me to set up TFSAs for both of us and also to use up all of the remaining RRSP room, while investing the balance in stocks. Others tell me the RRSP contributions I already make are too high and I should buy their mutual fund products. Any guidance?

A – To begin with, you and your wife have obviously been diligent savers. Bank of Canada governor Mark Carney would approve! Now to your question.

Although you have provided a lot of information, you have left out some important elements. For example, do you and/or your wife have employer pension plans, and if so, how much do you expect to receive from them? That is critical to your decision. It may seem as though you have a lot of money in RRSPs, but if they will be the source of most of your future retirement income it may not be enough.

Your two plans are currently worth $410,000. If you stopped contributing now and the money earned 5 percent a year, the RRSPs would be worth about $850,000 in fifteen years, when presumably you'd be coming up to retirement. If inflation averages 2 percent over that time, the value of your RRSPs in current dollars would be about $640,000. Assuming a 5 percent annual withdrawal rate (until you reach age seventy-one, after which it would be higher), that would generate a before-tax income of about $32,000 in 2010 dollars. If that plus CPP/OAS would be enough for you to live comfortably in retirement and you have no pension, then your RRSPs are probably adequate. Your next logical step would be to set up Tax-Free Savings Accounts for both of you and maximize your contributions.

However, if after doing these calculations you feel you want to build a larger retirement fund, then continue to make RRSP contributions and invest the money conservatively. This way, you'll generate a tax refund (assuming you are both still working) that can be used for starting your TFSAs.

CASH IN RRSPS?

Q – Should I cash in my RRSPs to pay down debt? My debt-to-income ratio is about 46 percent.

A – Your debt-to-income ratio is actually quite reasonable—and well below the national average of 148 percent. However, what's really important is the type of debt you're carrying and whether it is putting a strain on your personal finances.

The worst type of debt to carry is a credit card balance because of the high interest rates imposed. If most or all of your debt is owed to Visa, MasterCard, etc., you are paying hundreds and perhaps thousands of dollars a year in interest. In that case, the RRSP option might be worth considering. If, on the other hand, most of the debt is in your mortgage, then I would not advise cashing in your RRSPs. Mortgage rates are very low right now, and you can probably get a better return by keeping the money in your retirement plan.

Remember that cashing in an RRSP means the withdrawal will be subject to tax. So you'll actually receive less (perhaps much less) than the value of the plan after the Canada Revenue Agency takes its cut.

RRSP STRATEGY

Q – Does it make sense to withdraw funds from my RRSP in years when my income level will be low and hence the withdrawals will be taxed at a lower rate? The big downside I can see to this approach is the loss of tax-free growth in my RRSP going forward. But then I guess one could transfer the funds to the TFSA (assuming the contribution room exists). Is this a good plan in your estimation, or is there something I am missing?

A – The logic is sound as long as you ensure that the RRSP withdrawals don't push you into a higher tax bracket. By all means, move the money into a TFSA, where you will continue to enjoy the advantages of tax-sheltering.

WANTS TO TRANSFER SPOUSAL RRSP

Q – I contributed to a spousal RRSP for my husband. Due to the new income-splitting tax rules, we would like to close that account. Is it possible for him to transfer the holdings in that account into his own regular RRSP?

A – Unfortunately, no. A spousal plan must retain its separate status. Your husband can also have his own personal RRSP, but the spousal plan must remain in place unless it is cashed out.

WHO OWNS SPOUSAL PLAN?

Q – I've contributed to my wife's spousal RRSP; she has no earned income. The last such contribution was in the 1990s. I've always been under the impression that the funds in the plan are hers—that I have no claim on them and no control over them. Is this the case?

A – You are correct. RRSPs belong to the annuitant—in this case, your wife. The money is not yours, even though you originally contributed it, and you have no say over how it is invested or its disposition. There are tax implications if any withdrawals are made within three years after a contribution, but for you, that waiting period expired long ago. The bottom line is that your wife can do anything she wants with this money.

SPOUSAL RRSP WITHDRAWALS

Q – I have been told that after an absence of contributions for three years to a spousal RRSP, withdrawals can be made without tax penalty. This is before the termination age of seventy-one years. However, I could not find any information regarding this on Revenue Canada's website. Can you confirm or dispute this? Am I missing something here, such that I'm not looking for the correct information?

A – The rule is that if withdrawals from a spousal RRSP are made within three years of the last contribution, some or all of that withdrawal is attributed back to the spouse who made the contribution and he or she is taxed on it. The actual calculation of the amount attributed is based on the total withdrawal and the contributions made in the three-year period. After three contribution-free years, any withdrawals are taxed in the hands of the spouse who owns the plan.

BORROWING FOR RRSPS

Q – Is borrowing to invest in an RRSP a wise idea?

A – The math says yes, as long as the loan is repaid within a year, or two at the most. Suppose you have a marginal tax rate of 35 percent and you borrow $5,000 to put into an RRSP. You generate an immediate tax refund of $1,750, which is effectively a 35 percent return on your investment.

RRSP loans are available at very attractive rates, usually slightly more than prime, so the carrying cost of the loan will be much less than the value of the refund. Of course, every year the loan is outstanding erodes the initial differential between profit and cost, which is why I recommend paying it off as soon as possible.

OVERCONTRIBUTE TO RRSP?

Q – I earn $40,000 a year, and with a company pension adjustment amount of $4,900, it leaves me with an RRSP deduction limit of just $2,300, which I max out. Since there is $2,000 of overcontribution room, is it worthwhile to overcontribute by that amount (to $4,300/year) when the $2,000 is after-tax dollars and will be taxed again in the future when withdrawing? Even though there is no tax deduction on the $2,000, is there any tax benefit to do this, other than that the earnings are tax-sheltered? Would you encourage people to take advantage of the overcontribution limit? In future, when I withdraw the $2,000, do I need to report it as income, which wouldn't seem fair considering that tax has already been paid? (I max out my TFSA each year, so I can't put it there.)

A – To clarify, the RRSP overcontribution limit is $2,000 *lifetime*, not $2,000 *a year*. Yes, it will be taxed when it comes out of the plan, even though you receive no deduction for it. That seems perfectly fair to me considering that the money is not supposed to be in the RRSP at all. The overcontribution rule was created to avoid having penalty interest triggered by a small error or technical recalculation. It was never intended to encourage everyone to add an extra $2,000 to their plans.

Is it worth it? A lot depends on how the money is invested. Let's say you put an extra $2,000 into your plan and invest it conservatively, averaging 4 percent profit annually. At the end of thirty years, it will be worth $6,486.80. You then withdraw the money at a marginal tax rate of 30 percent. Your after-tax return is $4,540.76, for a gain of 127 percent over your original $2,000. That looks great at first glance, but your average annual compound rate of return is only 2.77 percent.

The higher the return within the RRSP, the better the strategy looks. But of course, you increase your risk by shooting for higher gains.

RRSP MONEY LEFT IN CANADA

Q – We have approximately $300,000 in RRSPs in Canada. We became U.S. citizens twenty years ago. We would like to pay our mortgage off with these funds. What is the process and the "good and bad" of doing it?

A – I can't understand why you would leave your money in Canadian RRSPs for so long. But since you have, you should probably take steps to get it out sooner rather than later. However, there will be significant tax involved. The Canadian government will withhold tax at source on the withdrawals, and the money will be treated as income by the U.S. government. My advice is to hire an accounting firm that specializes in cross-border taxation to help you work out the best solution.

RRSP FRUSTRATION

Q – Ten years ago I had about $110,000 in my RRSP. I became a single mom and my finances changed considerably. I have not contributed any more than a few thousand dollars max per year since then.

I had expected that the interest from my funds would reinvest itself, and that although I wasn't contributing, I would see an increase over a ten-year period. (I understand the long-term ups and downs.) Today, ten years later, my RRSP is worth $87,000.

The first five years after I stopped contributing, my advisor and I rearranged my portfolio a couple of times a year. The last three years, I haven't touched it. I am not sure if my advisor gets paid each time we rearrange the portfolio. There is no statement that specifies how he gets paid, and I don't really understand front- and rear-end loads. I don't know if his suggestions to redistribute my portfolio are for his benefit or mine. It doesn't seem to be working in my favour. I have all the statements for the past fifteen years and it seems that any growth I have gained was equal to what I contributed myself (a shoebox under the bed would have had the same result, or maybe better). It seems that once you stop contributing to RRSPs, they stop growing.

My home and RRSPs are the only big assets I have, so I am eager to get some good counsel. I need to know what questions to ask. Is my advisor working in my best interests? Is there a better way to invest that money, in other funds or real estate, without penalty?

A – It may be time to switch to a new advisor. Certainly the current one hasn't done you any favours. A net loss of that magnitude over a decade is more than enough to justify a move. You could have simply put the money into GICs and done much better.

I don't know what was in your portfolio, but based on the results, it appears it was overweighted in higher-risk stocks or equity funds. A balanced portfolio that included a decent bond weighting would likely have done much better.

I suggest you interview three or four prospective new advisors. Be upfront with them. Show them the results over the past decade and ask what they could have done differently. Then ask how they would reconfigure the portfolio going forward. Also, be sure to find out how they are compensated. Make your selection after you've heard all the answers. Good luck.

RRSP LIMITS

Q – I would like to know how to calculate my RRSP contribution limits after I retire and am receiving pension income. I know that pension income cannot be used for contributions, but can it be used to determine the percentage I can contribute from other sources? Also, can I include the grossed-up amount from dividends when calculating my total income? I haven't been able to find this information anywhere.

A – RRSP contribution limits are calculated on "earned income" only. Pension and investment income does not qualify. Unless you have income from employment sources, even if it is freelance or consulting work, you won't be able to create any RRSP contribution room. But you can still use a Tax-Free Savings Account.

MOVING ASSETS

Q – Will I be penalized if I move my RRSPs from one advisor to another?

A – There may be an account-closing fee, but it shouldn't be more than $100 or so. Just be sure that you transfer the assets from the old RRSP to a new one—don't sell the assets, close the old RRSP, and then open another one. Choose the new advisor first, open an RRSP with that company, and then instruct them to transfer the existing assets directly from the old plan.

MORTGAGING A COTTAGE

Q – Can we use our RRSPs to mortgage a cottage?

A – In theory, yes. In practice, it's questionable. As long as the cottage is located in Canada, there is no legal obstacle to placing an RRSP mortgage on it. But you must be able to obtain loan insurance from Canada Mortgage and Housing or Genworth MI Canada, and you'll have to find an RRSP administrator that allows mortgages to be held in a self-directed plan (many don't because of the administrative complexities). You refer to "RRSPs," plural, but the mortgage would have to be held in a single plan—you cannot split one mortgage among two or more plans. Finally, remember that RRSP mortgages must carry commercial interest rates. There is no financial advantage to going this route.

RRSP WITHDRAWALS

Q – I am sixty-eight years old and recently was advised to withdraw some of my RRSP money (specifically $5,000 a year) and deposit it into a Tax-Free Savings Account. I have $108,000 in RRSPs. I was told that if anything happened to me, my RRSPs would be taxed at 46 percent but my TFSA would not be taxable to my survivors. What do you think about this proposal?

A – It may be a good idea, depending on how much income you have. The RRSP withdrawals will be taxable, so you won't have the full $5,000 to put into a TFSA. Since this money will be on top of your other income (e.g., CPP, OAS), it will be taxed at your marginal rate. If that is 25 percent, you will have to pay the government $1,250 on a $5,000 withdrawal, which means you will keep only $3,750. Still, that's better than a 46 percent tax rate.

But your estate may not have to pay 46 percent. For Ontario residents, that rate does not kick in until taxable income exceeds about $127,000, and then it applies only to the amount above that. If you live a long life, you may draw down the RRSP/RRIF over the years, so that the amount remaining when you die is much less. You have to decide if you want to pay tax now on the chance that your estate will pay less tax in the future. I have always preferred to defer tax as long as possible.

PROFITING FROM AN RRSP

Q – I have a question for you, and if I am correct, I wonder why everyone doesn't do this. Let's say I have $100,000 in my RRSP and I am in the 40 percent tax bracket. In December, I borrow $10,000 from my bank and put the money into the RRSP. Come tax time I would receive a refund of $4,000.

In March, I withdraw the same $10,000, which was sitting in my RRSP in cash, not invested, and repay the loan. Interest cost would be very low due to the current low rates. The penalty for withdrawing the money is the withholding tax of 20 percent, thus $2,000. Am I not more or less ahead of the game by $2,000 (the tax refund minus the withholding)?

A – No. You'll end up losing money on the transaction. The withholding is only a down payment on your final tax bill. The $10,000 you withdraw must be added to your income when you file the tax return for that year. So you will end up paying tax at your marginal rate. All that will happen is that the withdrawal will offset the contribution for tax purposes, and you'll pay the bank interest for nothing.

RRSP WITHDRAWAL STRATEGY

Q – I am sixty-two and retired. My current income is $14,000/year (CPP and dividends). My RRSP is worth approximately $500,000. Assuming the amount remains the same, I will have to transfer to a RRIF when I turn seventy-one and start withdrawing 7.38 percent, or $36,900. Wouldn't it make sense for me to start depleting my RRSP (withdraw, say, $10,000/year) and pay tax at a lower rate on $24,000 than to pay tax at a higher rate on $36,900? Also, the amount that I must withdraw will continue to increase each year after age seventy-one.

A – There is certainly some logic to your idea, but a lot depends on where you live. For example, in Ontario the 2011 marginal rate on taxable income of $24,000 was 20 percent. It jumps to slightly more than 31 percent on $50,900 in taxable income, so there would be a significant savings of 11 percentage points using your strategy. In British Columbia, however, you would save only about 6 percentage points of tax, and much or all of that could be offset by the early RRSP withdrawal and the loss of compounding on what otherwise would have continued to be tax-sheltered money.

Your example assumes no growth in the RRSP between now and age seventy-one. But let's say you invest conservatively and earn 5 percent annually. A $10,000 withdrawal this year if you live in Ontario will cost you about $2,000 in tax. Over nine years, that money would grow to more than $3,100—a 55 percent increase. So if you don't need the RRSP money to live on, you need to weigh the options carefully before proceeding.

WORTHLESS SHARES

Q – I have shares of a company that is dissolving, and the shares are worthless. The last dividend payout was a $1.46 per share, and that same day they dropped by the same amount, to zero. The stock is in an RRSP account, and I am being charged a 1 percent penalty on the $1.46 rate [even though the shares] are worthless. What is my best option?

A – It's not clear to me why you are being charged penalty interest on the shares, but the obvious course of action is to swap them out of the account at fair market value, which in this case is zero. Your broker should be able to handle this for you.

RRSP ELIGIBILITY

Q – Are all ETFs trading on designated American exchanges eligible for an RRSP? If not, what is the best way to obtain a reliable answer for a given U.S.-listed fund? I have read Internet postings of people being given conflicting answers by their discount brokers for common ETFs such as the SPDR Gold Trust (NYSE: GLD) and the iShares Silver Trust (NYSE: SLV).

A – The short answer is yes. All ETFs that trade on any stock exchange recognized by the Canada Revenue Agency are RRSP-eligible. The conflicting answers you are reading may relate to old rules that did not allow physical metals such as gold and silver to be held in registered plans.

SEVERANCE PAYMENTS

GETTING SACKED

Q – After twenty years with my employer, I found out that he was going to terminate my employment. I am hoping to receive severance from them. What is the best way to defer taxation and get my best bang for my buck? Let's say $50,000 is the amount.

A – In tax legalese, a severance payment is known as a "retiring allowance." You may be able to transfer some or all of the money directly to an RRSP and avoid paying tax until you withdraw money from the plan.

You say you have worked for the company for twenty years. Let's assume you started in 1990. You can transfer to an RRSP a total of $2,000 for each year or part of a year you worked from 1990 to 1995—so six years. That gets $12,000 into the RRSP—you don't need to have any contribution room available to do that. For the rest, you can ask your employer to transfer enough of the sever- ance to your RRSP to cover all your available contribution room. You can find that amount on your latest notice of assessment from the Canada Revenue Agency.

So to sum up, if you receive $50,000, you can have your employer transfer $12,000 directly, leaving $38,000. If you have another $15,000 in available RRSP contribution room, ask him to transfer that amount as well. That would leave $23,000 as taxable income.

SEVERANCE TRANSFER

Q – I will be receiving a severance package from my employer upon retirement, and I was wondering whether I would be able to transfer some of it directly into my husband's RRSP if all my RRSP room is used up.

A – No. You cannot transfer money to another person's RRSP, even when that person is your spouse, except in cases of marriage breakdown. However, if you worked for the employer prior to 1996, you can transfer $2,000 for each year or part year of service until the end of 1995 to your own RRSP, even if you have no contribution room.

TAX-FREE SAVINGS ACCOUNTS

TFSA TAXATION

Q – How are interest income, dividend income, capital gains, and capital losses handled within a Tax-Free Savings Account? Are capital losses within the TFSA handled exactly like they are in RRSPs?

A – Profits earned with a TFSA are not taxed, no matter what form they take, and there is no limit on the amount of money you can earn tax-free. The downside is that any capital losses within the plan cannot be claimed and the dividend tax credit does not apply. The rules are exactly the same as they are for RRSPs in this regard.

WIFE'S TFSA CONTRIBUTION

Q – I wish to pay for my wife's TFSA contribution this year. Is it better to send my cheque directly to her plan on her behalf, or can I simply give her the money and let her send her own cheque to the company?

A – Give her the money. You are not allowed to contribute to someone else's plan.

TFSA OR RRSP?

Q – We are both around fifty-three years of age and to date we have $20,000 in TFSAs. My husband has $50,000 in his RRSP, and I have about $29,000 in my RRSP. We have been advised that we should contribute to non-registered investments because we are late bloomers and would then qualify for the GIS (Guaranteed Income Supplement). Any advice? We hear so many different opinions; some say yes to RRSP and others say no.

A – It's true that TFSAs are the better choice if you expect to qualify for the GIS. But do you really expect your income after retirement to be that low? Currently, only couples with a combined annual income of less than $20,880, not including Old Age Security, are eligible. To put this in perspective, if you both qualify for the maximum Canada Pension Plan benefit, your combined income would exceed the GIS maximum. I suggest you do a projection of what your approximate income will be after you retire. If it is unlikely to be below the GIS threshold, then keep adding to the RRSPs.

TFSA TRANSFERS

Q – How can I "deregister" a TFSA at one financial institution and transfer it to another institution?

A – This must be done as a direct transfer from one TFSA to another. Open a new plan at the financial institution of your choice and give them the details of the existing TFSA. Ask them to complete the necessary paperwork to execute the transfer. Do not, under any circumstances, close the existing account, withdraw the money, and deposit it elsewhere in a new plan. That will be construed as an overcontribution by the Canada Revenue Agency unless you wait until the new calendar year. Note that there may be an account-closing fee charged by the institution that currently holds the TFSA.

TFSA TO RRSP?

Q – This year the value of my TFSA has grown by $2,000. If I transfer $2,000 from my TFSA to an RRSP before the end of the year, will I get a tax credit for the $2,000 RRSP contribution? Also, will I be able to contribute an additional $2,000 more into my TFSA next year?

A – There is no mechanism for transferring assets from a TFSA to an RRSP. But there is no need to do that, and no benefit, since TFSA withdrawals are tax-free. Simply arrange with the company that administers your TFSA to withdraw $2,000 from the plan. Then use that money to make the RRSP contribution. You will be allowed a tax deduction for the full $2,000. Assuming you do that before year-end, you will have $2,000 in additional TFSA contribution room next year.

TAXES

U.S. WITHHOLDING TAX

Q – I have a question regarding the withholding taxes on U.S. investments. For holdings in an RRSP, I know interest payments are not subject to withholding tax, but I am unclear as to the status of dividends.

A – Under the Canada–U.S. Tax Treaty, dividends from American companies paid into RRSPs or RRIFs are not subject to withholding tax. Note that this protection does not apply to dividends from foreign companies that trade in New York as American Depository Receipts (ADRs). Also, dividends paid to TFSAs are not exempt from the tax.

WINDFALL PROFIT IN RRSP

Q – I am a retired pensioner and have within my RRSP shares of a small mining company that have grown in value from $34,000 to over $300,000 and have the potential to rise considerably higher. I am wondering if I could take the shares out of the RRSP and replace them with $300,000 cash (a switch) without paying tax on the capital gain of some $260,000. I would then put the shares into my margin account, where only 50 percent of the capital gain would be taxed when the shares are sold. Also, the book value of these shares in the margin account would be $300,000. I also like the idea of having a smaller RRIF at age seventy-one, with smaller required withdrawals. I would so appreciate your response.

A – The idea looks good at first glance, and you can indeed make the switch you describe. But you are forgetting one small detail: when everything is said and done, you'll be left with $300,000 cash in the RRSP. That money will be taxed at your marginal rate when it comes out of the plan. One way or another, you are going to pay tax at your marginal rate on the capital gain. The only advantage of this move would be to reduce the tax liability on any future capital gains. By the way, congratulations for picking such a terrific stock!

APPENDIX 1
PERSONAL LIFESTYLE PLANNER

	SELF	SPOUSE
Target retirement age		
Number of working years remaining		

HOUSING	YES	NO	NOT SURE
Continue to live in present house	☐	☐	☐
Move to a less expensive house	☐	☐	☐
Move to a more expensive house	☐	☐	☐
Move to a condo	☐	☐	☐
Move in with children	☐	☐	☐
Own more than one residence and will continue to do so	☐	☐	☐
Will acquire a second residence or RV	☐	☐	☐
Will acquire more than one additional residence	☐	☐	☐

LIFESTYLE GOALS

	YES	NO	NOT SURE
Spend more time with family	☐	☐	☐
Travel frequently	☐	☐	☐
Spend winters in the Sunbelt	☐	☐	☐
Be more active in sports (e.g., golf, tennis, fishing)	☐	☐	☐
Spend more time gardening	☐	☐	☐
Devote time to reading, TV watching	☐	☐	☐
Take educational courses	☐	☐	☐
Spend time with computers, the Internet	☐	☐	☐
Devote time to hobbies	☐	☐	☐
Begin a second career, consulting, part-time work	☐	☐	☐
Have a more active social life (e.g., dinners, parties)	☐	☐	☐
Join a club	☐	☐	☐
Play bridge, canasta, or similar	☐	☐	☐
Take up or do more boating	☐	☐	☐
Do volunteer work	☐	☐	☐

Other (fill in your own priorities):

_____

_____

_____

_____

MATERIAL GOALS

	YES	NO	NOT SURE
Buy a new car at least every three years	☐	☐	☐
Renovate the house	☐	☐	☐
Dine out frequently	☐	☐	☐
Buy the latest high-tech equipment (e.g., TV sets, computers, smartphones)	☐	☐	☐
Provide for grandchildren's education	☐	☐	☐
Help children or other relatives financially	☐	☐	☐
Give large amounts to charities	☐	☐	☐
Leave a large estate for heirs	☐	☐	☐

Other (fill in your own priorities):

_____

_____

_____

_____

APPENDIX 2
EXPENSE ESTIMATOR

Before you begin filling in this worksheet, you'll need to know approximately how much your family is already spending annually in each category. If you don't have a current budget, this is a good time to create one. You can download a free family budget spreadsheet in Excel format at www.buildingwealth.ca.

Use today's dollars when completing the Expense Estimator. Leave taxes aside for the present, except for Canada Pension Plan and Employment Insurance premiums.

Here's how to complete the worksheet: On the line "This Year's Cost," write down how much you expect to spend on the specific item over the next twelve months. The "Retirement Percentage" line represents how much you think you'll spend on the item after you stop work. For example, you might enter 0 percent for CPP/QPP/EI premiums but 120 percent for medical costs. The number on the last line, "Retirement Cost," is calculated by multiplying the figure in line one by the percentage in line two.

If you are unsure about any line, check the notes that follow.

PRINCIPAL RESIDENCE

CATEGORY	THIS YEAR'S COST	RETIREMENT PERCENTAGE	RETIREMENT COST
Mortgage/rent	_____	_____	_____
Property taxes	_____	_____	_____
Maintenance/repairs	_____	_____	_____
Utilities	_____	_____	_____
Improvements/ replacements	_____	_____	_____

RECREATIONAL PROPERTY

CATEGORY	THIS YEAR'S COST	RETIREMENT PERCENTAGE	RETIREMENT COST
Mortgage/rent	_____	_____	_____
Property taxes	_____	_____	_____
Maintenance/repairs	_____	_____	_____
Utilities	_____	_____	_____
Improvements/ replacements	_____	_____	_____

FOOD

CATEGORY	THIS YEAR'S COST	RETIREMENT PERCENTAGE	RETIREMENT COST
At home	_____	_____	_____
Meals out	_____	_____	_____

CLOTHING

CATEGORY	THIS YEAR'S COST	RETIREMENT PERCENTAGE	RETIREMENT COST
You			
Spouse/partner			
Other person (e.g., parent)			
Laundry/cleaning			

TRANSPORTATION

CATEGORY	THIS YEAR'S COST	RETIREMENT PERCENTAGE	RETIREMENT COST
Car(s)			
Public			
Reserve			

HEALTH CARE

CATEGORY	THIS YEAR'S COST	RETIREMENT PERCENTAGE	RETIREMENT COST
Insurance premiums			
Medical costs			
Prescriptions			
Dental care			
Eye care			
Hearing care			
Physiotherapy			
Other			

PERSONAL CARE

CATEGORY	THIS YEAR'S COST	RETIREMENT PERCENTAGE	RETIREMENT COST
(Haircuts, manicures, etc.)	_____	_____	_____

LIFE/DISABILITY INSURANCE

CATEGORY	THIS YEAR'S COST	RETIREMENT PERCENTAGE	RETIREMENT COST
Premiums	_____	_____	_____

FAMILY

CATEGORY	THIS YEAR'S COST	RETIREMENT PERCENTAGE	RETIREMENT COST
Children	_____	_____	_____
Other relatives	_____	_____	_____

TRAVEL/HOLIDAYS

CATEGORY	THIS YEAR'S COST	RETIREMENT PERCENTAGE	RETIREMENT COST
Total cost	_____	_____	_____

RECREATION

CATEGORY	THIS YEAR'S COST	RETIREMENT PERCENTAGE	RETIREMENT COST
Memberships/fees	_____	_____	_____
Equipment	_____	_____	_____
Hobbies	_____	_____	_____
Other	_____	_____	_____

PET CARE

CATEGORY	THIS YEAR'S COST	RETIREMENT PERCENTAGE	RETIREMENT COST
Vet, food, etc.	_____	_____	_____

DEBT REPAYMENT

CATEGORY	THIS YEAR'S COST	RETIREMENT PERCENTAGE	RETIREMENT COST
Credit cards	_____	_____	_____
Loans	_____	_____	_____

PROFESSIONAL SERVICES

CATEGORY	THIS YEAR'S COST	RETIREMENT PERCENTAGE	RETIREMENT COST
(Legal fees, accounting fees, etc.)	_____	_____	_____

DONATIONS/GIFTS

CATEGORY	THIS YEAR'S COST	RETIREMENT PERCENTAGE	RETIREMENT COST
Charity	_____	_____	_____

CPP/QPP/EI PREMIUMS

CATEGORY	THIS YEAR'S COST	RETIREMENT PERCENTAGE	RETIREMENT COST
Premiums	_____	_____	_____

SAVINGS

CATEGORY	THIS YEAR'S COST	RETIREMENT PERCENTAGE	RETIREMENT COST
Amount saved	_____	_____	_____

OTHER EXPENSES

CATEGORY	THIS YEAR'S COST	RETIREMENT PERCENTAGE	RETIREMENT COST
Miscellaneous	_____	_____	_____
Total	_____	_____	_____

These notes may be helpful in completing some of the lines:

PRINCIPAL RESIDENCE. You may still be paying off a mortgage, but look to the future. Based on the current amortization schedule, or on any mortgage pay-down plans you have, will it be fully discharged by the time you stop work? If so, the mortgage component can be eliminated from your retirement spending estimates.

Under Utilities, include the costs of heating, hydro, water, cable TV, telephone (including long-distance charges, cellphones, etc.), and your Internet service provider. And don't forget any special costs you may have, such as a water softener, water filter, or security system.

The Improvements/replacements line is for the cost of renovations or new furniture and appliances. Don't underestimate these expenses: many people like to spend time after retirement fixing up their home or buying new furniture, drapes, and carpets. If your lifestyle plans call for you to move to a less (or more) expensive home after retirement, adjust your spending estimates accordingly. Do not include any allowance for the profit you may make on the sale of your present home. That isn't real money until it happens.

RECREATIONAL PROPERTY. You may not own a cottage, Sunbelt condo, or vacation property now, but if you want one after you retire, you'll have to build in the cost. Many retirees buy a place in the sun to spend the winter months. If this is part of your desired retirement lifestyle, start planning for it now. If you want a rough rule of thumb on the annual costs of carrying such a property, assuming it's mortgaged, use 15 to 20 percent of your estimated purchase price. A condo in the Sunbelt will usually cost at least as much to carry as a comparable residence in Canada—what you save in heating bills, you'll pay out in higher costs for electricity (mainly air conditioning), property taxes, insurance, and maintenance charges.

FOOD. Your current food costs may not be indicative of what you can expect to pay after retirement. Your children will probably have left home by the time you stop work, and many people also find they eat smaller portions as they age. Meals out may cost less, especially if you and your spouse both work now and have lunch away from home five days a week. On the other hand, if your desired lifestyle calls for more socializing and entertaining, budget accordingly.

CLOTHING. If you and your spouse have to dress for work, whether it's in an office or on a construction site, those costs will be eliminated. You may have to build up your leisure wardrobe, but casual clothes usually cost less than business wear. If you have children living at home now, eliminate the cost of their clothing from the calculation unless you expect them to still be living with you after your retirement. If you think you may have others living with you, such as an aged parent, factor that in.

TRANSPORTATION. For most people, the family car is the largest single expense in this category. You'll almost certainly want to retain at least one car when you stop work, so you'd better plan for it. Remember to include all relevant costs:

gas, oil, insurance, licence, and maintenance. I've also added a line for public transportation (many communities offer seniors' discounts) and one marked "Reserve." This is for putting aside money to purchase a new car every five years or so.

HEALTH CARE. This is a tough one to estimate. Your personal health costs will almost certainly be higher after you retire, and you may not have ongoing group plan protection. Dental care and glasses may cost more, and you may have to purchase hearing aids. However, if you're currently paying large sums for health care—perhaps your daughter just got braces on her teeth—the increase may not be overly dramatic. Make inquiries about the cost of individual health insurance for older people and include this in your post-retirement projection. Note that some provinces subsidize prescription costs for older people. Ontario, for example, picks up most of the expense for qualified prescription drugs for all people over sixty-five, regardless of income.

PERSONAL CARE. Cosmetics, hair care, perfumes, and the like all cost money. Allow for it here. Also include any spending on tobacco and alcohol on this line.

LIFE/DISABILITY INSURANCE. If you have a young family, your annual premiums may be quite high at present. However, you shouldn't need as much insurance after the kids have grown up, especially if you've built a solid retirement plan that will comfortably support both you and your spouse through the rest of your lives. Unless you want to use life insurance to leave a big estate to your children, plan to reduce your costs once you stop work. Disability insurance is valuable as long as you're working, but once you retire, there is no point continuing it. Any money you're now spending on disability premiums can be directed elsewhere.

FAMILY. Take a close look at what your dependants are costing you now. If you have children in university, for example, you're probably laying out thousands of dollars annually that won't be required in a few years. But you must also consider your parents or other close family relatives. Are they in good financial shape, or are they likely to need help from you in later years? And don't lose sight of the grandchildren who may come along (or be here already). They can cost a lot of money in gifts and visits.

TRAVEL/HOLIDAY. If you want to see the world, or at least the sunny south, after you retire, this is the time to start planning for it. If you don't spend a lot on holidays now, this may be the component of your budget that shows the largest percentage increase. Remember to factor in the cost of out-of-province travel insurance; the older you get, the more it will cost. A five-month winter stay for a couple over seventy could carry an insurance premium of several thousand dollars.

RECREATION. You're probably going to want to be active in your spare time, so don't skimp here. If you're a golfer, you may want to join a club (if you don't belong to one already) or purchase new clubs. Hobbies can be costly—I happen to enjoy collecting fine wines, and I don't intend to give it up when I stop work. Many retirees like gardening, which can be expensive. You may want to buy some music or rent some movies. How about some nights on the town? Will you be doing more reading? Do you plan to buy a boat? A state-of-the-art home entertainment system? A new computer? This is your chance to do all those things you complain you never have time for, so make sure the money is available in your budget.

PET CARE. Many retired people like the companionship of a dog, cat, or other pet. If that sounds like you, put some money in your budget at this line. Don't underestimate the cost. Vet fees can be expensive, and if your pet requires regular grooming the way our shaggy Sheltie did, that will set you back as much as $100 every month or two.

DEBT REPAYMENT. You may be servicing a lot of debt right now: credit card balances, a car loan, investment loans, etc. Include the annual interest cost of everything except your mortgage in the Present Cost column. Your target should be to pay off all your debts before retirement to reduce that outlay to zero, thereby freeing up cash for other post-retirement needs.

PROFESSIONAL SERVICES. You may need the services of a lawyer, accountant, financial planner, and/or investment counsellor when you retire. Budget for those costs at this line.

DONATIONS/GIFTS. If you give regularly to charitable organizations, you'll want to continue doing so when you retire. Include an appropriate amount here.

CANADA PENSION PLAN/EMPLOYMENT INSURANCE PREMIUMS. You're probably paying several hundred dollars each year in premiums, and the higher your income, the greater the amount deducted. This expense will disappear when you retire.

SAVINGS. You should be contributing several thousand dollars each year to savings plans, including pension plans, RRSPs, and TFSAs. This outlay will be reduced once you retire, although you can contribute to your TFSA for as long as you live.

OTHER EXPENSES. Most people find they spend at least 10 percent of their income on items for which they can't readily account. Make an appropriate allowance on this line. If you have any unusual expenses, such as alimony payments, also add them at this point.

TOTAL. The total amount in the Retirement Cost column represents your estimated expenses *in today's dollars* once you stop work.

APPENDIX 3
THE INFLATION FACTOR

Use this table to determine your post-retirement expenses in terms of current purchasing power. Select a target rate of inflation to find out how much your current dollar expenses will increase over time. For example, the inflation adjustor for ten years at a 2 percent average annual inflation rate is 1.22. That means for every $10,000 in projected retirement expenses, you'll need $12,200 after a decade to maintain your standard of living.

YEARS TO RETIREMENT	INFLATION ADJUSTOR					
	1%	2%	3%	4%	5%	6%
1	1.01	1.02	1.03	1.04	1.05	1.06
2	1.02	1.04	1.06	1.08	1.10	1.12
3	1.03	1.06	1.09	1.13	1.16	1.19
4	1.04	1.08	1.13	1.17	1.22	1.26
5	1.05	1.10	1.16	1.22	1.28	1.34
6	1.06	1.13	1.19	1.27	1.34	1.42
7	1.07	1.15	1.23	1.32	1.41	1.50
8	1.08	1.17	1.27	1.37	1.48	1.58
9	1.09	1.20	1.31	1.42	1.55	1.69
10	1.11	1.22	1.34	1.48	1.63	1.79
11	1.12	1.24	1.39	1.54	1.71	1.90
12	1.13	1.27	1.43	1.60	1.80	2.01
13	1.14	1.29	1.47	1.67	1.89	2.13
14	1.15	1.32	1.51	1.73	1.98	2.26
15	1.16	1.35	1.56	1.80	2.08	2.40
16	1.17	1.37	1.61	1.87	2.19	2.54
17	1.18	1.40	1.65	1.95	2.29	2.69
18	1.20	1.43	1.70	2.03	2.41	2.85
19	1.21	1.46	1.75	2.11	2.53	3.03
20	1.22	1.49	1.81	2.19	2.65	3.21
21	1.23	1.52	1.86	2.28	2.79	3.40

YEARS TO RETIREMENT	INFLATION ADJUSTOR					
	1%	2%	3%	4%	5%	6%
22	1.25	1.55	1.92	2.37	2.93	3.60
23	1.26	1.58	1.97	2.47	3.07	3.82
24	1.27	1.61	2.03	2.56	3.23	4.05
25	1.28	1.64	2.09	2.67	3.39	4.29
26	1.29	1.66	2.16	2.77	3.56	4.55
27	1.31	1.67	2.22	2.88	3.73	4.82
28	1.32	1.69	2.29	3.00	3.92	5.11
29	1.33	1.71	2.36	3.12	4.12	5.42
30	1.35	1.72	2.43	3.24	4.32	5.74
31	1.36	1.85	2.50	3.37	4.54	6.09
32	1.38	1.89	2.58	3.51	4.77	6.45
33	1.39	1.92	2.65	3.65	5.00	6.84
34	1.40	1.96	2.73	3.79	5.25	7.25
35	1.42	2.00	2.81	3.95	5.52	7.69
36	1.43	2.04	2.90	4.10	5.79	8.15
37	1.45	2.08	2.99	4.27	6.08	8.64
38	1.46	2.12	3.08	4.44	6.39	9.15
39	1.47	2.17	3.17	4.62	6.71	9.70
40	1.49	2.21	3.26	4.80	7.04	10.29

APPENDIX 4
SOME USEFUL WEBSITES

Assuris
www.assuris.ca

British Columbia Securities Commission
www.bcsc.bc.ca

Canada Revenue Agency
www.cra-arc.gc.ca

Canadian Foundation for Advancement of Investor Rights
www.faircanada.ca

Canadian Institute of Actuaries
www.actuaries.ca

C.D. Howe Institute
www.cdhowe.org

Dinkytown.net (financial calculators)
www.dinkytown.net

E.E.S. Financial Services (life expectancy calculator)
www.ees-financial.com

Ernst & Young (tax calculators)
www.ey.com

Financial Advisors Association of Canada (commonly known as Advocis)
www.advocis.ca

Financial Consumer Agency of Canada
www.fcac-acfc.gc.ca

Financial Planning Standards Council (Directory of CFP Professionals in Good Standing)
www.fpsc.ca

Fiscal Agents
www.fiscalagents.com

Franklin Templeton (retirement calculator)
www.franklintempleton.ca

Globe Investor
www.globeinvestor.com

Globe Investor Funds
www.globefund.com

Intuit Canada (tax software)
www.intuit.ca

Investor Education Fund
www.getsmarteraboutmoney.ca

MoneySense
www.moneysense.ca

Quebec Pension Plan
www.rrq.gouv.qc.ca

Red Flag Deals (credit card comparison tool)
www.creditcards.redflagdeals.com

Retirement Advisor
www.retirementadvisor.ca

Saskatchewan Pension Plan
www.saskpension.com

Service Canada
www.servicecanada.gc.ca

Task Force on Financial Literacy
www.financialliteracyincanada.com

Tax Chopper (tax software)
www.taxchopper.ca

Vanier Institute of the Family
www.vifamily.ca

The Wealthy Barber
www.wealthybarber.com

ACKNOWLEDGMENTS

I have to begin by thanking my wife, Shirley, for her patience in putting up with my long absences in my office while this book was being written. Her love and support has always been a vital factor in my success, and I want her to know how much I appreciate it.

I also want to thank my daughter, Kim Pape-Green, for the incredible amount of research material she compiled for me in preparation for this book. Her work enabled me to draw on a wealth of information with just a mouse click. Every writer will know how important that is.

My thanks to Anne Clark-Stewart, who provided me with the details of the plight faced by Nortel pensioners in the wake of the company's bankruptcy. She also put me in touch with Nortel retirees Robert Dowson and Bill Nickerson, whose stories appear in the chapter titled "Pension Plans Are Dying." I wish to thank them for granting me permission to include their personal accounts of the difficulties faced by people who have had their lives turned upside down by forces over which they had no control.

Finally, thank you again to the team at Penguin Canada, led by my editor, Andrea Magyar, with a lot of help from senior production editor Sandra Tooze and copyeditor Janice Weaver. The Penguin people have had confidence in me and helped me so much over the years. I can only write the words. These folks do everything else!

FOR MORE INFORMATION

THE ULTIMATE TFSA GUIDE. Tax-Free Savings Accounts are the most powerful investment tool made available to Canadians since RRSPs. And Gordon Pape has written the definitive guide to using them successfully.

This book provides all the information you need to choose the right type of TFSA for your needs and maximize your investment returns. Should you use a TFSA or an RRSP? The answer is here. Want to know the best investment choices? They're in the book. Wondering how much a plan will cost? You'll find reviews of the plans from dozens of companies.

Whether you already have a TFSA or are planning to open one, this book is a must-read resource. Available at all bookstores and online book sellers.

NEWSLETTERS

Gordon Pape is the editor and publisher of several invest-ment newsletters. They include the following:

INTERNET WEALTH BUILDER. This weekly email newsletter covers all aspects of investing and money management, including stocks, bonds, mutual funds, income trusts, taxes, and general economic comment. The seasoned team of contributing editors includes some of Canada's best investment minds. The newsletter takes a conservative approach to money management, focusing on high-quality securities with minimal risk.

THE INCOME INVESTOR. This twice-monthly newsletter covers income-generating securities with the goal of providing readers with above-average returns consistent with reasonable risk. At a time when interest rates are low and income trusts have all but disappeared, the guidance provided by this letter is vital to anyone seeking steady cash flow from their investments.

MUTUAL FUNDS/ETFs UPDATE. Now in its seventeenth year of publication, this monthly newsletter continues to represent the gold standard in sound, sensible mutual fund and ETF advice. One of its most popular features is the "Ideal Portfolios," which provides models for investors of all types, from ultra-conservative to growth-oriented.

For information on these newsletters, visit www.building wealth.ca or call toll-free 1-888-287-8229.

WEBSITE

More financial information from Gordon Pape can be found at www.buildingwealth.ca. You'll find free investment articles, a Q&A feature, valuable budget and net worth spreadsheets, book excerpts, and more. There's also complete information on how to subscribe to Gordon's newsletters.

INDEX